THE FINANCIAL ECONOMY MYTHS

PRIVATE PLACEMENT
PROGRAM

THE COMPLETE GUIDE

SIR PATRICK BIJOU

DEDICATION

I dedicate this book to the loving memory of my late mother, Esther, the inspiration of my life and the most remarkable woman I have ever known. I know that she is looking down on me from heaven and smiling. Thank you for your kindness and love. I couldn't have asked for more. I dedicate this book to her with all my love.

ABOUT THE AUTHOR

Sir Patrick lives and writes in the UK and is an Investment banker, UN Ambassador, and author. He is a renowned leading specialist in the debt capital markets, private placement, derivatives, and futures trading and is considered the world's leading expert in Private Placement Programs. He is undoubtedly the world's greatest private placement banker and world authority in Private Placement programs. As a distinguished trader on Wall Street, Tire 1 and level 17 banker, he has worked with multiple top banks such as Wells Fargo, Deutsche, Credit Agricole CIB, Merrill Lynch, and others. He has established and managed Hedge Funds such as The Tiger Fund and became a notable Fund Manager at Blackstone. Sir Patrick was responsible for setting up the MTN & Private Placement Desk and dealer function at Lloyds Bank Plc. He was the first trader for Lloyd's treasury to increase self-led deals significantly from 4% to 32% in 2002.

His journey into content writing has allowed him to become an exceptionally motivated and enthusiastic author and professional communicator.

Sir Patrick is an avid lover of literature, and he has published more than 45 books across several genres. He excelled on his journey to become a highly educated and intellectual academic. Aside from being a notable investment banker, he is also a professional communicator and philanthropist.

Work History and Career

From his humble beginnings at Wells Fargo Bank on wall street, he has served as a private banker, fund manager, and an outstanding bond, futures, and derivatives trader on the trading floors. He established himself in his specialist field in the debt markets and private placement. His financial architecture and creative skills have seen him work with some of the best minds. Many consider him an enigma in his field and the most extraordinary in structuring financial products and private placement, the very best in his field.

He has helped large corporations create new credit structures for international supply chains, SMEs for the public sector, private clients, and governments. His innovative and leadership skills have tailored funding and investments for various clients. His methods are sustainable, and he can boast one of the highest return ratios in the banking sector, assuring clients impressive profits and capital returns.

He is the creator and designer of the economic phenomenon of Contract For Difference (CFD), a concept regarded as truly pioneering that today banks and trading institutions now adopt. Using clever leverage ratios, CFD has changed how trading is implemented across capital markets. He has written journals and books about CFD and how to become wealthy by executing his strategies and concepts in wealth creation. He is also a renowned and sought-after wealth manager, managing his trading platforms at his desk at Credit Suisse Bank and DBS Bank. He has published several books on Private Placement Programs and Investment trading strategies, all of which have become notable best sellers.

Beliefs

Sir Patrick believes that when people are learning, then they are growing. He is on a quest to make excellence a part of the people he meets. He considers every day as an opportunity to improve the world. He helps people to turn an idea into an opportunity. He teaches how to utilise creative thinking and innovative strategies to become an expert in wealth creation and a humanitarian. He believes no mountain is too high to climb if you have the right tools. Additionally, every obstacle has a solution, and the most challenging dream can be realised with imagination, creativity, and resilience.

Table of Content

INTRODUCTION/1

CHAPTER 1/3

1. Epitome Of Medium-Term Note Market (MTNs)/3

2. Background Of The MTNs Market/6

3. Mechanics Of The Market/8

4. The Economics Of Mtns And Corporate Bonds/10

5. The Federal Reserve Board's Survey Of Us. Corporate MTNs/14

6. The Volume of Corporate MTNs Outstanding and the Components of Net Borrowing/16

7. The Relative Size of the MTN market/17

8. RECENT DEVELOPMENTS IN THE MTN MARKET/19

9. Book-Entry Clearing and Settlement of MTNs/24

10. Developments in the Distribution of MTNs/27

CHAPTER 2/31

1 EURO-MTNs/31

2. The Primary Market/34

3. MTNs and corporate bonds/37

4. MTN issue options/39

5. Issue mechanism/41

6. The Secondary Market/44

7. MANAGED BUY/SELL PROGRAMS/49

8. PROCESS OF MANAGING BUY/SELL MTNs PROGRAM/54

9. Why do banks issue MTNs?/59

110. MTN Programs: SEC-Registered and Exempt/63

11. Medium Term Note Programs/70

12 How Do We Update Our MTN Descriptions?/76

CHAPTER 3/89

1. Introduction To Private Placement Program?/89

2. Historical Background Of Private Placement Programs/90

3. Understanding Private Placement Trade Programs/95

4. Prominence Of Private Placement Trading MTNs As A Debt Instrument/100

5. Private Placement Programs For the Creation Of Credit/106

6. The Beauty Of A Private Placement Trade Platform 111

7. Normal Trading vs. Private Placement/113

8. Arbitrage And Leverage/115

9. Analysis Of Risk Involved In Ppo Contracts/123

10. From The Broker's And Intermediary's Side/127

11. How Private Placement Programs / Trade Platforms Work/133

12. Are Private Placement Programs/Trade Platforms Real Or A Scam?/139

13. Steps To Private Placement Success/142

14. The Basic Options:/146

CHAPTER 4/159

1. The Concept Of Hedge Funds/159

2. Features Of Hedge Funds./161

3. Types Of Hedge Fund Investments./164

4. General Classification/172

5. Fund of Hedge Funds:/179

6. Comparison Between Hedge Funds And Private Equity:/179

7. Comparison between Hedge Funds and Mutual Fund:/180

8. Regulatory Environment:/181

9. Risk of Hedge Funds:/189

CHAPTER 5/190

1. Arbitrage Trading/190

2. Why Is Arbitrage So Important?/192

3. The Nature and Significance of Arbitrage/194

4. The Relationship Between the Law of One Price and Arbitrage/195

5. Mispricing, Convergence, and Arbitrage/196

6. Identifying Arbitrage Opportunities/198

7. The Essence of Arbitrage/202

8. Feasibility of Futures Arbitrage/204

9. Arbitrage Trading Strategies/212

CHAPTER 6/216

1. Derivative Instruments/216

2. Financial Derivatives/217

3. Classes of Financial Derivatives/221

4. Recording of Financial Derivative Transactions and Positions/223

5. Valuation of Positions/223

6. Resale of Derivatives in Secondary Markets/225

7. Treatment of Selected Financial Derivatives/227

8. Major types of derivatives/230

9. The Effect Of Financial Derivatives On Enterprises/237

10. Hedging and speculation arbitrage/237

11. Function of financial derivatives/237

12. Role Of Derivatives In Recent Credit Events And Regulatory Issues/241

CHAPTER 7/243

1. Futures Contract/243

2. TYPES OF FINANCIAL FUTURES CONTRACTS/245

3. Foreign currency futures/245

4. The Clearing House/247

5. Hedging using futures contract/248

6. Payoff Of Futures Contract/251

7. Types of Futures Traders/251

8. The Futures Contract And The Futures Exchange/252

9. Advantages Of Futures Contract/255

10. Disadvantages Of Futures Contract/256

11. Difference Between Forwards And Futures Contract/257

CHAPTER 8/259

1. Investing In CFD Contract/259

2. What is a CFD?/260

3. Features And Benefits Of CFDs/262

4. The Cost Of Using CFDs/263

5. How CFDs Work A Step-By-Step Guide/264

6. CFD positions in share register analyses/269

7. Investment Market Capitalization/270

8. Why Market Cap Matters/271

9. What Are Large-Cap Stocks?/272

10. What Are Mid-Cap Stocks?/273

11. What Are Small-Cap Stocks?/273

12. Difference Between Large-Cap, Medium-Cap and Small-Cap companies/274

13. Mutual Funds And Market Capitalisation/275

14. The Limitations of Market Cap/276

CHAPTER 9/277

1. What Is Money?/277

2. Massive Confusion Exists About Money/281

3. Money is not Gold/283

4. The Myth of Corrupt Governments/284

5. Bank Created Credit as Money/285

6. How the Bank of England Came Into Being/286

7. Private Control of Money Creation/288

8. The Function of Banks/290

9. Bankers' Stratagems/292

10. Some Crucial Historical Facts/294

11. Moneyless Economy/298

12. The Three Key System Entities/303

13. Historical Evidence And Current Practice/311

14. Money Creation By Commercial Banks Today/318

CONCLUSION/322

INTRODUCTION

In the real financial world, talking is cheap, and you must "show your muscle" through buying and selling. Therefore, a good theory should lead to profitable trading strategies. The stock market is a battlefield among traders with different beliefs and it is the winner's belief that determines the destiny of the stock prices. Therefore, our basic trading philosophy is to follow the winners. But who are the winners? In this book we concentrate on the type of traders who we believe are very likely to be the winners: the big buyers and the big sellers. the institutional investors (pension funds, mutual funds, hedge funds, money managers, investment banks, etc.) who manage large sums of money, and often buys or sell a stock in large quantity.

The internet and the evolution of technology have enabled many folks to become seriously successful traders. The whole process has become so simplified that most successful traders these days trade from the comfort of their own homes. As more people have leveraged this technology, the fat commissions paid by small investors to Brokerage Houses are almost forgotten. Online trading is by far the most convenient cost effective and accessible platform for anyone contemplating buying and selling shares.

All trading programs in the Private Placement arena involve trade with discounted debt notes in some fashion. Further, in order to bypass the legal restrictions, this trading can only be done on a private level. This is the main difference between PPP trading and 'conventional' trading, which is highly regulated. This is a Private Placement level business transaction that is free from the usual restrictions present in the securities market. It is based on trusted, long established private relationships and protocols. Conventional trading activity is performed under the 'open market' (also known as the 'spot market') where discounted instruments are bought and sold with auction-type bids. To participate in such trading, the trader must be in full control of the funds, otherwise he has no means of buying the instruments before reselling them.

Money has always been associated in varying degrees of closeness with religion, partly interpreted in modern times as the psychology of habits and attitudes, hopes, fears and expectations. Thus, the taboos which circumscribe spending in primitive societies are basically not unlike the stock market bears which similarly reduce expenditures through changing subjective assessments of values and incomes, so that the true interpretation of what money means to people requires the sympathetic understanding of the less obvious motivations as much as, if not more than, the narrow abstract calculations of the computer. To concentrate attention narrowly on 'the pound in your pocket' is to devalue the all-pervading significance of money.

CHAPTER 1

Epitome Of Medium-Term Note Market (MTNs)

Medium-term notes (MTNs) are corporate bonds that have evolved into an important source of corporate funding. They are not exclusively corporate instruments, however, and have been issued by sovereigns, supranational, and federal and local authorities. The first MTN was issued by the General Motors corporation in 1972, and was sold directly to investors rather than via an agent bank. During the 1970s the MTN market was largely illiquid, and in 1981 the volume of outstanding issues were less than $1 billion. In that year, Merrill Lynch issued an MTN for Ford Motor Credit and also undertook to make a secondary market in the paper. Since then the MTN market has grown into a major corporate finance instrument, traded both domestically and internationally, and at the end of 1998 the outstanding volume of MTN issues around the world was approaching $1 trillion.

A medium-term note is essentially a plain vanilla debt security with a fixed coupon and maturity date. The term "medium-term" is something of a misnomer, as the bonds range in maturity from nine months to 30 years or more; however the first MTNs generally had maturities of five years or less. They were originally designed to bridge the gap between commercial paper and long-dated bonds. An MTN is an unsecured debt, therefore the majority of MTNs are investment grade quality. In terms of the way they trade in the market, MTNs are virtually identical to conventional corporate bonds, and the main difference between an MTN and a corporate bond is the manner in which it is issued in the primary market. The unique characteristic of MTNs is that they are offered to investors continually over a period of time by an agent of the issuer, as part of an MTN programme. MTNs are usually offered in the market by investment banks acting as agents, and sold on a "best efforts" basis. The issuing bank does not act as an underwriter of the bonds, unlike with a conventional bond issue, and, therefore, the borrowing company is not guaranteed to place all its paper. As MTNs are usually offered as part of a continuous program, they are issued in smaller amounts than conventional bonds, which are generally sold in larger amounts at one time. Notes can be issued either as bearer securities or registered securities. A Euromarket in MTNs developed in the mid-1980s. Euro MTNs (EMTNs) trade in a similar fashion to Eurobonds; they are debt securities issued for distribution across markets internationally.

The majority of MTNs are conventional bonds with fixed coupon rate and single maturity date. There is a wide range of structures available however, and MTNs have been issued with floating rate coupons, call and put features, amortising nominal amounts, multi-currency structures or as part of more exotic structures such as asset swaps. Certain MTN issues are underwritten by investment banks as well, making them indistinguishable from conventional corporate bonds.

Medium-term note ("MTN") programs enable companies to offer and sell a wide range of debt securities, which may have similar or different terms, on a periodic and/or continuous basis, by using pre-agreed offering and distribution documents and a simplified clearing process. With an MTN program, the issuer is able to use streamlined documentation for each offering and rely on the master program documentation and disclosure documents. MTN programs were historically developed by the commercial paper departments of investment banks and often were administered by a bank's specialty group rather than through the typical relationship bankers. Most of these offerings are made on a principal or agency basis through the MTN broker-dealer's trading desk. MTNs having tenors of between two to five years were conceptualized as a means to bridge the gap between short-term commercial paper maturing in nine months or less, and long-term debt securities maturing 30 years or more from the issuance date. However, it is not unusual for issuers to issue both short-term and long-term securities under an MTN program.

In light of the convenience offered by shelf registration and MTN programs, issuers use MTN programs

(i) to effect small and medium-sized offerings of debt securities to investors that seek specific terms such as a specified principal amount, with a specified credit rating and a specified maturity (known as reverse inquiry trades);

(ii) to effect large syndicated offerings of debt securities that might, in the absence of an MTN program, be offered through a traditional shelf takedown;

(iii) to offer structured notes, such as equity-linked, index-linked, currency-linked and commodity-linked securities; and

(iv) to operate a retail MTN program wherein an issuer offers MTNs with small minimum denominations to the retail investor market, while limiting administrative costs to the issuer to acceptable levels.

In one type of retail MTN program, an issuer will post rates weekly with retail and/or regional brokers. During the week that these rates are posted, the brokerage firms that market the securities to retail investors will place orders in the applicable minimum denominations. At the end of the week, the retail and regional brokerage firms will contact the issuer and indicate the aggregate amount of orders for notes at each maturity, and the issuer will issue one series of notes for each maturity.

Background Of The MTNs Market

General Motors Acceptance Corporation (GMAC) created the MTN market in the early 1970s as an extension of the commercial paper market. To improve their asset-liability management, GMAC and the other auto finance companies needed to issue debt with a maturity that matched that of their auto loans to dealers and consumers. However, underwriting costs made bond offerings with short maturities impractical, and maturities on commercial paper cannot exceed 270 days. The auto finance companies, therefore began to sell MTNs directly to investors. In the 1970s, the growth of the market was hindered by illiquidity in the secondary market and by securities regulations requiring approval by the Securities and Exchange Commission (SEC) of any amendment to a registered public offering. The latter, in particular, increased the costs of issuance significantly because borrowers had to obtain the approval of the SEC each time they changed the posted coupon rates on their MTN offering schedule. To avoid this regulatory hurdle, some corporations sold MTNs in the private placement market.

In the early 1980s, two institutional changes set the stage for rapid growth of the MTN market. First, in 1981 major investment banks, acting as agents, committed resources to assist in primary issuance and to provide secondary market liquidity. By 1984, the captive finance companies of the three large automakers had at least two agents for their MTN programs. The ongoing financing requirements of these companies and the competition among agents established a basis for the market to develop. Because investment banks stood ready to buy back MTNs in the secondary market, investors became more receptive to adding MTNs to their portfolio holdings. In turn, the improved liquidity and consequent reduction in the cost of issuance attracted new borrowers to the market.

Second, the adoption by the SEC of Rule 415 in March 1982 served as another important institutional change. Rule 415 permits delayed or continuous issuance of so called shelf registered corporate securities. Under shelf registrations, issuers register securities that may be sold for two years after the effective date of the registration without the requirement of another registration statement each time new offerings are made. Thus, shelf registration enables issuers to take advantage of brief periods of low interest rates by selling previously registered securities on a moment's notice. In contrast, debt offerings that are not made from shelf registrations are subject to a delay of at least forty-eight hours between the filing with the SEC and the subsequent offering to the public.

The ability of borrowers to sell a variety of debt instruments with a broad range of coupons and maturities under a single prospectus supplement is another advantage of a shelf-registered MTN program. Indeed, a wide array of financing options have been included in MTN filings. For example, MTN programs commonly give the borrower the choice of issuing fixed or floating rate debt. Furthermore, several "global" programs allow for placements in the U.S. market or in the Euro market. Other innovations that reflect the specific funding needs of issuers include MTNs collateralized by mortgages issued by thrift institutions, equipment trust certificates issued by railways, amortizing notes issued by leasing companies, and subordinated notes issued by bank holding companies. Another significant innovation has been the development of asset-backed MTNs, a form of asset securitization used predominantly to finance trade receivables and corporate loans. This flexibility in types of instruments that may be sold as MTNs, coupled with the market timing benefits of shelf registration, enables issuers to respond readily to changing market opportunities.

In the early and mid-1980s, when finance companies dominated the market, most issues of MTNs were fixed rate, noncallable, and unsecured, with maturities of five years or less. In recent years, as new issuers with more diverse financing needs have established programs, the characteristics of new issues have become less generic. For example, maturities have lengthened as industrial and utility companies with longer financing needs have entered the market. Indeed, frequent placements of notes with thirty-year maturities have made the designation "medium term" something of a misnomer.

Mechanics Of The Market

The process of raising funds in the public MTN market usually begins when a corporation files a shelf registration with the SEC. Once the SEC declares the registration statement effective; the borrower files a prospectus supplement that describes the MTN program. The amount of debt under the program generally ranges from $100 million to $1 billion. After establishing an MTN program, a borrower may enter the MTN market continuously or intermittently with large or relatively small offerings. Although underwritten corporate bonds may also be issued from shelf registrations, MTNs provide issuers with more flexibility than traditional underwritings in which the entire debt issue is made at one time, typically with a single coupon and a single maturity.

The registration filing usually includes a list of the investment banks with which the corporation has arranged to act as agents to distribute the notes to investors. Most MTN programs have two to four agents. Having multiple agents encourages competition among investment banks and thus lowers financing costs. The large New York based investment banks dominate the distribution of MTNs.

Through its agents, an issuer of MTNs posts offering rates over a range of maturities: for example, nine months to one year, one year to eighteen months, eighteen months to two years, and annually after that. Many issuers post rates as a yield spread over a Treasury security of comparable maturity. The relatively attractive yield spreads posted at the maturities of three, four, and five years discussed indicate that the issuer desires to raise funds at these maturities. The investment banks disseminate this offering rate information to their investor clients. When an investor expresses interest in an MTN offering, the agent contacts the issuer to obtain a confirmation of the terms of the transaction. Within a maturity range, the investor has the option of choosing the final maturity of the note sale, subject to agreement by the issuing company. The issuer will lower its posted rates once it raises the desired amount of funds at a given maturity. The issuer might lower its posted rate for MTNs with a five-year maturity to 40 basis points over comparable Treasury securities after it sells the desired amount of debt at this maturity. Of course, issuers also change their offering rate scales in response to changing market conditions. Issuers may withdraw from the market by suspending sales or, alternatively, by posting narrow offering spreads at all maturity ranges. The proceeds from primary trades in the MTN market typically range from $1 million to $25 million, but the size of transactions varies considerably. After the amount, of registered debt is sold, the issuer may "reload" its MTN program by filing a new registration with the SEC.

Although MTNs are generally offered on an agency basis, most programs permit other means of distribution. For example, MTN programs usually allow the agents to acquire notes for their own account and for resale at par or at prevailing market prices. MTNs may also be sold on an underwritten basis. In addition, many MTN programs permit the borrower to bypassfinancialintermediaries by selling debt directly to investors.

The Economics Of Mtns And Corporate Bonds

In deciding whether to finance with MTNs or with bonds, a corporate borrower weighs the interest cost, flexibility, and other advantages of each security. The growth of the MTN market indicates that MTNs offer advantages that bond do not. However, most companies that raise funds in the MTN market have also continued to issue corporate bonds, suggesting that each form of debt has advantages under particular circumstances.

Offering Size, Liquidity, And Price Discrimination

The amount of the offering is the most important determinant of the cost differential between the MTN and corporate bond markets. For large, standard financings (such as $300 million of straight debt with a ten-year maturity) the all in interest cost to an issuer of underwritten corporate bonds may be lower than the all in cost of issuing MTNs. This cost advantage arises from economies of scale in underwriting and, most important, from the greater liquidity of large issues. As a result, corporations that have large financing needs for a specific term usually choose to borrow with bonds. From an empirical point of view, the liquidity premium, if any, on small offerings has yet to be quantified. Nevertheless, the sheer volume of financing in the MTN market suggests that any liquidity premium that may exist for small offerings is not a significant deterrent to financing. According to market participants, the interest cost differential between the markets has narrowed in recent years as liquidity in the MTN market has improved. Many borrowers estimate that the premium is now only about 5 to 10 basis points.

Furthermore, many borrowers believe that financing costs are slightly lower in the MTN market because its distribution process allows borrowers to price discriminate. Consider, a stylized example of a company that needs to, raise $100 million with a bond offering, the company may have to raise the offering yield significantly, for example, from 6 percent to 6.25 percent, to place the final $10 million with the marginal buyer. In contrast, with MTNs the company could raise $90 million by posting a yield of 6 percent; to raise the additional $10 million, the company could increase its MTN offering rates or issue at a different maturity. Consequently, because all of the debt does not have to be priced to the marginal buyer, financing costs can be lower with MTNs.

The Flexibility of MTNs

Even if conventional bonds enjoy an interest cost advantage; this advantage may be offset by the flexibility that MTNs afford. Offerings of investment-grade straight bonds are clustered at standard maturities of two, three, five, seven, ten, and thirty years. Also, because the fixed costs of underwritings make small offerings impractical, corporate bond offerings rarely amount to less than $100 million. These institutional conventions impede corporations from implementing a financing policy of matching the maturities of assets with those of liabilities. By contrast, drawdowns from MTN programs over the course of a month typically amount to $30 million, and these drawdowns frequently have different maturities and special features that are tailored to meet the needs of the borrower. This flexibility of the MTN market allows companies to match more closely the maturities of assets and liabilities.

The flexibility of continuous offerings also plays a role in a corporation's decision to finance with MTNs. With MTNs, a corporation can "average out" its cost of funds by issuing continuously rather than coming to market on a single day. Therefore, even if bond offerings have lower average yields, a risk-averse borrower might still elect to raise funds in the MTN market with several offerings in a range of $5 million to $10 million over several weeks, rather than with a single $100 million bond offering.

The flexibility of the MTN market also allows borrowers to take advantage of funding opportunities. By having an MTN program, an issuer can raise a sizable amount of debt in a short time; often, the process takes less than half an hour. Bonds may also be sold from a shelf registration, but the completion of the transaction may be delayed by the arrangement of a syndicate, the negotiation of an underwriting agreement, and the "preselling" of the issue to investors. Furthermore, some corporations require that underwritten offerings receive prior approval by the president of the company or the board of directors. In contrast, a corporate treasurer may finance with MTNs without delay and at his or her discretion.

Discreet Funding with MTNs

The MTN market also provides corporations with the ability to raise funds discreetly because the issuer, the investor, and the agent are the only market participants that have to know about a primary transaction. In contrast, the investment community obtains information about underwritten bond offerings from a variety of sources.

Corporations often avoid the bond market in periods of heightened uncertainty about interest rates and the course of the economy, such as the period after 1987 stock market crash. Underwritings at such times could send a signal of financial distress to the market. Similarly, corporations in distressed industries, such as commercial banking in the second half of 1990, can use the MTN market to raise funds quietly rather than risk negative publicity in the high profile bond market. Thus, during periods of financial turmoil, the discreet nature of the MTN market makes it an attractive alternative to the bond market.

"Reverse Inquiry" In The MTN Market

Another advantage of MTNs is that investors often play an active role in the issuance process through the phenomenon known as "reverse inquiry." For example, suppose an investor desires to purchase $15 million of A-rated finance company debt with a maturity of six years and nine months. While such a security may not be available in the corporate bond market, the investor may be able to obtain it in the MTN market through reverse inquiry. In this process, the investor relays the inquiry to an issuer of MTNs through the issuer's agent. If the issuer finds the terms of the reverse inquiry sufficiently attractive, it may agree to the transaction even if it was not posting rates at the maturity that the investor desires.

According to market participants, trades that stem from reverse inquiries account for a significant share of MTN transactions. Reverse inquiry not only benefits the issuer by reducing borrowing costs but also allows investors to use the flexibility of MTNs to their advantage. In response to investor preferences, MTNs issued under reverse inquiry often include embedded options and frequently pay interest according to unusual formulas. This responsiveness of the MTN market to the needs of investors is one of the most important factors driving the growth and acceptance of the market.

The Federal Reserve Board's Survey Of Us. Corporate MTNs

The Federal Reserve surveys U.S. corporations with MTN programs. These companies provide data on a confidential basis on the amount of MTNs they issue; respondents report monthly, quarterly, or annually depending on how active they are in the market. At year-end, all MTN issuers are asked to provide data on the amount of their outstandings. The data on gross issuance begin in January 1983, and the data on outstandings have been collected since year-end 1989. The Federal Reserve obtains information on new programs from announcements of SEC Rule 415 registrations and contacts with MTN agents.

Because the participation rate in the Federal Reserve survey is 100 percent, it provides an accurate measure of the volume of MTN financing by U.S. corporations in the U.S. public market. However, while the U.S. corporate sector is the largest segment of the MTN market, MTNs have been issued in other markets and by non-U.S. corporations. For example, several U.S. corporations have issued MTNs in the Euro-market. Also, the survey does not include MTNs issued in the U.S. public market by government-sponsored agencies, such as the Federal National Mortgage Association, by supranational institutions, and by non-U.S. corporations. Furthermore, although the database includes MTNs issued by bank holding companies, it does not include deposit notes and bank notes offered by banks because these securities are exempt from SEC registration. Perhaps most important, the database does not include privately placed MTNs. The private placement market is particularly attractive to issuers who wish to gain access to U.S. investors without having to obtain SEC approval for a public offering. According to MTN agents, non-U.S. corporations are the largest borrowers in the market for privately placed MTNs.

Because the financing costs are usually lower in the public market than in the less liquid private market, most U.S. corporations choose to issue public, SEC-registered MTNs.

Issuance Volume and Industry of the Issuers

From 1983 through 1992, the volume of MTN issuance in the public market increased in each year, rising from $5.5 billion in 1983 to $74.2 billion in 1992, and totaled $330 billion over the ten-year period. Similarly, the number of borrowers increased from 12 in 1983 to 208 in 1992, and totaled 402 corporations for the period.

Borrowers in the MTN market span a wide array of industry groups. In the financial sector, major borrowers include auto finance companies, bankholding companies, business and consumer credit institutions, and securities brokers. In the nonfinancial sector, participants in the MTN market include utilities, telephone companies, manufacturers, service firms, and wholesalers and retailers. Within industry groups, the auto finance companies have been the heaviest borrowers, raising $88 billion over the period. In relative terms, however, issuance by auto finance companies declined from an 87 percent share of the MTN market in 1983 to 18 percent in 1992.

In the early to mid-1980s, financial companies dominated the MTN market. Indeed, in 1983, only two nonfinancial companies issued MTNs, and they accounted for less than 1 percent of the issuance volume. In recent years, however, nonfinancial companies have increased their share of the market, and from 1990 through 1992, they accounted for about one-third of MTN issuance.

The increase in the volume of MTN issuance reflects a dramatic increase in the number of new borrowers in the market. In each year from 1984 through 1992, at least twenty companies issued MTNs for the first time, and most of the new entrants have been nonfinancial companies. In 1991, for example, sixty-six new borrowers entered the market, of which fifty-five were nonfinancial companies. As a result of this trend, in each year beginning in 1990, the total number of nonfinancial firms issuing MTNs has exceeded the total number offinancial issuers.

The Volume of Corporate MTNs Outstanding and the Components of Net Borrowing

Outstanding MTNs and issuer use of MTN programs have increased sharply since 1989. In the aggregate, outstanding MTNs increased from $76 billion in 1989 to $176 billion in 1992. Over this period, outstandings of non-financial firms increased from $18.5 billion to $67.6 billion, while outstandings of financial corporations increased from $57.5 billion to $108.2 billion. For individual firms, outstandings of MTNs averaged $504 million in 1992, compared with $350 million in 1989.

The data on net borrowing, that is the year-over-year change in outstandings, can be dissected to determine the sources of growth in the market. For the market as a whole, new entrants accounted for about one-third of net borrowing in 1990, one-fourth of net borrowing in 1991, and less than one-fifth in 1992. Thus, firms that had already issued MTNs accounted for most of the recent growth in the market. In the financial sector, in particular, new entrants accounted for only a small proportion of the growth. These simply because a large share of the financial firms could enter the MTN market did so in the 1980s. Among nonfinancial firms, in contrast, new entrants have continued to fuel a significant share of the growth in the market.

Credit Ratings

The corporations issuing MTNs have had high credit ratings. Since 1983, more than 99 percent of MTNs have been rated investment grade (Baa or higher) at the time of issuance. In

1992, $51 billion of the $74 billion in MTN offerings were rated single A, and six firms, issuing a total of $540 million, had Ba ratings. Outstanding MTNs also tend to have high credit ratings, but not as high as the ratings on new offerings because of the preponderance of rating downgrades in recent years. Nevertheless, 98 percent of outstanding MTNs were rated investment grade at year-end 1992.

Maturities and Yield Spreads

Maturities on MTNs reflect the financing needs of the borrowers. Financial firms tend to issue MTNs with maturities matched to the maturity of loans made to their customers. Consequently, in the financial sector, maturities are concentrated in a range of one to five years, and only a small proportion are longer than ten years. Nonfinancial firms, in contrast, often use MTNs to finance longlived assets, such as plant and equipment. As a result, maturities on MTNs issued by non-financial corporations cover a wider range, and in 1992, 25 percent to 30 percent were longer than ten years.

Yields on fixed-rate MTNs, commonly quoted as a yield spread over a Treasury security of comparable maturity, reflect the credit risk of the borrower. Other factors held constant, Baa-rated MTNs have higher yield spreads than A-rated MTNs, which in turn have higher yield spreads than A-rated MTNs. Yield spreads also varies over time, particularly over the course of the business cycle. Spreads on A-rated MTNs increased from 60 basis points over Treasury securities in July 1990, a cyclical trough, to 140 basis points in January 1991.

The Relative Size of the MTN market

The MTN market accounts for a significant share of borrowing by U.S. corporations. One measure of the size of the market is the ratio of outstanding MTNs to the amount of outstanding public debt (MTNs plus public corporate bonds). According to this definition of market share, MTNs accounted for 16 percent of public corporate debt in 1992, compared with 9 percent in 1989. This ratio understates the size of the MTN market; however, because the market is still relatively new, and outstandings are growing rapidly.

An alternative measure of the size of the market is the volume of investment-grade MTN issuance as a percentage of total investment-grade debt issuance (MTNs plus underwritten straight bonds). By this definition, the share of investment-grade debt issued as MTNs rose from 18 percent in 1983 to a peak of 42 percent in 1990. In 1992, the ratio fell to 37 percent, a decline that mainly reflects the heavy volume of refinancing in the corporate bond market, especially in the nonfinancial sector. This ratio of debt issuance may overestimate the size of the MTN market because MTNs typically have shorter maturities than corporate bonds.

MTNs represent an increasingly important source of credit to nonfinancial corporations, as companies have shifted funding from alternative credit markets. In general, nonfinancial corporations that borrow in the MTN market have access to other major credit markets: corporate bonds, commercial paper, bank loans, and privately placed bonds. From 1989 through 1992, net borrowing by nonfinancial corporations in the MTN market increased $49 billion, while borrowing in the other four markets increased an estimated $102 billion. Notably, corporate borrowing in the public bond market rose $100 billion, while borrowing at banks fell $35 billion. The shift to long-term financing (MTNs and bonds) over this period is a typical, cyclical phenomenon that occurs in periods of slow economic growth and falling long term interest rates. However, some of the growth of the MTN market reflects a secular decline in the role of banks as financial intermediaries.

RECENT DEVELOPMENTS IN THE MTN MARKET

In recent years several changes have occurred in the MTN market as a result of innovations in other capital markets. Among the most important changes in the MTN market is the increasing use of "structured" MTNs, the increasing participation by banking organizations in the market, and the development of a system for book-entry clearing and settlement of MTN transactions. Also, foreign corporations have begun to use the MTN market more frequently since the adoption of SEC Rule 144A in April 1990.

Structured MTNs

In recent years, an increasing share of MTNs have been issued as part of structured transactions. In a structured MTN, a corporation issues an MTN and simultaneously enters into one or several swap agreements to transform the cash flows that it is obligated to make. The simplest type of structured MTN involves a "plain vanilla" interest rate swap. In such financing, a corporation might issue a three-year, floating-rate MTN that pays LIBOR plus a premium semiannually. At the same time, the corporation negotiates a swap transaction in which it agrees to pay a fixed rate of interest semiannually for three years in exchange for receiving LIBOR from a swap counterparty. As a result of the swap, the borrower has synthetically created a fixed-rate note because the floating-rate payments are offsetting. At first glance, structured transactions seem needlessly complicated. A corporation could simply issue a fixed-rate MTN. However, as a result of the swap transaction, the corporation may be able to borrow at a lower rate than it would pay on a fixed-rate note. Indeed, most MTN issuers decline to participate in structured financings unless they reduce borrowing costs at least 10 or 15 basis points. Issuers demand this compensation because, compared with conventional financings, structured financings involve additional expenses, such as legal and accounting costs and the cost of evaluating and monitoring the credit risk of the swap counterparty. For complicated structured transactions, most issuers require greater compensation.

Many structured transactions originate with investors through a reverse inquiry. This process begins when an investor has a demand for a security with specific risk characteristics. The desired security may not be available in the secondary market, and regulatory restrictions or bylaws prohibit some investors from using swaps, options, or futures to create synthetic securities. Through a reverse inquiry, an investor will use MTN agents to communicate its desires to MTN issuers. If an issuer agrees to the inquiry, the investor will obtain a security that is custom-tailored to its needs. The specific features of these transactions vary in response to changes in market conditions and investor preferences. For example, in 1991, many investors desired securities with interest rates that varied inversely with short-term market interest rates. In response to investor inquiries, several corporations issued "inverse floating-rate" MTNs that paid an interest rate of, for example, 12 percent minus LIBOR. At the time of the transaction, the issuers of inverse floating-rate MTNs usually entered into swap transactions to eliminate their exposure to falling interest rates.

While structured transactions in the MTN market often originate with investors, investment banks also put together such transactions. Most investment banks have specialists in derivative products who design securities to take advantage of temporary market opportunities. When an investment bank identifies an opportunity, it will inform investors and propose that they purchase a specialized security. If an investor tentatively agrees to the transaction, the MTN agents in the investment bank will contact an MTN issuer with the proposed structured transaction.

Most investors requires that issuers of structured MTNs have triple-A or double-A credit ratings. By dealing with highly rated issuers, the investor reduces the possibility that the value of the structured MTN will vary with the credit quality of the issuer. In limiting credit risk, the riskiness of the structured MTN mainly reflects the specific risk characteristics that the investor prefers. Consequently, federal agencies and supranational institutions, which have triple-A ratings, issue a large share of structured MTNs. The credit quality profile of issuers of structured MTNs has changed slightly in recent years, however, as some investors have become more willing to purchase structured MTNs from single-A corporations. In structured transactions with lower-rated borrowers, the investor receives a higher promised yield as compensation for taking on greater credit risk.

Market participants estimate that structured MTNs accounted for 20 percent to 30 percent of MTN volume in the first half of 1993, compared with less than 5 percent in the late 1980s. The growth of structured MTNs highlights the important role of derivative products in linking various domestic and international capital markets. Frequently, the issuers of structured MTNs are located in a different country from that of the investors.

The increasing volume of structured transactions is testimony to the flexibility of MTNs. When establishing MTN programs, issuers build flexibility into the documentation that will allow for a broad range of structured transactions. Once the documentation is in place, an issuer is able to reduce borrowing costs by responding quickly to temporary opportunities in the derivatives market. The flexibility of MTNs is also evident in the wide variety of structured MTNs that pay interest or repay principal according to unusual formulas. Some of the common structures include the following:

1) floating-rate MTNs tied to the federal funds rate, LIBOR, commercial paper rates, or the prime rate, many of which have included caps or floors on rate movements;

2) step-up MTNs, the interest rate on which increases after a set period;

3) LIBOR differential notes, which pay interest tied to the spread between, say, deutsche mark LIBOR and French franc LIBOR;

4) dual currency MTNs, which pay interest in one currency and principal in another;

5) equity-linked MTNs, which pay interest according to a formula based on an equity index, such as the Standard & Poor's 500 or the Nikkei; and

6) commodity-linked MTNs, which have interest tied to a price index or to the price of specific commodities such as oil or gold. The terms and features of structured MTNs continue to evolve in response to changes in the preferences of investors and developments in financial markets.

Bank Notes

Banking organizations are major participants in the MTN market. Like other corporations, bank holding companies must file registration documents with the SEC when issuing public securities. Consequently, the Federal Reserve survey captures MTNs issued by bank holding companies. Over the ten-year survey period, thirty-five bank holding companies raised funds in the MTN market, and from 1989 to 1992, outstanding MTNs of bank holding companies increased from $8.3 billion to $17.9 billion. Although most of these MTNs have senior status in relation to other debt outstanding, a few bank holding companies have issued subordinated MTNs. Subordinated MTNs of bank holding companies typically have long maturities of about ten years. Under regulatory capital requirements, subordinated debt with a maturity of five years or longer qualifies as tier 2 capital.

In contrast to public offerings by bank holding companies, securities issued by banks are exempt from registration under section 3(a)2 of the Securities Act of 1933. In recent years, a growing number of banks have issued exempt securities, called bank notes, that have characteristics in common with certificates of deposit (CDs), MTNs, and short-term bonds.

Like CDs, most bank notes are senior, unsecured debt obligations issued by the bank. In the event of the insolvency of the issuing institution, bank notes are likely to rank equal with deposits, except in states where deposits have priority over other debt obligations. As with institutional CDs, nearly all bank notes are sold to institutional investors in minimum denominations of $250,000 to $1 million. Bank notes are not covered by FDIC insurance, nor are they subject to FDIC insurance assessments. CDs, in contrast, are insured for $100,000 per depositor. Furthermore, in the event of a bank failure, the FDIC could choose to protect the financial interests of some or all depositors or other creditors without treating bank notes in the same manner.

Like MTNs, bank notes may be offered continuously or intermittently in relatively small amounts that typically range from $5 million to $25 million. In addition, as with MTNs, most medium-term bank notes have maturities that range from one to five years. However, ratings on senior bank notes are typically one notch higher than the ratings on senior MTNs, which are issued at the holding company level. Reflecting these differences in ratings and priority in the firms' capital structures, the yields on banks notes usually are significantly lower than the yields on MTNs of comparable maturity.

Some bank notes, which are similar to corporate bonds, are sold in large, underwritten, discrete offerings that range from $50 million to $1 billion. However, they differ from corporate bonds in that they are not registered with the SEC. From 1988 through 1992, banks issued $14.3 billion of underwritten, senior bank notes, including $7.8 billion in 1992. In the first half of 1993, they issued $6.3 billion.

Book-Entry Clearing and Settlement of MTNs

In the early and mid-1980s, high administrative costs deterred some issuers from establishing MTN programs. Among the most significant of the administrative costs were those arising from transferring physical securities to investors. These costs specifications included printing, delivery, safekeeping, messengers, insurance, and recordkeeping. Moreover, issuers incurred significant costs in the disbursement of interest and principal payments to each individual noteholder. According to market estimates, the direct costs of transferring physical securities range from $5 to $30 per transaction. For small offerings, the costs of physical delivery can add significantly to the all-in cost of borrowing. As a result, many issuers refused to sell MTNs in denominations of less than $1 million.

Since 1988, the costs of clearing and settlement of MTNs have decreased substantially as a computer-based system of book-entry record keeping has supplanted physical certificates when an MTN is issued under the book-entry system, an agent bank for the issuer uses a computer link with The Depository Trust Company (DTC) to enter the descriptive information and settlement details of the transaction. The sales agent receives a copy of the computer record from DTC, and the investor receives a trade confirmation from the sales agent and periodic ownership statements from the custodian bank, in lieu of physical certificates. Secondary market trades are likewise recorded with computer entries. Under the book-entry system, an issuer makes one wire transfer to DTC that covers all interest payments on each interest payment date. This payment process contrasts with the process for physical certificates in which issuers make separate payments to each investor. Similarly, under the book-entry system, when the MTN matures, the issuer makes only one funds transfer to DTC. The DTC book-entry process costs $4 for each issuance, and each participant in a transaction pays between $1.29 and $1.54 for subsequent deliveries in the primary and secondary markets. Besides reducing the direct cost of issuance, the book-entry system also lowers the likelihood of delayed delivery because of logistical problems and reduces the chances of failed trades arising from paperwork errors.

Book entry has become the preferred method of clearing and settlement in the MTN market. According to DTC, issuance of book-entry MTNs rose from $600 million in 1988 to $80 billion in 1992. Moreover, outstanding MTNs under the book-entry system amounted to $160 billion at year-end 1992, a total that includes 16,495 individual securities.

Borrowing by Foreign Entities in the MTN Market and SEC Rule 144A14

In the 1980s, SEC disclosure requirements associated with public offerings discouraged foreign corporations from issuing MTNs in the U.S. public market. For foreign corporations, the most burden some requirement is that financial statements conform to U.S. generally accepted accounting principles. Most foreign issuers would have to incur considerable legal and accounting expenses to meet this requirement, and many would have to disclose more information about their operations than is required in their home markets. The expense of registering securities and satisfying ongoing reporting requirements has also deterred foreign entities from borrowing in the U.S. market. Foreign issuers could avoid the costs of a public offering by selling MTNs in the U.S. private placement market. However, yields on most private placements included an illiquidity premium resulting from regulatory restrictions on trading.

The adoption of SEC Rule 144A in April 1990 effectively created an alternative market in which foreign corporations could gain access to U.S. investors without having to satisfy the disclosure requirements for public offerings. Rule 144A allows institutional investors to trade private placements among themselves with few restrictions. To protect less sophisticated investors, the SEC requires that 144A securities be sold only to "qualified institutional buyers," which own and invest in a minimum of $100 million in securities. This definition is broad enough to include most of the institutions that buy MTNs, such as banks and bank trust departments, insurance companies, pension funds, mutual funds, investment advisers, and state and local governments.15 A foreign issuer of a 144A security must provide, upon demand by a security holder or potential purchaser, a brief description of the business and financial statements for the three most recent fiscal years, which can be in the accounting format used in the issuer's home country. Privately placed MTNs are an example of a security that may be eligible for resale under Rule 144A.

Since the adoption of Rule 144A, issuance of MTNs by foreign corporations in the U.S. private market has increased markedly. According to the Securities Data Corporation, issuance increased from $2.2 billion in 1990 to $10 billion in 1992. In general, MTNs issued by foreign corporations under Rule 144A have similar characteristics to those sold by U.S. corporations in the public market. Both typically are dollar denominated and investment grade, with standard covenants.

Developments in the Distribution of MTNs

In the early and mid-1980s, the major difference between MTNs and corporate bonds was in their primary method of distribution: Typically, agents placed MTNs in relatively small amounts continuously or intermittently, while underwriters placed large, discrete amounts of corporate bonds. This strict classification no longer applies, however. A growing number of MTN offerings have the characteristics of traditional corporate bonds, and regional dealers now sell a significant percentage of MTNs. Thus, as the MTN market has matured, it has become harder to define the securities and to describe their mode of distribution.

Large, discrete offerings of medium-term notes in the U.S. corporate market, 1984-92

Principal Transactions

One important change in the distribution process is that a larger share of MTNs are now sold on a principal basis, rather than on an agented basis. In a principal transaction, the MTN dealer purchases an MTN for its own account and later resells it to investors. In a "riskless principal" transaction, when the dealer buys the MTN, it has already lined up an investor that has agreed to the terms of the resale. Riskless principal transactions often involve structured MTNs. In other principal transactions, dealers underwrite MTNs when they have not lined up investors but expect to do so easily and quickly.

Large, Discrete Offerings

Corporations now more often sell MTNs that are nearly indistinguishable from corporate bond offerings. These MTN offerings typically have large face amounts of $100 million or more, the typical size of corporate bond offerings. They are sold on an underwritten basis, and they often have relatively long maturities of ten or thirty years. Furthermore, announcements of such offerings appear along with announcements of corporate bond offerings in financial publications. In 1992, thirtyone corporations issued $7.14 billion of MTNs in large, discrete, underwritten offerings, compared with less than $1 billion between 1983 and 1989.

Despite the similarities to corporate bonds, these large, discrete, underwritten securities technically are MTNs because they are issued from MTN shelf registrations. To most investors, this technical difference is largely irrelevant because the securities have the essential features of corporate bonds. As a result, the securities reportedly do not command a yield premium relative to the yield on corporate bonds.

As large, discrete offerings of MTNs have become more common, the distinction between MTNs and corporate bonds has blurred. As a result, the arguments for financing with MTNs have become more compelling. By setting up an MTN program, a corporation does not give up the advantages of issuing large, underwritten securities that typically would be accomplished with a corporate bond offering. However, unlike a shelf registration for corporate bonds, an MTN program gives the corporation the flexibility to issue in small amounts continuously and to participate more actively in structured transactions.

Distribution through Regional Dealers

Through the mid-1980s, the major New York investment banks distributed nearly all MTNs to investors. As the market has matured, regional dealers have placed an increasing volume of MTNs. According to market estimates, placements through regional dealers now account for 5 to 15 percent of MTN issuance volume. In these placements, regional dealers receive information about issuers' offering rate schedules from MTN agents. In turn, the regional dealers communicate this information to their investor clients. When an investor buys an MTN through a regional dealer; the regional dealer receives a selling concession from the MTN agent. Placements through regional dealers improves efficiency in the market by broadening the investor base for MTNs. Many regional dealers have contacts with smaller institutional investors, such as small banks, municipalities, and individuals with high net worth, that represent a relatively stable source of funding.

Distribution of MTNs with Small Denominations to "Retail" Investors

When the market first developed, most MTNs were sold primarily to institutional investors. Indeed, most MTN programs had minimum denominations of $100,000, which precludes small investors, sometimes called retail investors, from purchasing MTNs. In addition, some issuers declined to issue MTNs in denominations below $1 million because bookkeeping and administrative costs become more burdensome with smaller offerings. In recent years, however, book-entry clearing through DTC and advances in computer bookkeeping have decreased the cost of issuing in small denominations. As a result, many issuers have registered MTN programs with minimum denominations of $1,000, the standard in the corporate bond market. Although most MTNs are still sold to institutional investors, the lowering of minimum denominations has broadened the investor base to include smaller investors. Regional dealers place a significant proportion of the smaller offerings with small institutional investors.

Several MTN programs have recently been designed specifically to tap the retail market without significantly increasing the administrative costs to issuers. The process of issuing retail MTNs may differ slightly from that of MTNs sold to institutions. In one type of retail MTN program, an issuer will post rates weekly with retail brokers. For example, an issuer might post a rate of 4 percent for two-year MTNs and 5 percent for five-year MTNs. During the week that these rates are posted, regional brokerage firms market the securities to retail investors, who place orders in minimum denominations of $1,000. At the end of the week, the regional brokerage firms will contact the corporate issuer and indicate the aggregate volume of orders for notes at each maturity, and the corporation will issue one security at each maturity. In the example, several hundred retail investors could place orders for MTNs with maturities of two and five years, but the administrative costs for the corporate issuer would reflect only two issues from the shelf registration. While this system has the potential to broaden the investor base for MTNs, the size of the retail MTN market is still small relative to the institutional market.

Although the size of MTN offerings has always varied considerably; the variation has become wider as a result of developments in the distribution of MTNs. In 1992, the size of MTN offerings ranged from less than $5,000 to more than $500 million. In terms of dollar volume, about 65 percent of MTNs had an issue size between $5 million and $100 million. However, several firms have issued a large volume of MTNs with denominations of less than $5 million. While these offerings account for less than 5 percent of the dollar volume of total proceeds, they represent 45 percent of the number of issues.

CHAPTER 2

EURO-MTNs

MTNs have become a major source offinancingin international financial markets, particularly in the Euro-market. Like Euro-bonds, Euro-MTNs are not subject to national regulations, such as registration requirements. However, Euro-MTNs and Euro-bonds can be sold throughout the world, the major underwriters and dealers are located in London, where most offerings are distributed. Although the first Euro-MTN program was established in 1986, the market represented a minor source of financing throughout the 1980s. In the 1990s, the Euro-MTN market has grown at a phenomenal rate, with outstandings increasing from less than $10 billion in early 1990 to $68 billion in May 1993. New borrowers account for most of this growth, as a majority of the 190 entities that have established Euro-MTN programs did so in the 1990s. As in the U.S. market, flexibility is the driving force behind the rapid growth of the Euro-MTN market. Under a single documentation framework, an issuer with a Euro-MTN program has great flexibility in the size, currency denomination, and structure of offerings. Further-more, reverse inquiry gives issuers of Euro-MTNs the opportunity to reduce funding costs by responding to investor preferences. The characteristics of Euro-MTNs are similar, but not identical, to MTNs issued in the U.S. market. In both markets, most MTNs are issued with investment grade credit ratings, but the ratings on Euro-MTNs tend to be higher. In 1992, for example, 68 percent of Euro-MTNs had Aaa or Aa ratings, compared with 13 percent of U.S. corporate MTNs. In both markets, most offerings have maturities of one to five years. However, offerings with maturities longer than ten years account for a smaller percentage of the Euro-market than of the U.S. market. In both markets, dealers have committed to provide liquidity in the secondary market, but by most accounts the Euro-market is less liquid.

In many ways, the Euro-MTN market is more diverse than the U.S. market. For example, the range of currency denominations of Euro-MTNs is broader, as would be expected. The Euro-market also accommodates a broader cross-section of borrowers, both in terms of the country of origin and the type of borrower, which includes sovereign countries, supranational institutions, financial institutions, and industrial companies. Similarly, Euro-MTNs have a more diverse investor base, but the market is not as deep as the U.S. market.

In several respects, the evolution of the Euro-MTN market has paralleled that of the U.S. market.

Two of the more important developments have been the growth of structured Euro-MTNs and the emergence of large, discrete offerings. Structured transactions represent 50 percent to 60 percent of Euro-MTN issues, compared with 20 percent to 30 percent in the U.S. market. In the Euro-MTN market, many of the structured transactions involve a currency swap in which the borrower issues an MTN that pays interest and principal in one currency and simultaneously agrees to a swap contract that transforms required cash flows to another currency. Most structured Euro-MTNs arise from investor demand for debt instruments that is otherwise unavailable in the public markets. To be able to respond to investor driven structured transactions, issuers typically build flexibility into their Euro-MTN programs. Most programs allow for issuance of MTNs with unusual interest payments in a broad spectrum of currencies and with a variety of options.

Large, discrete offerings of Euro-MTNs first appeared in 1991, and about forty of these offerings occurred in 1992. They are similar to Euro-bonds in that they are underwritten and are often syndicated using the fixed-price reoffering method. As a result of this development, the distinction between Euro-bonds and Euro-MTNs has blurred, just as the distinctions between corporate bonds and MTNs has blurred in the U.S. market.

The easing of regulatory restrictions by foreign central banks has played an important role in the growth of the Euro-MTN market. For example, over the past year MTNs denominated in deutsche marks have emerged as a major sector in the Euro-market as a result of regulatory changes made by the Bundesbank in August 1992. Under the previous rules, foreign borrowers could only issue debt denominated in deutsche marks through German subsidiaries or other German financial firms, and maturities could not be shorter than two years. Debt denominated in deutsche marks also had to be listed on a German exchange, and these offerings were subject to German law, clearing, and payment procedures. These rules effectively precluded issuers from establishing multicurrency Euro-MTN programs with a deutsche mark option.

In the August 1992 deregulation, the Bundes-bank removed the minimum maturity requirement on debt denominated in deutsche marks issued by foreign nonbanks, and it eliminated or simplified issuance procedures for all issuers. However, the new rules require that a "German bank" act as an arranger or dealer, the definition is broad enough to include German branches and subsidiaries of foreign banks.

The arranger is required to notify the Bundesbank monthly of the volume and frequency of issues denominated in deutsche marks. As a result of the Bundesbank's de-regulation, from 1991 to 1992, the share of Euro-MTN offerings denominated in deutsche marks increased from 1.4 percent to 4.8 percent, while the volume of issuance in deutsche marks rose from $268 million to $1.69 billion. Other central banks have instituted similar liberalizations that may result in rapid growth of MTNs denominated in other currencies, such as the Swiss franc and the French franc.

The Primary Market

MTN issues are arranged within a program. A continuous MTN programme is established with a specified issue limit, and sizes can vary from $100 million to $5,000 million or more. Within the programme MTNs can be issued at any time, daily if required. The programme is similar to a revolving loan facility; as maturing notes are redeemed, new notes can be issued. The issuer usually specifies the maturity of each note issue within a programme, but cannot exceed the total limit of the program.

EXAMPLE 21.1 ABC plc

- ABC plc establishes a five-year $200 million MTN programme and immediately issues the following notes: $50 million of notes with an one-year maturity $70 million of notes with a five-year maturity

ABC plc can still issue a further $80 million of notes; however in one year's time when $50 million of notes mature, it will be able to issue a further $50 million if required. The total amount in issue at any one time never rises above $200 million.

The first step for the borrower is to arrange shelf registration with the SEC. This ensures the widest possible market for the programme; there are also no resale or transfer restrictions on the bonds themselves. The shelf registration identifies the investment bank or banks that will be acting as agents for the programme and who will distribute the paper to the market. A domestic program may have only one agent bank, although two to four banks are typical. Global and Euro-MTN programmes usually have more agent banks. Once registration is complete the borrower issues a prospectus supplement detailing the terms and conditions of the programme. Often a draft prospectus is issued first, and only issued in final once the issuing bank has gauged market reaction. A draft prospectus is known as a red herring. Within a programme a borrower may also issue conventional corporate bonds, underwritten by an investment bank, but there is none of the flexibility available compared to an MTN issue, which can be arranged at very short notice, so conventional bond offerings within a programme are rare.

The exact date of a particular maturity issue is not always known at the time the program is announced, so yields are often given as a spread over the equivalent maturity government bond. If the borrower has a particular interest to tap the market at specific points of the yield curve, the spread offered at that point is increased in order to attract investors. Once the required funds have been raised, offer spreads are usually reduced. If the full amount stated in the registration details is raised, US domestic market borrowers need to file a new registration with the SEC. The size of individual issues within a programme varies with the funding strategy of the borrower. Certain companies have a preference to raise large amounts at once, say $100 to $200 milion, and raise funds using fewer issues. This also maintains a "scarcity value" for their paper compared to borrowers who tap the market more frequently. Other companies adopt the opposite approach, with small size issues of between $5 to $10 million spread over more dates.

Domestic market MTNs are primarily offered on an agency basis, although issues within a program are sometimes sold using other methods. Agent banks sometimes acquire the paper for their own book, trading it later in the secondary market. Specific issues may be underwritten by an agent bank, or sold directly to investors by the corporate treasury arm of the borrowing company.

The main issuers of MTNs in the US market are:

- general finance companies, including automobile finance companies, business credit institutions and securities houses;
- banks, both domestic and foreign; governments and government agencies; supranational bodies such as the World Bank;
- domestic industrial and commercial companies, primarily motor car and other industrial manufacturing companies, telecommunications companies and other utilities;
- savings and loan institutions.

During the 1980s, the MTN market was dominated by financial institutions, accounting for over 90% of issue volume. This share was reduced to approximately 70% by 1992 (Crabbe 1992), the remainder of the issues being accounted for by other categories of borrower.

There is a large investor demand in the US for high-quality corporate paper, much more so than in Europe where the majority of bonds are issued by financial companies. This demand is particularly great at the short to medium-term maturity end. As the market has a large number of issuers, investors are able to select issues that meet their requirements for maturity and credit rating precisely. The main investors are:

- investment companies;
- insurance companies;

- banks;
- savings and loan institutions;
- corporate treasury departments;
- state institutions.

It can be seen that the investor base is very similar to the issuer base!

All the main US investment banks make markets in MTNs, including Merrill Lynch, Goldman Sachs, Morgan Stanley, CSFB and Salomon Smith Barney. In the UK active market makers in MTNs include RBS Financial Markets and Barclays Capital.

MTNs and corporate bonds

A company wishing to raise a quantity of medium-term or long-term capital over a period of time has the choice of issuing MTNs or long-dated bonds. An MTN programme is a series of issues over time, matching the issuer's funding requirement, and therefore should be preferred over a bond by companies that do not need all the funding at once, nor for the full duration of the programme. Corporate bonds are preferred where funds are required immediately. They are also a better choice for issuers that expect interest rates to rise in the near future and wish to lock in a fixed borrowing rate for all the funds required. The decision on whether to raise finance using MTNs or corporate bonds will be taken after consideration of the interest cost and flexibility offered by each instrument. That MTNs offer financing advantages over conventional bonds under certain circumstances is reflected in the growth and current size of the market; however the same borrowers are evident in both markets, which implies that both instruments possess advantages over the other under specific conditions.

The main difference between MTNs and corporate bonds is the process by which they are sold and distributed. There are other differentiating features, however. MTNs are almost invariably sold at par on the issue, whereas conventional bonds are usually offered at a slight discount to par. The proceeds on the day of issue are settled on the same day for MTNs (making them similar to money market instruments in this respect), while the settlement for new issue traditional bonds is the following day, or T+3 for international issues. In the US market, corporate bonds pay semi-annual coupon on either the 1st or the 15th of the month; the latter is identical to Treasury securities. MTNs, however, have coupon dates payable on a fixed cycle basis, irrespective of their issue or maturity date. This payment convention means that MTNs have a long or short first coupon, and a short final coupon, whereas conventional bonds would always have a regular final coupon. MTNs pay interest on a 30/360 day count basis, similar to Eurobonds and US domestic corporate bonds.

EXAMPLE 21.2

- An MTN programme pays semi-annual interest on 1 June and 1 December each year and on maturity of the individual note. An issue within the programme of £10 million 6.75% bonds with a two-year maturity on 1 July would pay a short first coupon of £281,250 on the first coupon date in December, regular coupons of £337,500 on the next three coupon dates and a short final coupon of £56,250 on the maturity date.

Issue size and liquidity

The size of an issue has the most significant impact on the relative cost of an MTN issue versus a straight bond. For large issues, which are regarded as nominal amounts of over $400 million borrowed over a medium or long term, the all-in cost of a straight bond issue is generally lower than the all-in cost of an MTN programme. This reflects the economies of scale that may be achieved when issuing such an amount on one date, as well as the greater secondary market liquidity of larger-sized issues. For this reason borrowers who have a heavy funding requirement for a specific period in time will usually prefer to raise the funds with a straight bond issue. The liquidity premium associated with large volume issues is not known with certainty, but is estimated at around 5 to 10 basis points (Kitter 1999); for large amounts this saving would be substantial. However, this premium is indicative of the improved liquidity in the MTN market.

Another factor that borrowers consider is the cost saving associated with the distribution process for MTNs. To fully place a large bond issue, perhaps because the whole issue has not been taken up by customers, the bond may need to be offered at a higher yield, which raises the coupon for the borrower. If an individual bond within an MTN programme is not fully placed, borrowers have the option of raising the remaining sum by offering another bond at a different maturity, or as part of a different structure to another group of investors. Since, all the funding from an MTN issue need, not be priced at the coupon required by the marginal buyers, and may be raised at slightly different times, the financing costs for MTNs are often below those of a straight bond issue.

MTN issue options

The flexibility afforded by an MTN programme is often behind the corporate treasurer's decision to employ them as funding instruments, irrespective of the interest cost advantage of straight bonds. A major flexibility of MTNs is their term to maturity. It is common for MTNs to be issued with non-standard terms to maturity, such as 15 months, 3.5 years and so on. This contrasts with straight bonds which are usually issued with maturities of 2, 5, 7, 10, and 30 years in the US market and often just 5 or 10 years in the Euro market.

This makes MTNs the preferred instrument when exact maturity terms are required, for example when a borrower wishes to precisely match assets with liabilities. The cost of a bond underwriting makes small issues prohibitively expensive, and it is rare to see a bond offered with total nominal value outstanding of less than $100–150 million. If a corporate has a requirement for a smaller amount, it is more practical to issue an MTN. Some individual issues within MTN programs have been for as little as $5 million; again, this flexibility allows companies to meet their funding requirements more precisely.

A continuous program of MTN issues has the potential benefit of a lower average interest cost, compared to a single straight bond issue. For example, over a six-month period, five MTN issues of $20 million each may have a lower average interest cost than a single issue of $100 million in the same period. This may compensate for the lower interest cost of straight bonds mentioned earlier, and is more likely during periods of relatively high interest rate volatility.

Once a programme has secured shelf registration, the process of issuing an MTN can be very quick, often less than half a day. This enables agent banks to issue debt on behalf of a borrower in response to specific investor requirements, or to changes in the yield or swap curves. In fact a substantial amount of MTN issues originate as a result of reverse enquiry. This is when investors have a requirement for debt products of a certain maturity and credit quality. For example a bond fund manager may be interested in 10-year paper with an A-rating, paying at least 50 basis points above the government yield. This is detailed to their investment bank, who is also an MTN agent bank, and if the requirements suit the borrower, there will be an issue of bonds from within the borrower's MTN program. Bonds issued in response to reverse enquiry are often the most exotic instruments in the MTN market, due to investor requirements. This includes some of the example bonds described later in this chapter. This flexibility again makes MTNs an attractive option for borrowers.

Finally, a significant volume of MTNs are placed privately with investors, directly or via an agent bank. An advantage of this distribution method is that it avoids publicity, as the transaction details may be known only to the investor and borrower (and agent). Companies may wish to avoid raising funds in the bond market, and the publicity associated with this, during times of market correction or volatility, or if they are in a state of financial distress. This makes the MTN market particularly attractive during recessions and market downturns. The private placement market is also used by overseas borrowers that seek to place paper in the US market, as SEC approval is only required for a public offering. However, generally the financing costs are lower in the public market than the private placement market, with its lower liquidity, so the majority of domestic borrowers use the public offering method.

Issue mechanism

The issue process

Issuers of MTNs usually specify an Issuing and Paying Agent (IPA) responsible for providing investors with the ability to present interest coupons and notes in various locations around the world. The IPA function required for medium term note programmes is usually viewed as a processing and administration function, and is therefore normally of most interest to the settlements and processing areas of an issuing organisation.

Once an agent has been selected as the IPA for a new programme, and draft legal documentation is available, it will allocate the transaction to a documentation department.

This department will review the documentation from a legal perspective, and often calls in external legal firms to assist in the review. However the primary functions that the IPA performs is to receive an issuer's instructions, arrange for the issuance of the security to the relevant dealer via the international clearing systems, and then to service the security throughout it's term. Generally Euro-MTN transactions are represented by single security, known as the global note. When an issuer and underwriting bank agree a new transaction, both parties will advise the IPA of the transaction details, such as the currency, amount, issue date, interest basis, maturity, issue price and so on. Although the dealer is not obligated to advise the IPA of the trade details, market practices are such that this has now become the norm. The IPA issues the security after receiving the instructions of the issuer together with an authorized pricing supplement, which is the term sheet listing the issue details. Once trade details have been received the IPA will contact Euroclear and Clearstream and advise them of the trade information. The clearing systems will then advise the IPA of the unique security codes, known as International Securities Identification Number (ISIN) and the Common Code, which are used to identify the security during its term. The IPA will then input the trade and settlement information into a "new issuance account", while the dealer will input its instructions into the relevant clearing system. The IPA's instruction will be a securities delivery versus payment instruction, while the dealer's will be a securities receipt versus payment instruction. Processing the transaction on this basis means that all parties are protected and that the securities will never be issued unless the correct issue proceeds are paid. On the actual issuance date, the IPA will receive the cash proceeds from the dealer and will make onward payment to the issuer; it also creates the global note that represents the issue and delivers this to the common depositary for Euroclear and Clearstream. The common depositary is usually called the custodian.

Servicing the issue

The IPA is responsible for servicing the MTN during its life. Approximately ten business days before an interest payment date, or before the maturity date of an issue, it will advise the issuer of the forthcoming interest payment and provide them with payment details for the repayment amount due. On the installment due date, the IPA will pay the clearing system(s) the amount due to the investors holding via their computer systems, and will also credit the proceeds to the relevant investor's account. Investors holding securities outside of a clearing system have to physically present their EMTNs (and Eurobonds as well) for payment at one of the designated paying agents for the issue.

The activities described above summarise the core function that is performed by an IPA; in addition throughout the life of a programme the IPA also performs numerous other activities on behalf of the issuer. Such activities include:

- being responsible for the safekeeping of the master global notes;
- the submission of any reports required by regulatory entities, such as the Bank of England, Japanese Ministry of Finance and the Bundesbank;
- acting as the calculation agent service for cash flows paid by floating rate, indexed linked, and dual-currency note issues;
- arranging for the listing of the note issues at a relevant stock exchange; arranging for the publication of notices in the financial press; maintaining comprehensive details of all transactions on its computer systems; and

responding to external enquiries, such as requests made by auditors.

The Secondary Market

A liquid secondary market in MTNs was first established in the US market by Merrill Lynch which undertook to quote bid prices to any investor wishing to sell MTNs before maturity provided that the investor had originally bought the notes through them. In other words Merrill Lynch was guaranteeing a secondary market to borrowers that issued notes through it. This undertaking was repeated by other banks, resulting in a market that is now both large and liquid. That said, MTNs are not actively traded, and market makers do not quote real-time prices on dealing screens. The relatively low volume of secondary market trading stems from a disinclination of investors to sell notes they have bought, rather than a lack of market liquidity.

There is a wide range of maturities available for MTNs in the secondary market. The maturity of individual issues reflects the funding requirements of their issuers; for example bonds issued by motor car finance companies usually match the duration of loans to their customers, so they tend to have three-year to five-year maturities. Bonds issued by industrial and manufacturing companies have longer maturities.

The yield on MTNs is a function of the credit quality of the issuer, as well as the liquidity of the paper in the secondary market and market maker's support. In the US domestic market, MTNs are quoted on a yield basis, often as a spread over the equivalent maturity Treasury security. The highest yield spread is observed on the lowest rated bonds.

The MTN market is a major instrument of corporate finance in the US market, and is growing in importance in the Euro market. An indication of its significance is given by its growing share of total investment-grade debt issuance. For instance in the US debt market, MTNs accounted for 47% of total investment grade debt issued in 1995, where total debt comprised MTNs and straight bond issues. This is an increase from around 12% in the early 1980s.

Credit rating MTNs are unsecured debt. A would be issuer of MTNs will usually seek a credit rating for its issue from one or more of the main rating agencies such as Moody's or Standard & Poor's. The rating is given by the agency for a specific amount of possible new debt; should the issuer decided to increase the total amount of MTNs in issue it will need to seek a review of its credit rating. As MTNs are unsecured paper only the higher rated issuers, with an "investment grade" rating for their debt, are usually able to embark on a revolving facility. Although there are "junk" rated MTNs, there is no liquid market in them, and they account for less than 1% of outstanding volume. Companies issuing MTNs generally have high ratings within the "investment grade" category. During 1995, $65 billion of the $99 billion of MTNs issued in the US domestic market represented debt with a rating of "A" or higher, while at the end of that year approximately 98% of the outstanding debt in the US market was rated at investment grade level.

EXAMPLE

Reverse FRN with swap

- A subsidiary of a global integrated banking house that engages in investment activity requires US dollar funding. A proportion of its funds is raised as part of a $5 billion Euro-MTN programme. Due to demand for sterling assets, they issue a five-year pounds sterling reverse floating rate medium-term note as part of the MTN programme, with the following details. Issue size £15 million Issue date 20 January 1998 Maturity 21 January 2003 Rate payable 9% from 20/1/98 to 20/7/98 19% – (2 × LIBOR6mo) after that to maturity Price at issue 99.92

Proceeds £14,988,000 As the issuer requires US dollar funding, it swaps the proceeds into dollars in the market in a cross-currency swap, and pays US dollar three-month Libor for this funding. On termination, the original currencies are swapped back and the note redeemed.

The Euro-MTN market

The development of a market in offshore or internationally-traded MTNs was originally due to US companies seeking sources of finance overseas. The Euro-MTN market has since expanded dramatically and it is now an important source of corporate funding for US, European, Japanese and Asian domiciled companies. Euro-MTNs trade essentially as Eurobonds, that is they are international bonds that can be bought and sold across international boundaries. There is also a domestic market in MTNs in the UK, France, Germany and several other European countries, as well as Japan. The main trading centre is in London, where most of the major underwriters and market making banks trade out of. The growth of the Euro market has been even more rapid than the US one, rising from approximately $10 billion in 1990 to just under $500 billion in 1998. The flexibility of an MTN programme, which was behind much of the growth in the US domestic market, is the key reason behind the expansion of the Euro market. Euro-MTNs are essentially identical to MTNs in the US domestic market, with the key exception that they are not subject to national regulations or national registration requirements. The issuer base in the Euro market is much more concentrated among financial institutions and banks, and there is a lower appetite for lower-grade credit quality paper. In 1998 over 65% of Euro-MTNs were rated at AAA or AA, compared to just 13% of domestic US MTNs. Another slight difference is in the maturity structure; most Euro-MTNs have maturities of 5 to

10 years, and it is rare to encounter maturities of 30 years. However, there is a diverse range of structured Euro-MTNs in the market, according to Roland in 1999 structured transactions account for up to 60% of Euro-MTN issues, compared to under half of that in the US market. As one might expect, currency swap structures such as those described in Example are more common in the Euro market; note that the bonds in that example are part of the Euro-MTN program of a major integrated banking house.

Structured MTNs The application of financial engineering techniques has resulted in the introduction of exotic MTN structures. As a result both borrowers and investors have had their requirements met precisely through the use of tailor-made bond structures. Put simply, in a structured MTN, the borrowing company issues an MTN, which may or may not be a plain vanilla instrument itself, that is part of a swap agreement that changes the nature of the interest payments that the borrower makes. The first structured notes involved the issue of a conventional MTN in conjunction with an interest-rate swap. If the MTN was a fixed-coupon bond, the issuer would enter into an interest-rate swap whereby it received fixed interest and paid floating-rate interest; the end result would be that the issuer now had a floating-rate interest rate liability and, not a fixed-rate one. The relevant swap terms are identical to the MTN ones, that is the fixed-rate payments are on the same date as the MTN coupon dates, and on the same interest basis. The borrower might do this because such an arrangement saves it interest payments not available through the issue of a straight floating-rate MTN. For borrowers, the primary motivation for entering into structured note arrangements is because a reduction in interest costs can be achieved. The interest savings must be sufficient to offset the increased transaction costs of structured deals, because these frequently require additional tax, accounting and legal advice, which may be supplied by the agent bank or by a separate advisory firm. The flexibility of the MTN market has resulted in many structured transactions being created as a result of a reverse enquiry. An investor who has an interest in acquiring an instrument with specific terms, such as a link to an exotic exchange rate, equity index or commodity, may not be able to meet their requirements in the conventional market. If, via an agent bank, a borrower is able to issue an instrument that meets the specific needs of the enquiry, the investor will be able to purchase an instrument that fulfills its requirements precisely. The establishment of the inverse-floater MTN market in the US in the early 1990s was in response to investor needs; the issuer's of inverse floaters usually hedged their interest-rate risk exposure in the swap market. The other drivers of structured deals are the investment banks themselves, who may present an idea for a particular deal to their investor clients. Often this occurs when the structured finance team at the bank has spotted an area of the market where value may be obtained for the client, or a price anomaly may be exploited. According to Crabbe (1993), structured deals in the US market accounted for between 20% to 30% of MTN issue volume in the first six months of 1993, from a figure of under 5% ten years previously. The growth of structured deals is further evidence of the flexibility of the MTN market, although of course many of the structures have also been observed in the conventional bond market. In the remainder of this section we present examples of structured MTNs that have been issued as part of a global US dollar Euro-MTN programme by an investment banking group. They illustrate the wide range of features available to investors; in fact it is probably accurate to say that the range of arrangements available is limited only by market participants' imagination.

MANAGED BUY/SELL PROGRAMS

The term "Bank Trade" or "Managed Buy/Sell Program" represents a private category of investments that are not available on the open market.

This special type of trade is part of the process that brings International Bank Instruments from the Primary Market to the Secondary Market, usually involving Medium Term Notes (MTNs). Sometimes intermediaries refers to these as "Private Placement Programs" (PPPs), although that is a broad category of non-public investments includes many other investments besides just Bank Trades.

These are private "invitation only" investments. They are not available to the general public, which is why regulatory bodies who govern investments for the general public state that these programs do not exist. There are only five "Tier 1" Large Floors (Platforms) in the world. There are over 100 sub-floors or "Tier 2" or "Tier 3" groups that claim to be "Platforms", but they all bring the files back to the top. Managed Buy-Sell Programs are unlike any other investment because the returns are not speculative but are contractual, thereby making them immune to negative public market conditions.

Trading does not take place in the US, but occurs primarily in Europe (London, Zurich, Geneva) and Asia (Hong Kong, Singapore, Taiwan) among top-tier, AAA rated transaction banks such as JP Morgan Chase, Credit Suisse, Barclays, HSBC, Standard Chartered, and others. They generally are only available to Ultra High-Net-Worth Individuals or qualified Institutional Investors and only occur at the upper echelons of the world financial system. These are by invitation only are not available to the general public. For this reason, Financial Planners and Financial Advisors are not privy to these investments.

Even the transaction banks who execute the managed buy/sell trades do not offer these programs to their Private Wealth clients because of disintermediation, because once an investor gets access to these Manage Buy/Sell programs with high contractual returns and no risk to investment principal, none of the other financial products offered by Private Wealth Managers seem appealing.

The returns can be contractually as high as double-digit monthly returns and the capital is not put at risk in the trading. With "Large Cap" Programs ($100 million USD or more), the Investor's capital never even leaves their own bank account, as the investor is acting only as a 3rd party investment partner for the Trade Platforms. However, with "Small Cap" Programs ($1 million USD to $99 million USD) the investors usually have to move their funds to the licensed asset manager so that they can internally "piggyback" on the larger trades

Traders and Transaction Banks cannot legally trade their own funds. Therefore, to satisfy the rigid International Banking Regulations that govern this process, the Trade Platform must have 3rd party investors. The Platform is able to "block" the investor funds at the investor's existing bank account, becoming a Blocked Cash Funds Instrument. The Platform then monetizes or gets a loan against the Blocked Cash Funds Instrument and uses those monetization proceeds for the trading, usually at a Loan to Value (LTV) of about 85%. This is why only Investors with cash funds at highly rated banks will qualify to being invited into a Managed Buy/Sell Trade Program. Investors with funds in poorly rated banks will be rejected because a Blocked Cash Funds Instrument from a poorly rated bank would have a very low LTV ratio.

The fees and expenses associated with monetizing blocked funds can be in the 7 figures, which is why Small Cap investors have to piggyback on larger investors in order to be able to get into a real trade program. The trade proceeds are used to repay the monetization loan and to disburse profits to the Platform and the 3rd party Investor.

There are 40 international banking weeks in one 12 month calendar year, so the trade contracts are usually for 1 year (40 banking weeks). During that period of time, the Investor funds simply sit in the Investor/Client's own bank account and are blocked from being withdrawn until the end of the Trade Contract.

These bank trades are regulated by strict guidelines established by the International Chamber of Commerce (ICC), the Federal Reserve, European Central Bank, the Bank of International Settlement (BIS) and both Traders and participating financial institutions require special licenses in order to participate.

Intermediaries in the form of a Facilitator and a Program Manager/Intake Officer serve to pre-qualify investors, answer their questions, and get all the necessary compliance documents. After the Know-Your-Customer (KYC) Anti Money-Laundering (AML) compliance documents are submitted by the Applicant and accepted by the Platform, the Applicant will then receive a call directly from the Platform's Compliance Officer to review the KYC and to get the Asset Management Agreement (Trade Contract) which details terms of the trade program.

Due to the Trade Platform's strict non-solicitation rules, the Applicant has to go through Intermediaries in order to make the connection to the Platform, but once that connection is made, all communication is direct between the Platform and the Applicant.

Due diligence can be undertaken by the Investor only after they have passed compliance and have received the Asset Management Agreement from the Platform stipulating the terms and procedures. This gives the Investor full transparency and makes due diligence very easy.

The International Monetary Fund (IMF) monitors all trades and assigns each Trade Contract a serial number/ tracking code. The serial number of that contract and the banking license of the Trader can easily be verified by the Investor's own banker. After reviewing the contract and performing banker due diligence, the Investor then decides if they want to move forward or not. Because of this, the Investor has full transparency before making any decisions.

The "United States Department of the Treasury" (US Treasury), fulfilling its responsibilities under the Bretton Woods Agreement, developed the Medium Term Note (MTN) by employing established European financing methods through which banks and financial institutions commonly finance long-term loans by selling Letters of Credit or Bank Notes of medium term to provide funding for loans.

The MTN bank issues are debt instruments that are legally allowed to be excluded from the debit side of their ledger or "off-balance sheet", but count towards the bank's capital reserves. Funds received by issuing these instruments rank at equal rate with depositors accounts, but these are long-term "contractual obligations" and as such are allowed to be listed in the footnotes instead of on the balance sheet itself.

As banks have the ability to borrow funds on a leveraged ratio against their capital reserves, in order to engage in fractional reserve lending, this method of financing can be very profitable.

In the post World War II era, the Bretton Woods Agreement created a stable international financial system and a mechanism to finance macroeconomic projects to re-build parts of Asia and Western Europe. The US Treasury and the "Federal Reserve System" (Federal Reserve) developed an instrument that may be traded to create new credit and that credit would be used in specific approved macroeconomic projects, allowing such funds and credit to be applied in geographical areas requiring credit and cash infusions to survive and grow.

While that understanding or intent remains true today, it is no longer always a necessary requirement to involve an economic project / humanitarian project. Investors can engage in either wealth creation or project funding, depending on the client's goal and the terms of the trade program.

The contracts to purchase and sell these MTNs are managed and/or approved by the US Treasury and are administered by prime US and European bank syndicates.

The US Treasury or the Federal Reserve may price these instruments at whatever price is necessary to provide the needed new credit in the geographical location or for the project(s) for which they have been approved.

Not all applicants or projects are approved. Both the applicant and the funds that will be used to purchase and sell the financial instruments must be screened according to US Patriot Act and Anti-Money Laundering (AML) Guidelines and their European equivalents.

Generally, there is just one Investor Principal (or Asset Provider). That Principal is the owner of the Funds and the Principal is the Applicant to the "Trade Platform", which must also have the approval to trade from the US Treasury or the Federal Reserve.

These programs are a very low-risk opportunity for an "Investor" who can provide a cash deposit, a fully cash-backed Bank Guarantee (BG), or a cash-backed Standby Letter of Credit (SBLC) for a minimum of 100 Million USD or Euro (100,000,000.00).

The notional returns to the Investor/Asset Provider are historically over 20% per month. However, returns are contractually agreed upon by the Investor and the Trader before the trading begins, and can vary on a case-by-case basis.

The Investor's capital is not put at risk in the trading. The investor's capital is not physically involved (prohibited use) with the buy and resale exchange activities generating the profit. An Investor's capital always sits in their own back account, without liability of lien, encumbrance, transfer of control, or subject to first call by anyone. The bank protects the Investors' account from call in that the contracts for the buy and sell of securities is subject to bank-to-bank confirmation of a "closed book" sale only.

The trader must have confirmed evidence of contracts with exit buyers (closed book) for the securities before the bank will execute the trade contract. The sale itself is managed and scrutinized by the bank at all times.

In other words, the investor's funds are not directly involved in the buy/resale transactions. The Investor's cash deposit, as a security commitment, is non-callable and not subject to loss liability because of the terms and conditions of the trade contracts in which the transaction resale funds are in place prior to release of the purchase funds.

PROCESS OF MANAGING BUY/SELL MTNs PROGRAM

The prime banks that offer credit facilities are governed by the Basel II and Basel III Accords, which became effective in September 2006 and January 2010, respectively, which impose strict requirements on bank lending and borrowing. Most notably, a bank's credit lines must be "capitalized" by an acceptable form of collateral (of sufficient value) held "in the care, custody and control" of the credit issuing facility. The collateral is the Investor's cash deposit or Bank Instrument.

Successful trade programs, besides having unique access to established bank lines-of-credit, require the expertise of qualified licensed traders capable of engaging in the purchase and sale of investment-grade bank debentures in the wholesale market. Traders are licensed by European regulatory agencies, and trades proceed according to strict procedural and legal guidelines. Under present rules, traders cannot use their own assets to trade. This is why third-party investors are necessary.

This trading operation is generally referred to as a "controlled", "managed", "closed" bank debenture trading effort because the Supply Side of the financial instruments and the Exit Buyer for the financial instruments have already been pre-arranged and the price of the instruments already established. In other words, the licensed traders contractually manage the buy and the resale of the financial instruments before any trading actually takes place, thus the term, "Managed Buy/Sell".

Therefore, each and every completed trade will result in a net gain (and never a net loss) to the trader.

The following procedural protocol are normally be followed:

- The investor's funds are never touched (funds verification only).
- Targeted 20% yield per tranche to clients (maximum allowable by authorities).
- Four tranches a week - with settlements on Friday – there may be multiple trades on a given day.
- No Powers of Attorney.
- No surprises (the Investor/Asset Provider is to be a Signatory to the Buy-Sell Trading Contract).

The crucial distinction, however, is that under a properly managed "buy-sell" transaction, the Investor does NOT transfer any funds to an intermediary escrow attorney or

PRIVATE PLACEMENT PLATFORM | 56

trader, nor are the funds required to be pledged or subjected to a lien.

When moving an MTN into the secondary market, through trading,

1)   Master Commitment Holders are first in line;
2)   Commitment Holders are second in line;
3)   The secondary market comes after that.

A newly issued or "fresh cut" instrument is issued by a bank at a steep discount to face value, for example 58% of face value. It can only be purchased by a Fed authorized Master Commitment Holder, who has a certain quota they have to fill annually in order to keep their Fed appointment.

They line up a number of Commitment Holders who have the exclusive right to purchase these MTNs from the Master Commitment Holders, each in smaller volume and at a slight markup. This is the popular business model of "buy wholesale, sell retail" ... buy wholesale in bulk, then sell in smaller quantities at a higher price.

These Commitment Holders can then sell it as a live seasoned instrument into the secondary market, at 98.5% of face value or similar. The resulting spreads can be substantial. They get contractual commitments from the exit buyers before the initial fresh-cut transaction with the Master Commitment Holder is ever triggered.

It is all done digitally... authentication, verification, invoicing and close-out can be done in seconds, using Bloomberg or similar.

Again, BIS regulation is that banks cannot sell their authorized issues to each other, which is where the third-party Investor comes in. The Investor is the key for the trader to unlock the credit line from the trade bank.

The traders who do these trades use credit lines from banks, but the credit line has to be fully underwritten before it can be triggered. In other words, the trader must have confirmed evidence of contracts with exit buyers for the MTNs, what they call a "closed book" before the bank will release the credit line. This is risk-free arbitrage... the simultaneous purchase and sale of the exact same asset, at the exact same time, but at different prices.

The trader keeps a large percentage of that profit and shares the rest with the investor, based upon their contractual agreement.

Payouts are usually weekly, but can be bi-weekly or monthly, depending on what the Trade Platform and the Investor agree to. Returns are contractually agreed upon by the Trader and the Investor, based upon what paper issues he has lined up, and it is usually listed as a minimum or as a "best efforts" basis. Facilitators can only state "notional double digit returns per month" and must let the trader disclose to the Investor if it ends up being higher, sometimes as high as 100% per month. Facilitators are not allowed to specify returns, as that is privately contracted between the trader and the Investor, after the Investor passes AML compliance.

Because of the high returns, investors with large sums will eventually reach the Wealth Accumulation threshold and will be required to engage in Project Funding, which requires them to donate around 80% of their profits to an economic project (can be as low as 40% or as high as 95%), as non-recourse project funding. However, traders are allowed to make more profit per trade if the client engages in project funding, and because of this higher profitability per trade, the net profit to the Investor can be about the same if they do Wealth Accumulation or Project Funding.

When doing a "Project Funding" trade, the Federal Reserve requires an accounting of those project funds so that they are released only against invoices certified by the accounting entity, similar to how construction loans function. United

Nations approval is also necessary for most projects. We have a United Nations Advisor available to fast-track this process if required.

Experts are also available to assist in helping qualified applicants access Pre-Structured Humanitarian Projects to fit the precise and rigid guidelines covered by International Banking Law and the United Nations.

Risks and Risk Management

There should be no material risks to the cash deposit or BI, given that the absolute priority is the preservation of its value and that the BI remains under the control of the Investor at all times.

Since the cash deposit or BI is required to be a top 25 bank, there is nominal Financial Institution risk, should there be a bank bail-in. However, these trade programs only occur among top 25 banks with AAA credit ratings, which is better than the US Federal Government, and the US Treasury is considered to be the "risk-free rate".

Investor Funds

Investor funds cannot be borrowed funds and have to be of commercial origin, free of any liens or encumbrances. During the term of the Bank Trade, there cannot be any withdrawal of funds from the Client Account, nor shall any loans, credit lines, pledges, hypothecations, liens or encumbrances be placed against it. The cost of doing business is the opportunity cost of that capital just sitting there, not being deployed into other investments.

Institutional investors such as U.S. pension funds are prohibited under ERISA from purchasing anything that is not on-screen (anything other than live MTNs or registered securities which are screen able). A fresh-cut MTN can only become live or seasoned after its title changes and it receives an ISIN or CUSIP number, and it is registered for screening on Bloomberg or Reuters.

MTNs pay much higher yields than US treasuries, a 10 year MTN can pay 5% to 8% whereas the 10 year treasury is only around 1% to 2%, and the MTNs from the top banks have AAA credit rating, unlike the downgraded credit rating of the US treasuries.

The secondary market is dominated by institutional buyers, like pensions funds, sovereigns, and foundations, who buy and hold until maturity while collecting their annual coupon interest. They have to match cash outflows with cash inflows, and this is a reliable way for them to be able to do that, without the volatility of market speculation in equity markets. These are part of their conservative allocation, while equities and private equity funds are part of their riskier higher yield allocations.

Why do banks issue MTNs?

Banks issue MTNs because they can leverage the funds 10:1 and loan it out at interest for 10 years, turning a hefty profit. Below is an illustrative example.

1) Full Face Value of MTN Issue (FFV): 10 Billion Euro
2) Sell at 58% of Face Value: 5.8 Billion Euro
3) Coupon value at 7.5% per annum for 10 yrs: 7.5 Billion Euro
4) Liability (Point 2-{1+3}): -11.7 Billion Euro
5) Leverage (Point 2) at 10:1: 58 Billion Euro
6) Interest by bank at 3% per annum for 10 yrs on Point 5: 17.4 Billion Euro
7) Profit made by Bank (Point 4+6): 5.7 Billion Euro

Costs

The Investor/Asset Provider is not required to make any upfront fee payments. Because the invitation only Managed Buy/Sell Programs are under strict non-solicitation rules, it is customary to have facilitating intermediaries involved in the introduction. Those intermediaries are compensated with a small referral fee (usually 1% to 2%) paid out of the trading profits by the Paymaster, before net profits are distributed to the Investor/Asset Provider. On Small Cap trades, the intermediary fee is usually higher, around 5% to 10%.

Rules of Participation

Traditional investments involve a solicitation using a Prospectus or a Private Placement Memorandum that give potential investors all relevant information of the Investment Sponsor and the investment offer prior to the investor submitting any paperwork. However, due to the strict non-solicitation rule associated with Managed Buy/Sell Programs, the traditional procedure is reversed.

Potential Investors/Asset Providers must first submit a Client Information Summary (CIS) and Proof of Funds (Tear Sheet, Bank Statement, or Bank Confirmation Letter) to the Facilitator and Program Manager in order to pass AML compliance. Only AFTER an Applicant passes AML Compliance can a Trade Platform disclose their name or their offer to that specific applicant. The Applicant is never put at risk in this process because they have full disclosure from the Platform and a written offer with clear contractual returns and capital protections before they enter any obligations. This procedure keeps these elite trade programs out of the view of the general public and weeds out most investors who do not have the right connections to get in.

It is considered a "privilege" to be invited to participate in a Fiduciary Trade, not a "right." The trading administrators and managers have a virtually endless supply of financially qualified applicants.

Program Managers favor the applicants who provide the best paperwork, promptly respond to all requests for updated information or clearer copies of documents, and does not attempt to modify or dictate variations to the standard procedures. An applicant should never underestimate what the trading entities know about them. Failure to provide full disclosure upfront will disqualify the disingenuous.

Applicants must first prove that they are qualified, not the other way around. Until the applicant has passed the AML compliance required by the Trading Banks, no placement can occur nor will any offer be made. The U.S. Patriot Act has introduced obligatory compliance procedures. Program Managers are legally not allowed to discuss yield schedule nor contract terms until AFTER a potential Investor/Asset Provider has passed compliance, or else they could lose their license.

Corporate applicants must empower an Officer or Director as sole/exclusive signatory by using a Corporate Resolution. Not only do the funds have to be on deposit in an acceptable bank, they must also be in an acceptable jurisdiction. Trading does not occur in the US, but funds can be in certain US banks with corresponding branches in Europe or Hong Kong (JP Morgan Chase, Citibank, etc.).

It is felony fraud to submit documents or Financial Instruments that are forged, altered or counterfeit. Such documents (including attempting to submit assets that are, not under direct control) are promptly referred to the appropriate law enforcement agencies for immediate criminal prosecution. The practices, procedures and rules are determined by the U.S. Federal Regulatory Authorities, Western European Central Banks program management, the International Chamber of Commerce (ICC), licensed traders and trading banks. It is their decision whom to accept and whom to reject. Contract terms, yield, schedules, etc., are made to fit their needs and schedules – and not the demands of the investors.

This marketplace is highly regulated and strictly confidential, and absolute confidentiality by the investor is a key element of every contract, with strict Non-Disclosure Agreement that is enforced. A client who breaks confidentiality will precipitate instant cancellation and may be required to repay profits received.

Finally, submission of the application documents to more than one management group at a time is termed "shopping." If an Investor "shops," he/she can expect that this fact shall be quickly disseminated and known among the program management groups who maintain close communication – and will then be accepted by none and rejected by all. Shopping a file can get an applicant and their intermediaries blacklisted.

Offered Securities

MTN securities historically were principally fixed-rate, non-redeemable senior debt securities and eventually evolved to include other types of debt securities, including floating rate, zero coupons, non-U.S. dollar denominated, amortizing, multi-currency, subordinated or indexed securities. Common reference rates for floating rate securities issued under MTN programs include secured overnight financing rate ("SOFR"), the interbank offered rates ("IBORs") (though, of course, these are being phased out), the prime rate, the Treasury rate, the federal funds rate and the constant maturity swap ("CMS") rate. Most MTN programs are rated investment-grade by one or more nationally recognized credit rating agencies.

MTNs are usually sold on a best efforts basis. However, competitive pressures may sometimes lead a dealer to purchase MTNs securities as principal, and large syndicated MTN offerings often are effected on a firm commitment basis. In both cases, the MTN dealer is usually regarded as an "underwriter" for liability purposes under Section 11 of the Securities Act of 1933 (the "Securities Act").

The traditional market for MTNs is investor-driven wherein dealers continuously offer MTNs within a specific maturity range, and an investor can negotiate to have the dealer meet its particular investment needs. In making their investment decisions, MTN investors consider credit ratings, an evaluation of the issuer and its business, and the maturity and yield of the MTNs

MTN Programs: SEC-Registered and Exempt

MTN programs generally are limited to larger public companies with at least a $75 million public equity float and are usually registered on a shelf registration statement under Rule 415 of the Securities Act, specifically under Rule 415(a)(1)(x) for continuous or delayed offerings of issuers that are eligible to use Form S-3 or Form F-3 on a primary basis, or under Rule 415(a)(ix) for continuous offerings of issuers that are not eligible to use Form S-3 or Form F-3 and cannot undertake delayed offerings. MTN programs may also be registered on Form S-1 or Form F-1, but this is rare.

Non-SEC reporting companies can also issue MTNs. MTN programs that are not required to be registered with the SEC include (i) bank note programs exempt from registration under Section 3(a)(2) of the Securities Act; (ii) Rule 144A programs in which the securities are offered exclusively to qualified institutional buyers; (iii) private placements made through continuous Section 4(a)(2) offerings; and (iv) Regulation S programs in which the MTNs are offered outside the United States. The issuer and the selling agents for these offerings may use a variety of term sheets to offer these MTNs, which are not subject to the filing requirements of the Securities Act.

Even though MTN offerings under Section 3(a)(2) are exempt from registration under the Securities Act, they are public securities offerings conducted by banks and must be filed with the Financial Industry

What's the Deal? Medium-Term Note Programs |

Regulatory Authority, Inc. ("FINRA") for review under Rule 5110(a)(2) when there is a FINRA member involved in the distribution, unless the issuer has outstanding investment grade rated unsecured non-convertible debt with a term of issue of at least four years, or the non-convertible debt securities are so rated. Transactions under Section 3(a)(2) and Rule 144A must also be reported through FINRA's Trade Reporting and Compliance Engine, or TRACE, to provide greater transparency for investors.

MTN Program Participants

The working group involved in establishing an MTN program generally includes:

1) Issuer, which usually will be a large corporate or financial services issuer, which has an ongoing need for capital and that is eligible to file a shelf registration statement for delayed and continuous offerings, as well as government-sponsored entities, such as Fannie Mae and Freddie Mac;

2) Guarantor (in some cases), such as the issuer's subsidiary or a special purpose finance subsidiary, which may have a higher credit rating on its indebtedness than the issuer;

3) Arranger, which is usually an investment bank that (i) serves as principal selling agent for the MTNs; (ii) advises the issuer as to potential financing opportunities in the MTN market; (iii) communicates to the issuer any offers from potential investors to buy MTNs; (iv) advises the issuer as to the form and content of the offering documents, including the types of securities to be included; (v) negotiates the terms of the agreements on its own behalf and on behalf of the other selling agents;

(vi) coordinates settlement of the MTNs with the issuer, the trustee and the paying agent; and (vii) makes a market in the issued and outstanding securities under the MTN program;

4) Selling Agents, other than the arranger, are often added to an MTN program if not at establishment, then, through an accession letter, which is a short form of agreement between the issuer and the new selling agents that makes the new selling agents parties to the existing MTN program agreement. Selling agents may be added for the entirety of the program or as dealers for a day to participate in a specific MTN offering. Having multiple selling agents fosters competition among the selling agents to market the issuer's MTNs, and helps to attract more reverse inquiry transactions that may likely bring down the issuer's financing costs;

5) Regional dealers (in some cases) may be included by the selling agents, and, if so, are paid by selling agents through selling concessions;

6) Law Firms acting as counsel to the issuer and to the investment banks and, at program establishment, to the trustee or fiscal and paying agent;

7) Accounting firm, which audits the issuer's financial statements and is expected to deliver a comfort letter at the establishment of the program and then from time to time as required under the distribution agreement;

8) Rating agencies (typically at least two) that will provide credit ratings to the issuer's indebtedness generally or credit ratings that are specific to notes issued pursuant to the MTN program;

9) Trustee or fiscal and paying agent serves variety of roles, including:

   i. processing payments of interest, principal and other amounts on the MTNs from the issuer to the investors;

ii. communicating notices from the issuer to the investors;

iii. coordinating settlement of the MTNs with the issuer and the selling agent;

iv. assigning security identification codes to the MTNs (in the case of U.S. programs, the trustee typically obtains a block of CUSIP numbers for the relevant issuer's MTN program and assigns them on an issue-by-issue basis);

v. processing certain tax forms that may be required under the MTN program; and

vi. in the case of a trustee of a series of U.S.registered MTNs, acting as representative of the investors in the event of any claim for payment if a default occurs;

10) Listing agent if the relevant MTNs are to be listed or the program is to be qualified for listing on a securities exchange, usually a European securities exchange;

11) Clearing systems such as DTC, Euroclear and Clearstream; and

12) Financial printer to the extent printing is required.

MTN Program Documentation

The offering documents for a registered MTN program may include a "universal" shelf registration statement for debt and other securities, or a shelf registration statement relating only to debt securities. The base prospectus, which is included in the registration statement, will include a general description of the issuer's debt securities that may be issued as well as the possible benchmark rates that may be referenced, and any other potential terms of the securities that are then known. For an exempt MTN program, the offering document will be an offering circular or offering memorandum, rather than a base prospectus, with a form of pricing supplement or final terms to be used for individual offerings made pursuant to the program. In the structured notes context, there may be a need to file a more detailed prospectus supplement describing the notes to be issued under the MTN program, and free writing prospectuses and/or pricing supplements, each of which will include the specific details of each offering or each type of note that may be issued pursuant to the program.

An issuer and the selling agent may also use several other disclosure documents in the offering process, including preliminary and final term sheets, subject to the filing requirements of Rule 433 and other SEC rules relating to "free writing prospectuses" to negotiate the terms of an offering with potential investors, to market an offering, or to set forth the agreed upon final terms of an offering; free writing prospectuses that may be brochures or other educational materials, and websites and other types of documents used to market potential offerings from an MTN program; product supplements for issuers of structured products to describe the detailed terms, risk factors and tax consequences of a particular type of product to potential investors; and press releases, particularly in the context of syndicated offerings.

If not otherwise filed with the registration statement, the issuer must also file: the distribution agreement entered into with the selling agents, which also may be called a "program agreement" or a "sales agency agreement" designed to provide for multiple offerings during the term of the MTN program, and typically includes

i.   representations and warranties of the issuer, deemed to be made both at the time of the signing of the agreement and at the time of each takedown, as to the accuracy of the offering documents, the authorization of the applicable issuance documents and the indenture or fiscal and paying agency agreement;

ii. the steps to be followed if the MTN prospectus supplement is amended or the size of the program is increased;

iii. the steps to be followed, and the approvals required, if any free writing prospectuses are to be used;

iv. requirements as to the conditions precedent, documents and deliverables required to establish the MTN program and/or conduct takedowns, which may be reverse inquiry transactions, or agented or syndicated takedowns;

v. requirements as to any subsequent deliverables from the issuer to the selling agents, such as periodic comfort letters, legal opinions and officer's certificates;

vi. provisions allocating program expenses among the issuer and the selling agents;

vii. indemnification of the selling agents for liabilities under the securities laws;

viii. provisions relating to the determination of the selling agents' compensation or a schedule of commissions; and

ix. provisions for adding additional selling agents, whether for the duration of the program or for a specific offering. Beginning on January 1, 2019, U.S. global systemically important banks and their subsidiaries began adding stay provisions in their securities contracts, such as the distribution agreement. These arose from the qualified financial contract ("QFC") stay rules requiring "covered entities" to include standardized contractual stay language in their QFCs in order to mitigate the risk of destabilizing closeouts of their QFCs, which could be an impediment to an orderly resolution of such financial institutions if there were a failure of such institutions. the indenture duly qualified under the Trust Indenture Act of 1939 (in the case of an SEC-registered program), which is usually open-ended, does not limit the amount of debt securities that can be issued, and may have restrictive covenants, affirmative covenants and events of default; or paying agency agreements (in the case of an exempt or unregistered program); an administrative procedures memorandum, which is usually an exhibit to the distribution agreement and describes the exchange of information, settlement procedures and responsibility for preparing documents among the issuer, the selling agents, the trustee or paying agent, and the applicable clearing system in order to offer, issue and close each series of securities under the MTN program; a calculation agency agreement wherein the calculation agent, oftentimes the trustee or the paying agent, agrees to calculate the rate of interest due on floating rate notes; an exchange rate agency agreement wherein the exchange rate agent, which may be the trustee or paying agent, will, in the case of notes with payments to be made in a non-U.S. currency, convert the non-U.S. currency into U.S. dollars; in the case of complex securities, an opinion on the disclosure of the US federal income tax consequences of investing in the MTNs; and the form of the master note or certificate representing the MTNs which typically is in global form, with a single master certificate representing each series, and for more efficient takedowns, containing detailed provisions that could apply to many different types of notes (fixed and floating; the calculation of different types of base rates) and a short leading page or cover page for the note that indicates (through check boxes and blank lines) which of those detailed terms are applicable to the specific issuance.

Depending upon the arrangements between the issuer and the selling agents, some or all of the comfort letters, opinions and officer's certificates called for by the distribution agreement will be required to be delivered to the selling agents on a periodic basis as part of the ongoing due diligence process because the selling agents are subject to liability as "underwriters" under Section 11 of the Securities Act as noted above. These "deliverables" will help the underwriters establish a "due diligence" defense against any potential Section 11 claims against them for misstatements or omissions in the offering documents.

An MTN program takedown is intended to be relatively straightforward since the distribution or program agreement and the principal governing documents were negotiated and agreed when the program was established. The issuer and the arranger (and the other selling agents, if applicable) will agree on the terms of the takedown, commonly done orally with written confirmation to follow; and the agents will deliver the base prospectus, MTN prospectus supplement and pricing supplement to investors (which may occur via "access equals delivery" under SEC Rule 172 in the case of a registered program). In the case of a syndicated MTN issuance, an updated comfort letter, legal opinions and one or more officers' certificate are also provided to the selling agents at the closing of the offering. For a registered offering, the issuer will file with the SEC under Rule 424 a pricing supplement containing the title of the securities, issue date, maturity date, interest rate, any redemption dates, the names of the underwriters or selling agents and their compensation for the offering, and the legal opinion language. The issuer will also instruct the trustee or issuing and paying agent to complete the form of the note or certificate representing the MTNs in global or certified form.

Medium Term Note Programs

- MTN Programs may be either registered with the Securities and Exchange Commission or exempt from registration there under:
  - Section 3(a)(2) bank note programs

- Rule 144A / Regulation S programs
- Regulation S EMTN programs

- At the launch of an MTN program, a set of program documents are executed: a distribution agreement (which provides a framework for continuous offerings, as opposed to an underwriting agreement used in individual offerings), a fiscal agency agreement or indenture, and ancillary documents, such as a calculation agency agreement and an exchange rate agency agreement.

Offering Documents

- The offering documents for an MTN program will include:
  - A base prospectus with a general description of the issuer's debt securities that may be issued under the issuer's existing debt indenture,
  - For an exempt program, the base offering document will be an offering circular or offering memorandum, rather than a base prospectus,
  - A more detailed prospectus supplement describing the notes to be issued under the MTN program, and
  - Free writing prospectuses and/or pricing supplements, each of which will include the specific details of each offering.
  - The prospectus supplement will usually include a description of the issuer's fixed and floating rate notes, and the various underlying rates for floating rate notes (e.g., SOFR, the constant maturity swap rate (CMS), the Euro Interbank Offered Rate (EURIBOR), the federal funds rate, and others).

Distribution Agreement

- The issuer will usually have multiple agents execute the MTN distribution agreement. The agents may act in the role of principal (i.e., underwriter/dealer) or as an agent for the issuer for direct sales by the issuer to the investor.

- Under the distribution agreement, the agents are entitled to receive diligence documentation from the issuer on a regular basis—usually quarterly, coinciding with the issuer's filing of its Form 10-K or 10-Q.

- The diligence documentation will consist of a comfort letter, officers' certificate of the issuer, and counsel's Rule 10b-5 letter confirming that the prospectus (which incorporates by reference the issuer's filings under the Securities Exchange Act of 1934) do not make any untrue statement of a material fact or omit to state a material fact necessary in order to make the statements made, in the light of the circumstances under which they were made, not misleading.

- Often the underwriter is an affiliated broker-dealer of the issuer.

- In that case, the MTN program must be rated investment grade by a rating agency, or the issuer's debt of the same class must be so rated.

- Having that rating will perfect an exemption from the requirement to use a qualified independent underwriter under the rules of the Financial Industry Regulatory Authority, Inc. ("FINRA")

  - This exemption is required for registered and Section 3(a)(2) MTN programs, but not Rule 144A or Regulation S programs.

- Some MTN programs are set up with only one agent signed up to the distribution agreement, which may be the issuer's affiliated broker-dealer.

- That broker-dealer will then, in turn, execute dealer agreements with other distributors. In that situation, when notes are issued, they are sold first to the affiliated broker-dealer and then to an unaffiliated distributor.

- At the time of a note offering, the agent, acting as an underwriter, will agree on the terms of the offering with the issuer, whether through a form terms agreement or a more informal process (such as an email or other confirmation).
- Issuer's counsel usually prepares the preliminary offering document, which will be either a free writing prospectus or a preliminary pricing supplement.

Risk Factors

- The uncertainty with respect to the timing of Term SOFR as a USD LIBOR replacement and the potential differences between the USD LIBOR rate for any particular tenor and the Benchmark Replacement rate and Benchmark Adjustment call out for clear risk factor disclosure.
- Risk factors have been, and should be, updated to reflect this uncertainty and to highlight the potential conflicts of interest between the calculation agent, which may be an affiliate of the issuer, and the note holders.

Section 3(a)(2) and Offerings by Banks

- Section 3(a)(2) of the Securities Act exempts from registration under the Securities Act any security issued or guaranteed by a "bank."
- Basis: banks are highly regulated and provide adequate disclosure to investors about their finances in the absence of federal securities registration requirements. Banks are also subject to various capital requirements that may increase the likelihood that holders of their debt securities will receive timely payments of principal and interest.
- Under Section 3(a)(2), the institution must meet both of the following requirements:

- It must be a national bank or any institution supervised by a state banking commission or similar authority; and
- Its business must be substantially confined to banking.
- Examples of entities that do not qualify:
  - Bank holding companies
  - Finance companies
  - Investment banks
  - Foreign banks
- Regulated US branches and agencies of foreign banks may qualify.
- Another basis for qualification as a bank: securities guaranteed by a bank.
  - Not limited to a guarantee in a legal sense, but also includes arrangements in which the bank agrees to ensure the payment of a security.
  - The guaranty or assurance of payment, however, has to cover the entire obligation; it cannot be a partial guarantee or promise of payment, and it must be unconditional.
  - Again, guarantees by foreign banks (other than those of an eligible US branch or agency) would not qualify for this exception.
  - The guarantee is a legal requirement to qualify for the exemption; investors will not be looking to the U.S. branch for payment/credit. Investors will look to the home office.
  - Finance companies can issue under Section 3(a)(2), if the securities are guaranteed by a bank.

Non-US Banks/US Offices

- US branches/agencies of foreign banks are conditionally entitled to rely on the Section 3(a)(2) exemption.

- 1986: The SEC takes the position that a foreign branch/agency will be deemed to be a "national bank" or a "banking institution organized under the laws of any state" if "the nature and extent of federal and/or state regulation and supervision of that particular branch or agency is substantially equivalent to that applicable to federal or state chartered domestic banks doing business in the same jurisdiction."

- As a result, US branches/agencies of foreign banks are frequent issuers or guarantors of debt securities in the United States. Most issuances or guarantees occur through the New York branches of these banks.

FINRA Requirements

- Even though securities offerings under Section 3(a)(2) are exempt from registration under the Securities Act, public securities offerings conducted by banks must be filed with the Financial Industry Regulatory Authority for review under Rule 5110(a)(2), unless an exemption is available.

  - Exemption: The issuer has outstanding investment grade rated unsecured non-convertible debt with a term of issue of at least four years, or the non-convertible debt securities are so rated.

- If an affiliated dealer is an agent for the offering, there is "prominent disclosure" in the offering document with respect to the conflict of interest caused by that affiliation and the bank notes are rated investment grade or in the same series that have equal rights and obligations as investment grade rated securities, then no qualified independent underwriter will be required.

- Transactions under Section 3(a)(2) must also be reported through FINRA's Trade Reporting and Compliance Engine. TRACE eligibility provides greater transparency for investors. Rule 144A securities are also TRACE reported.

How Do We Update Our MTN Descriptions?

- Drafting – how?
  - Old way: Copy description out of the 2006 ISDA Definitions
  - New way: Enter the Matrix
- How do we use the Matrix?
  - Lots of columns
  - Most of the first group are just simple identification, whether the rate is overnight or term, and where do we get it (screen rates are read off of screens, including H.15(519) fed reserve daily published rates) (calculated rates involve a calculation, mainly Fed Funds and US Treasury Bills (money market yield and bond equivalent yield, respectively)
  - CMS not included

The new fallbacks

- Fallbacks:
  - Big changes – no more polling (Reference Banks)
  - Obvious problems with polling, if no quotes, end up with a fixed rate note – nobody wants that anymore
    - Three situations covered: Temporary cessation, permanent cessation and "administrator/benchmark event."
- Temporary: The "Standard Temporary Non-Publication Trigger" is to simply use the previous day's rate – super simple
  - Permanent cessation: Index Cessation Event – uses the same descriptions as currently used for USD LIBOR and SOFR – public statements by the administrator or the regulatory supervisor for the rate that it will cease

- Has a third option, used in USD LIBOR, that the regulatory supervisor says that the rate is no longer representative, even if being published – zombie LIBOR

Administrator/Benchmark event:

- You receive a notice from the issuer or the trustee that under law or regulation, it's illegal to continue using the rate
- Now what?
- "Generic Fallback Provisions"
  - Agreement between the parties;
  - Application of Alternative Pre-nominated Index;
  - Application of Alternative Post-nominated Index;
  - Application of Calculation Agent Nominated Replacement Index; and
  - No fault termination
- For FRNS, only alternative pre-nominated index will work
- We will see issuers including fallback rates in their offering documents
- Goal is to get to an amendment to the FRN that allows the FRN to continue under the new rate

Rule 144A – Overview

- Rule 144A provides a clear safe harbor for offerings to institutional investors.
- Does not require extensive ongoing registration or disclosure requirements.
- "Benchmark" sized issuances have good liquidity in the Rule 144A market.
- A US bank may use a Rule 144A program for marketing reasons — a desire to be clearly identified with the QIB market.

- Rule 144A provides a non-exclusive safe harbor from the registration requirements of Section 5 of the Securities Act for resales of restricted securities to "qualified institutional buyers" (QIBs).
- The premise: not all investors are in need of the protections of the prospectus requirements of the Securities Act.
- The rule applies to offers made by persons other than the issuer of the securities (i.e., "resales").
- The rule applies to securities that are not of the same class as securities listed on a US securities exchange or quoted on an automated inter-dealer quotation system.
- A reseller may rely on any applicable exemption from the registration requirements of the Securities Act in connection with the resale of restricted securities (such as Regulation S or Rule 144).

Conditions for Rule 144A Offerings

- Reoffers or resales only to a QIB, or to an offeree or purchaser that the reseller reasonably believes is a QIB.
- The QIB must purchase for its own account or for the account of another QIB
- Reseller must take steps to ensure that the buyer is aware that the reseller may rely on Rule 144A in connection with such resale.
- The securities reoffered or resold (a) when issued were not of the same class as securities listed on a US national securities exchange or quoted on a US automated inter-dealer quotation system and (b) are not securities of an open-end investment company, UIT, etc.
- For an issuer that is not an Exchange Act reporting company or exempt from reporting pursuant to Rule 12g3-2(b) under the Exchange Act, the holder and a prospective buyer designated by the holder must have

the right to obtain from the issuer, upon the holder's request, certain reasonably current information.

- The following qualify as "QIBs":
  – Any corporation, partnership or other entity (but not an individual) that owns and invests on a consolidated basis $100 million in the aggregate in securities of non-affiliates (other than bank deposits and loan participations, repurchase agreements and securities subject thereto, and currency, interest rate and commodity swaps);
  – Registered dealers that own or invest $10 million of such non-affiliate securities or are engaged in "riskless principal transactions" on behalf of QIBs (to qualify, the QIB must commit to the broker-dealer that the QIB will simultaneously purchase the securities from the broker-dealer);
  – Any investment company that is part of a "family" that has the same investment adviser and together own $100 million of such non-affiliate securities; and
  – Any US or foreign bank or S&L that owns and invests on a consolidated basis $loo million in such non-affiliate securities and has a net worth of at least $25 million
  – Institutional Accredited Investors when these entities meet the $100 million in securities owned and invested

Rule 144A threshold

- A QIB can be formed solely for purpose of conducting a Rule 144A transaction
- A reseller may rely on the following (as long as the information is no more than 16 months old for a domestic entity or 18 months for a foreign entity):
  – The purchaser's most recent publicly available annual financial statements;

- Information filed with the SEC or another government agency or self-regulatory organization;
- Information in a recognized securities manual, such as Moody's or S&P;
- Certification by the purchaser's chief financial or other executive officer specifying the amount of securities owned and invested as of the end of the purchaser's most recent fiscal year; and
- A QIB questionnaire.

- The SEC acknowledges that the reseller may use other information to establish a reasonable belief of eligibility.
  - If alternative procedures are used, these should be documented.
- The reseller will make the buyer aware that the security is a Rule 144A security by:
  - Legending the security (i.e., the security must include language that it is not registered under the Securities Act);
  - Including an appropriate statement in the offering memorandum;
  - Obtaining an agreement that the purchaser understands that the securities must be resold pursuant to an exemption or registration under the Securities Act; and
  - By obtaining a restricted CUSIP number.

Current Information Requirements

- For securities of a non-public company, the holder and a prospective purchaser designated by the holder have the right to obtain from the issuer, upon request, the following information:
  - A brief statement of the nature of the business of the issuer and its products and services;
  - The issuer's most recent balance sheet and profit and loss and retained earnings statements, and similar

financial statements for such part of the two preceding fiscal years as the issuer has been in operation; and
- The financial statements should be audited, to the extent reasonably available.
- The information must be "reasonably current."

Rule 144A – The basic offering structure

- The issuer initially sells restricted securities to investment bank(s) in a Section 4(a)(2) or Regulation D private placement
- The investment bank immediately resells the securities to QIBs under Rule 144A

Issuer Initial Purchaser QIBs

- Often combined with a Regulation S offering and referred to as a Rule 144A/Reg S offering
- QIBs acquire restricted securities
  - May resell immediately to other QIBs
  - May resell in accordance with Rule 144 requirements

Rule 144A – MTN Programs

- Used for repeat offerings, often by financial institution and insurance company issuers, to institutional investors.
- Often used for structured products sold to QIBs.
- Advantages of a public MTN program:
  - No need to publicly disclose innovative structures or sensitive information such as underwriter compensation, investor's strategies.
  - Limit FINRA filing and other compliance requirements.
  - For financial institution issuers, greater flexibility as to timing of programs when the stock of an underlying security is on a "watch list."
  - No SEC filing fees.

- In principle, lower liability profile, and reduced possibility of regulatory review.

European/UK Areas of Interest on GMTN Programs Established in the US

- Offers of Securities and relevant private placement exemptions
- Marketing and financial promotion rules
- Participation of EU/UK Agents in the Syndicate
  - Product governance and disclosures to distributors and investors
  - Contractual recognition of bail-in
- MTN and ECB Eligibility/Collateral Recognition

Offers of Securities in the EEA and the UK

- Regulation (EU) 2017/1129 (as amended) – EU Prospectus Regulation
- Regulation (EU) 2017/1129 (as amended) as it forms part of UK domestic law by virtue of the European Union (Withdrawal) Act 2018 (as amended) – the UK Prospectus Regulation
  - Basic rule: Where there is an offer to the public in the EEA/UK of securities or securities are being admitted to a regulated market in the EEA/UK, a prospectus is required
  - The definition of "offer" is extremely broad and covers any "communication to any person which presents sufficient information on the transferable securities to be offered and the terms on which they are offered so as to enable an investor to decide to buy or subscribe to these securities"

Offers of Securities in the UK

- "Transferable securities" includes bonds, other forms of securitized debt and depositary receipts (but excludes money market instruments, such as commercial paper)

- Number of exemptions from the requirements to publish a prospectus apply (so called "public offer exemptions") for securities which, although being offered to the public, are not being admitted to trading on a regulated market in the UK – these include:
  - Offer solely to "qualified investors"
  - Offer where the minimum denomination of the securities is equal to or greater than Euro 100k
  - Offer to fewer than 150 natural or legal persons in the UK
- NB: There will still be a need to comply with rules of any other listing venue on which the securities are to be listed

PRIIPs Regulation and UK PRIIPs Regulation

- Regulation (EU) No 1286/2014 (as amended) on Key Information Documents for Packaged Retail and Insurance-based Investment Products (PRIIPs)
- "Investment ... where, regardless of the legal form of the investment the amount repayable to the investor is subject to fluctuations because of exposure to reference values or to the performance of one or more assets which are not directly purchased by the investor"
- Regulation applies to issuers and other persons selling PRIIPs – such person must provide a Key Information Document (KID) to retail investors in good time (free of charge) before he/she is bound by any contract of offer relating to the PRIIP
- KID intended to aid comparability of pre-contractual information across different types of product

PRIIPs Regulation and UK PRIIPs Regulation (cont'd)

- Certain categories of product expressly excluded, such as securities guaranteed by an EEA member state
- BUT plain vanilla MTN is not on the exclusion list:

- standard features (e.g., make-whole protection) where the payout on the MTN may be subject to fluctuation because of exposure to a reference obligation/value
- types of notes (credit/equity/commodity-linked securities) issued under MTN programmes?

- Lack of clarity as to scope of Regulation has resulted in many cases in prohibition of sales to EEA and UK retail investors
- Post-Brexit: UK Financial Conduct Authority recognized this problem and Financial Services Act 2021 provides FCA with power to clarify scope of regime
- No similar recognition by the European Securities and Markets Authority (ESMA) at this time

UK Financial Promotion

- Section 21 UK Financial Services and Markets Act 2000 (as amended):
  - A person must not, in the course of business, communicate an invitation or inducement to engage in investment activity unless:
- The promotion is exempt
- the promotion is communicated or approved by an authorised person
- Consequences of contravention of s.21 by unauthorised person:
  - Criminal offense (s.25 FSMA)
  - Unenforceability (s.30 FSMA)
- UK focus
  - In the UK
  - Originating overseas, but "capable of having an effect in the UK" (s21(3)) and directed at persons in the UK
- Promotion communicated or approved by an authorised person

- s.21 does not restrict communication by authorised persons, however, they must comply with FCA Handbook requirements in relation to the standard of communications (COBS 4)
- Promotion is exempt under The Financial Services and Markets Act 2000 (Financial Promotion) Order 2005 (the "FP order")
- Key exemptions in FP Order include:
- Article 12 – Communications to overseas recipients
- Article 19 – Investment professionals
- Article 49 – High net worth companies, unincorporated associations, etc.
- Article 70 – Promotions contained in listing particulars

Product Governance – MiFID II/UK MiFIR

- Markets in Financial Instruments Directive (2014/65/EU) (UK post-Brexit domestic version) created a new EU-wide and UK product governance regime
- Scope
- All investment firms established in the EEA (and its EEA branches) and to branches of non-EEA entities
- All types of clients (retail, professional, and eligible counterparties)
- All financial instruments, including structured products
- Covers both sides of the product development and sales process, namely to (if different):
- Product manufacturers: Investment firms that create, develop, issue and/or design investment products, including investment firms advising corporate issuers on the launch of new securities; and
- Product distributors: Investment firms that offer and/or recommend investment products and services

- Objective: Ensure that firms which manufacture and distribute financial instruments act in the clients' best interests during all the stages of the lifecycle of products
- Target Market:
  - The product approval process must specify an identified target market of end clients within the relevant category of clients for each financial instrument
  - Product manufacturers must provide sufficient information to distributors so they can understand and sell properly (disclosure of target market in prospectuses/pricing supplements/announcements of the offering, etc.)
  - Firms are required to review products on a regular basis to assess whether the product remains consistent with the needs, characteristics and objectives of identified target market (feed-back loop)
  - Mutual responsibilities must be outlined in writing where non-EEA/UK issuer/other parties used to create/ manage product (usually in the distribution or terms agreement)

Contractual Recognition of Bail-In

- Article 55 of the Bank Recovery and Resolution Directive (BRRD)
- Post-Brexit, Article 55 "onshored" in UK by Part I of UK Banking Act 2009
- Part of comprehensive powers given to EU/UK resolution authorities to deal with failing banks
- Bail-in tool allows resolution authority to write-down or convert to equity a failing bank's liabilities (actual debt liabilities and other unsecured liabilities)
  - Dealers based in the EU27 and the UK required to include "contractual recognition of bail-in" clauses in various MTN contracts (Distribution Agreements,

Terms Agreements, Agency Agreements etc.) that are governed by a non-EEA or non-English law (as applicable)

- New York law contracts will need to include (a) Article 55 bail-in language in their terms if an EU incorporated Dealer is party to the contracts and/or (b) Part I UK Banking Act bail-in language in their terms if a UK incorporated Dealer is party to the contracts

ECB Eligibility

- The European Central Bank (ECB) together with national central banks of the EU Member States (NCBs) who have adopted the Euro make up the Eurosystem
- Monetary policy of the Eurosystem includes providing standing facilities to / conducting open market operations with eligible counterparties, but credit operations must be based on the Eurosystem's assessment of credit risk and adequate collateral
  - Assets for use as collateral in Eurosystem credit operations must fulfil certain specified criteria to be included on the ECB's Single List of Eligible Assets
  - Eligible assets may be marketable assets such as MTN, subject to the ECB Eligibility Criteria for marketable assets being met (see Marketable assets (europa.eu) – these include:
    - o Issuer established in the EEA or non-EEA G10 country
    - o Senior debt securities
    - o Must be denominated in Euro (but occasionally currency scope widened)
    - o MTN must be listed on a regulated market in the EEA or traded on certain noon-regulated markets (Post Brexit: London Stock Exchange's (LSE) Main Market no longer meet ECB criteria, but can maintain ECB collateral eligibility via admission to

MTS BondVission Europe MTF – Italian MTF majority owned by the LSE)

- o Settled in the euro area (i.e., Euroclear/Clearstream, Luxembourg) and (a) Bearer Notes: issued in the form of New Global Notes (NGN) and, once authenticated, deposited with and effectuated by a common safekeeper (CSK) - either Euroclear or Clearstream, Luxembourg – and held in dematerialised / book-entry form and (b) Registered Notes: effectuated and held by a common safekeeper under the New Safekeeping Structure (but not dematerialised – a physical global note is retained)
- o Credit rating requirements of the debt instrument
- o NCB of the country where security is listed responsible for assessing and reporting eligible assets to the ECB
- o Assessment procedure starts only after the asset as been issued and all relevant documents have been delivered to the NCB (e.g. ISIN codes and brief description of the issuer)
- o NCBs/ECB will not confirm eligibility of an MTN before it is issued, though clarification on eligibility criteria can be obtained on a "no names basis" from NCBs.

CHAPTER 3

Introduction To Private Placement Program?

PRIVATE PLACEMENT PROGRAM or high-profit
investment programs are safe, private and "only invite-
to-join" trading programs for financial instruments
(especially MTN) They are offered by the banks. These
instruments are first bought early for their nominal value
with a significant discount, which are sold afterwards for a
higher price in the secondary market. The difference
between the selling price and the purchase price is the profit
of the supplier/investor. These programs are offered only to
customers with high purchasing power and such transactions
may only be carried out by licensed dealers. Most of the
revenues are used to finance humanitarian purposes and
business projects.

As explained in the previous chapter, PPP exist to 'create'
money and money is created by creating debt.

For example, you as an individual can agree to loan $100 to a
friend with the understanding that the interest for the loan
will be 10%, resulting in a total of $110 to be repaid. What you
effectively have done is creating $10, even though that money
can not be seen initially.

Banks do this sort of lending every day; however, when the
amount gets higher, it gives banks the power to create
money. PPP involves trading with discounted bank-issued
debt instruments which defer payment obligations, or debts.

Theoretically, any person, company, or organization can issue debt notes. Debt notes are, in a sense, deferred payment liabilities. The PPP market is changing and it is no longer limited to governments and MTN, also, industrial companies, and banks can issue their own debt instruments. Debt notes such as Medium Terms Notes (MTN), Bank Guarantees (BG), and Stand-By Letters of Credit (SBLC) are issued at the discounted prices by major world banks in the amount of $ billions every day.

All trading programs in the PRIVATE PLACEMENT PROGRAM area include trading with discounted debt notes. Furthermore, in order to bypass the legal restrictions, this trading can only be done on a private level. This is the main difference between trading with PPP and "normal" trading, which is highly regulated. PRIVATE PLACEMENT level business transactions are free from the usual restrictions in the securities market. It is based on reliable, essential, special relationships and protocols.

However, none of these programs can be started unless there are sufficient funds to support each transaction. At this point, the customer is needed, because the banks and the covenantees are not allowed to trade with their own capital or with the capital of the costumers, as long as they do not have the sufficient funds.

Historical Background Of Private Placement Programs

In the 1990s, the trading in bank instruments was and is presently a multitrillion dollars industry worldwide. The World's largest Holding Companies of North American and European Banks are authorized to issue blocks of debt instruments such as medium term notes, debenture instruments, and standby letters of credit at the behest of the United States Treasury for the United States Treasury Trust and Foundations and the United States Federal Reserve. The Instruments issued are backed by a Treasury undertaking.

The genesis of this marketplace was the 1944 Bretton Woods Conference of world's leaders. The principles originally championed as answers to post World War II economic stability are still the impetus for the operation of these transactions today. These transactions started some fifty years ago, have grown and been continuously modified, and as described in this article are Private Placement U.S. Treasury and Federal Reserve investment transactions administered by select Western Banks. A brief history will help to understand the origin of these transactions and how it has remained strong and viable although the great economic changes the world has experienced over the last half-century

With World War II having come to a close, the leading political and economic authorities of the world met in Bretton Woods, New Hampshire (USA). Their purpose was to formulate a common plan to rebuild the war's massive devastation and to impose global restraints upon forces which had twice led to world chaos during the first half of the Twentieth Century and left economic collapse in its wake. To accomplish this goal, these leaders sought to empower universally recognized international institutions capable of effectuating and preserving political order and capable of encouraging and facilitating world economic trade and cooperation.

Leading economists around the world advocated the creation of an international banking system that would administer a universally accepted "currency". It was believed that a centralized global authority, and a standard world currency, with fixed exchange rates between the different currencies of the world, was the formula for stimulating growth and maintaining world economic stability. The Bretton Woods Conference was held on July 1, 1944, with more than 700 participants representing 44 countries coming together and advocating for the establishment of an international banking system. The English economist John Maynard Keynes called for the adoption of a standard currency. However, the political realities of state autonomy have inevitably prevented the adoption of a uniform currency. As an alternative, international leaders have decided to adopt the US dollar as the standard global currency for international trade. It was backed by gold and the most stable currency. This adoption of the US dollar as the standard currency of international trade was the cornerstone that triggered the development of the banking instrument market. The Bretton Woods Conference also gave birth to the United Nations, the World Bank, the International Monetary Fund (IMF) and the Bank for International Settlements (BIS). The World Bank was structured to operate in a manner consistent with traditional commercial banks. It was created to serve as a lender to the poorest and least developed countries. World Bank funding came from the evaluation of the most industrialized countries. Today, it receives deposits from more than 140 member governments and lends to the least developed countries in need of international capital.

In its attempt to further solidify the universal acceptance of the U.S. Dollar as the standard world currency, the Bretton Woods Conference had fixed the price of Gold backing the U.S. Dollar at $35.00 an ounce. During the 1950s and the 1960s the price of gold in the open market had increased to a price nearly ten times that amount. The need to back the U.S. Dollar with gold valued at $35.00 an ounce while simultaneously providing sufficient U.S. Dollars to accommodate the increased needs of the international marketplace created significant stress on the United States Monetary system. The United States did not have enough gold to continue issuing the dollars necessary to continue to support international economic expansion. On August 15, 1971, facing a threatened speculative run on the U.S. gold reserves, President Richard Nixon renounced America's promise to convert paper dollars into gold upon demand. With this executive proclamation the United States abandoned the gold standard. In the absence of the gold backed standard currency, the idea of fixed exchange rates among all currencies of the world became passed, and by 1973 the IMF, the World Bank and the Bank of International Settlements (BIS) had abandoned the idea of fixed exchange rates. Within the territorial limits of the United States the U.S. Federal Reserve exerts influence upon the domestic economic trends by the regulation of domestic bank reserve requirements and the adjustment of the Federal Discount Rate. While these may be internally effective tools, they are inadequate to provide the international control demand in the global marketplace. The United States Treasury expanded the roll of the Federal Reserve System to monitor the International markets separate and apart from domestic duties.

The US Treasury needed to find a solution to continue creating US Dollars, so it created financial instruments, mainly Medium Term Notes (MTN's)*, which it sold to major global banks. The US Treasury through the validation of the Federal Reserve issues the largest financial instruments of the issuing banks of the World Bank in US dollars. These transactions are economically important because the banking instruments have such large dollar amounts that the effect of these sales will have a direct impact on the volume of the US dollar in circulation. Once the Federal Reserve cash out the sale of financial instruments in dollars, they can be reintegrated into targeted segments of the global economy in accordance with the US Treasury and policies determined by the G8 countries. The big world banks exchange their financial instruments. Private Placement Programs (PPP's) are born ...But reserved only for banks and governments... * Medium Term Notes are negotiable debt securities with an interest rate. They are issued by governments or companies in international debt markets to finance their medium and long-term capital needs.

This solution is very advantageous economically and financially for everyone, and it's something magical ... we always win upwards or downwards ... if the economy of a country is growing, we win in positive speculation, if the economy of a country collapse, the debt is erased ... but the US Dollars were created meanwhile ... everyone wins ... There is so much to gain from this system, that the banks have started to want to use this system to launder their own liquidity, and those of some of their clients obtained more or less in the legality (not respecting oil embargoes, money laundering. ...). Remember the file of HSBC a few years ago. Banks will therefore organize, and create "subsidiaries" so-called "trading platforms". They will offer their large clients to invest in programs through its platforms. The money returns gray and spring white with huge profits validated by the Federal Reserve (FED). But in this case, if there is any doubt about the origin of the funds, the Federal Reserve (FED) validate the transaction only if a part of the profits generated is donated to a humanitarian foundation, or a government project always humanitarian.

Compared to the yield from traditional investments, these programs can deliver a very high yield. 100% (or more) per week is possible. And this is how: Assume a leverage effect of 10:1, meaning the trader is able to back each buy-sell transaction with ten times the amount of money investor has deposited with the program. In other words, you have $10 million but the trader, because of his leveraged loan with the bank, is able to work with $100 million. Assume also the trader is able to complete three buy-sell transactions per week, with a 5% profit from each buy-sell transaction: " (5% profit/transaction) x (3 transactions/week) = 15% profit/week Assume 10x leverage effect = 150% profit...PER WEEK"

Understanding Private Placement Trade Programs

Private placement traders trade against non-depleting, tradeable lines-of-credit established on behalf of the client/investor. Traders are generally licensed by European regulatory agencies and trades proceed according to strict procedural and legal guidelines. Under present rules, traders cannot use their own assets to trade.

The trader's lines-of-credit are derived from prime banks that offer credit facilities. These credit-issuing banks, however, are governed by the Basil II and Basel III Accords which became are effective in September, 2006 and January 2010, respectively, which impose strict requirements on bank lending and borrowing. Most notably a bank's credit lines must be "capitalized" by an acceptable form of collateral (of sufficient value) held "in the care, custody, and control" of the credit issuing facility.

This is the acid test of a trade program's viability. The controlling variable is whether or not the trade group's procedures satisfy the credit issuing bank's "care, custody and control" standard for activating credit lines—the "control test", for short.

In other words, the trade program's procedures must meet the "control test" (i.e., the procedures do not place the client's assets sufficiently under the "care, custody and control" of the credit issuing bank).

Now trade programs today come in all shapes and sizes, offering clients a wide choice of procedures. Some of the more common procedures referenced in the PPP market place are as follows:

- "Pinging" of accounts,
- "blocked/reserved" funds Letters,
- internal (ledger-to-ledger) blocking, and
- SWIFT MT 760's.

Which of these procedures satisfy the credit-issuing banks' strict "control test" set forth in Basel II and Basel III?

Additionally, successful trade programs, besides having unique access to established bank lines-of-credit, require the expertise of qualified traders capable of engaging in the purchase and sale of investment-grade bank debentures in the wholesale market. This trading operation is generally referred to as "controlled" or "managed" bank debenture trading because the supply side of the financial instruments and the exit buyer for the financial instruments have already been pre-arranged and the price of the instruments already contracted for. Hence, each and every completed trade should result in a net gain (and never a net loss) to the trader. It is entirely true that the platform trade industry has become increasingly diluted in the last several years by a most varied assortment of illegitimate and unqualified parties who make uncorroborated and extravagant claims in hopes of capitalizing on unwary and ill-advised investors.

Rarely, if ever, do these illegitimate parties represent viable trade opportunities and these persons and/or groups of persons only serve to further convolute an already complex industry. As a direct result of the multitude of nefarious actors that have come forth, the US Securities and Exchange Commission (SEC) has issued an unequivocal statement disavowing these trade platforms as rife with fraudulent claims and misrepresentations.[1] The SEC and other regulatory agencies have filed suit in federal courts to enjoin many perpetrators and these court rulings are readily available on the internet.

To state, however, that all managed buy/sell programs are scams or pyramid schemes is simply, not true. Notwithstanding the many fraudulent offers in the market place today, actual private securities trading generates enormous amounts of money—legitimately— every day.

The Federal Reserve Bulletin for August 1993 provides insight and significant detail in an article entitled "Anatomy of the Medium-Term Note Market" where the economics of MTN's and corporate bonds are surveyed.

Shortly thereafter, however, the Board of Governors for the Federal Reserve System, and several other US law enforcement and regulatory agencies issued sharp rebukes against certain high-yield investment schemes. In an advisory letter entitled "Prime Bank and Other Financial Instrument Fraud Schemes" the Board of Governors states as follows:

In 1993 and 1996, the Federal Reserve issued advisories concerning illegal schemes purporting to involve "prime bank" financial instruments. In its alerts, the Federal Reserve advised banking organizations and the public that, among others things, it does not know of any legitimate use of any financial instrument called a "prime bank" note, guarantee, letter of credit, or debenture and that the Federal Reserve does not guarantee or enter into transactions with individuals and does not license anyone to trade "prime bank" financial instruments or act as the Federal Reserve's agent to sell or redeem such instruments.

Since 1996, fraudulent schemes involving financial instruments have proliferated in the United States and abroad, and investors have lost significant sums of money. Federal and state law enforcement agencies, as well as the U.S. Securities, and Exchange Commission, have investigated and prosecuted numerous individuals associated with supposed investment opportunities involving "prime bank" instruments or other financial instruments.

The Federal Reserve wants to again highlight the dangers associated with investing or participating in questionable transactions that promise unrealisticly (sic) high rates of return and involve other dubious characteristics. Over the past several years, Federal Reserve staff has reviewed numerous illicit transactions and provided assistance to U.S. and foreign law enforcement and securities regulators and, based on this experience, has identified the following hallmarks or "red flags" associated with many fraudulent financial instrument scams that can be used to avoid them:

- References to financial instruments issued by "prime banks," "top 100 world banks," "top 25 European banks," and similar references to categories or groups of banks that are not used in the banking industry.
- Promises of extremely high, unrealistic rates of return with little or no risk.
- Participation in an investment program often referred to as a "roll program (or programme)," "high yield investment program," or "bank debenture trading program."
- High rates of return are generated by repeatedly trading (or buying and selling) financial instruments (often over a 40-week period).

Legitimate financial instruments, such as letters of credit, guarantees, and medium term notes, are bought and sold or traded in manners that are not realistic -- for example, standby letters of credit are bought and sold.

Transactions are overly complex and nonsensical.

Terms that have no meaning in legitimate financial transactions are used repeatedly for example, "conditional SWIFT," "key tested telex," "pay order," "funds of good, clean, clear and non-criminal origin," "master commitment," "one-year and one day," and "commitment holder."

High Degree Of Secrecy - for example, the trading of financial instruments takes place on a secret market, your banker or investment adviser will not know about the investment opportunity because only a few special people around the world are aware of it or participate in the secret trading, or the investor is being allowed to participate in a secret trading program and, if he or she reveals any information about the program, the investor's participation will be terminated.

The investor's funds are absolutely safe and cannot be lost for example, a bank has issued a guarantee or an attorney is holding the funds in a special escrow fund.

Involvement of a well known governmental authority, such as the Federal Reserve, World Bank, or IMF.

Investor's funds will be used for "humanitarian" projects.

Supervisory Letter SR 02-13 the Board of Governors specifically references its previously published article "Anatomy of the Medium Term Note Market" in its advisory and states that "...[t]he article was written by Federal Reserve economists and describes the use of this type of legitimate debt instrument by corporations and banking organizations and how they are underwritten and priced by the market."

The reference warns, however, that "[s]ince the publication of [the] article and the issuance of the Federal Reserve's 1993 "prime bank" advisory, which alerted the public to the non-existence of "prime bank" instruments, many illicit scams purport to involve the trading of "medium term notes" (often referred to as "MTN's") rather than "prime bank" financial instruments."

The Board's advisory concludes that "...wrongdoers involved with illegal financial instrument scams try to convince their victims that the Federal Reserve Bulletin article proves the existence a market where MTNs can be traded for enormous profits."

The advisory concludes that "[n]o such market exists."

Managed "Buy-Sell" Programs

Still others contend that such trade program do exist and that they are to be distinguished from those schemes and fraudulent machinations referenced by the Board and other law enforcement and government regulatory entities.

Managed, (Closed-End) "Buy-Sell" opportunities are distinguished from "trading programs" by emphasizing the mechanics of discount buying that allow arbitrageurs, or speculators, to capitalize on purchase and sale spreads.

Managed, (Closed-End) "Buy-Sell" opportunities operate without a "trader" and the client's funds are not pledged or blocked.

No credit facility or SWIFT MT 760 (or SWIFT MT 103) is used.

The client's funds are merely verified by the "Provider" prior to each "buy-sell" tranche in order to ensure that sufficient funds are available to permit a legal "buy-sell" transaction to take place.

Prominence Of Private Placement Trading MTNs As A Debt Instrument

An MTN is a debt instrument similar to a bond usually issued by a corporate or increasingly a sovereign government where the issuer is authorized by the governing securities regulatory bodies to issue a limited amount of debt paper over a period of time and up to an authorized amount; each sporadic release can have a different maturity or yield and thus is highly flexible for the issuer allowing it to inject capital when it is most needed, rather than in one single large issue of bonds.

In addition, MTN's are not underwritten. MTN's are offered by corporate firms agents (brokerage or investment banks) on a best-effort basis thus the MTN issuing agents earn a fee from the issuer, not from the investor, so the agents are compelled to negotiate the MTN's.

When a corporation decides to generate additional capital, outside of the daily meanderings of business, corporate officers take an inclusive survey of their financial affairs and begin the process of further growth by a certain process. This process of generating additional liquidity can be done by filing a shelf registration with the SEC. Upon acceptance, MTN programs can be further perused, pursued and implemented into their modus operandi. Once an MTN program is established, this corporation is queued up to either enter the MTN market with frequency or on an intermittent level at both sizeable and moderate offerings and levels. MTNs provides much more flexibility than that more traditional underwritten corporate bonds that are also issued from shelf registrations because the entire debt issue is not made all at once through a single maturity and coupon rate.

MTNs are primarily offered on an agency basis. While this is the standard protocol, most programs consider additional distribution means. As one example, agents of these MTN programs acquire notes for their own accounts, as well as for resale, at par or the standing market rates. It is also common to see MTNs sold on an underwritten basis as well.

When a corporation has arranged to play the role of agent to apportion the notes to investors, their registration filing usually incorporates a list of investment banks. With MTNs, most will see four or less agents since the inclusion of additional agents emboldens competition amongst investment banks and decreases financing costs.

Once an MTN program is established, an investor can enter the MTN market with frequency or on an intermittent level at both sizeable and moderate offerings and levels.

MTN's provide much more flexibility than more traditional underwritten corporate bonds that are issued from shelf registrations simply because the entire debt issue is not made all at once through a single maturity and coupon rate. Instead, MTN's are primarily offered on an agency basis. While this is the standard protocol, most programs consider additional distribution means. For example, agents of MTN programs acquire notes for their own accounts, as well as for resale, at par or the standing market rates. It is also common to see MTN's sold on an underwritten basis as well, as this still substantiates the task at hand.

Agents, working together with their issuing MTN provider(s), post the offering rates through a range of maturities which could fall under the following classification: nine months to one year, a year to eighteen months, eighteen months to two years, and annually thereafter. It could also be a perpetual offering where it will remain 'open' for up to five (5) years at a time in certain scenarios. Many of these issuing MTN providers post rates as a yield spread over a US Treasury security with a comparable maturity rate.

The attractiveness of these posted yield spreads with maturities of three to five years indicate the issuers desire for fund raising at these maturity levels. When a corporation, or investor, shows willingness to perform on an MTN offering, the agent will then contact his issuer, gathering validation with regard to terms of the transactional contracts to be drafted. Within this maturity range, the corporation and/or investor can determine the end maturity of the note sale as long as it is acknowledged by the issuing company. The issuer will then lower its posted rates once it raises the desired amount of funds at a given maturity.

The issuer, for example, might lower its posted rate for MTN's with a five-year maturity to 40 basis points over comparable US Treasury securities after it sells the desired amount of debt at this maturity.

Bear in mind, issuers also change their offering rate scales in response to changing market conditions. Issuers may withdraw from the market by suspending sales or. Alternatively, by posting narrow offering spreads at all maturity ranges.

The proceeds from primary trades in the MTN market vary considerably dependent on the size of the transactions. After the amount of registered debt is sold, the issuer may "reload" its MTN program by filing a new registration with the SEC. Subsequently, the process begins again.

MTN Market In Flux

One writer comments that the MTN has evolved and is now the endangered species of debt instruments. He admits that in the MTN market "things are not how they used to be." His thesis is captured in the following text:

There is so much confusion regarding the purchasing of MTNs. Yes, there are many who want things to be the way they used to be prior to the last platform (Deutsche Bank) being closed in December of 2006 [when] over 350 Commitment Holders lost their opportunities to purchase MTNs' and resell these instruments...Now it is all about project funding, and it is a very closed business.

MTNs are tightly controlled now, very tightly controlled...[V]ery little business is being done at all, and that which is being done is for disaster relief, and it is very controlled.

We have also been told that until the new banking system comes on line, [they] will not be releasing these instruments, and even then, it will still be highly controlled and very specific, but never again for the profiteers to make money on, only for approved project funding.

The unnamed writer offers a strongly worded admonition against "ill-informed, poorly connected brokers who spawn misinformation and provide hope where there is no reality." The writer's psychological profile of the subject matter and its actors lends a unique perspective on the subject. The first person narrative offers advice and holds back nothing:

I am telling you more then you will ever hear anywhere else, and the specific reason is for your benefit and your... knowledge, and to inform the so many Investors who are running around chasing the impossible dream who are dealing with a bunch of ill-informed, poorly connected brokers who spawn misinformation and provide hope where there is no reality. Certain other groups also put out misinformation to keep the masses from ever getting close to a real transaction, because they do not have to monitor them or the proceedings while they are wandering in the massive desert of misinformation in this business. But when they really get close, then there is a real need for monitoring and much has to be done, and those who really do monitor this business are few in number and poorly funded. There go another reason why there is so much misinformation put out there to keep the confusion amongst the broker world and the Investors running wild. As everyone is chasing the impossible dream, i.e. MTN contracts, and entrances with no real connection to one of the four groups that can actually perform, there is little that really needs to be done, it is all very frustrating and confusing, and most drop out after a few attempts or years of trying without success.

Of the many who publish their views on the subject, this unnamed writer seems to project most forcefully. This writer's advice seems more precise and insightful than most of what is available on the subject. His "no-nonsense" tone is suggestive of something more than just technical commentary or editorial dicta. His passing references to Tier 1 (T1) and Tier 3 (T3) are either the fruit of creative disinformation campaigning or just reflexive allusions to the power brokers that manage the markets.

Because the piece is undated we cannot know for sure how the MTN market place might be different today from when the piece was authored. Despite these vagaries, certain insight may be gleaned from the unnamed writer's text which concludes as follows:

Tier 1 (T1) is the first answer to achieve project funding. Funding from T1 is very project specific, as T1 funds to fulfill the needs of the project requirements. There is little (1% for larger projects up to 4% on smaller projects) for life-style (profits) and administration on a T1 project funding, again, T1 funding is for project funding.

The minimum requirement is 500M for an entrance. If you can qualify for a T1 entrance, you will be doing business at the top of the financial world. Everything emanates from T1, plus, you will be a part of the new banking system, having a system account. At this level, you are doing business with the premier of all financial systems. Much can be done at this level to protect your assets, and you are always in control of your assets.

You will no longer be at the mercy and whims of the bankers and the governments who currently try every means to control your assets. T1 is enforcement over Central Banking in Europe. T1 controls the release of MTNs. You will be entered into a Managed Buy Sell, from which your projects will be funded. They control the instruments, they have the banking relationships, the settlement desks, they do they leveraging, and control all the exits, they do everything in the process and you get your projects funded.

Tier 3 (T3), is option number two. Tier 3 is geared for commercial funding, wherein asset enhancement and project funding is done by fulfilling contracts that Tier 3 already has in existence. T3 is licensed, authorized and approved to purchase instruments from certain banks they have relationships with (platforms). The Tier 3 Funder negotiates the paper for the Managed Buy Sells that they control, having the banking relationships in place to send the instruments to for the settlement and resell to the final exits. Through many years of experience and successful business transacting, they have complete knowledge of and relationships with those who can deliver at all levels. They control the reselling of the instruments also, in order to achieve the profits required to fulfill their existing contractual obligations and their contractual agreements with the Investor...

This is the manner in which this business is done in today's world. Through one of these two options, an Investor can achieve what [he or she desires] to accomplish.

Private Placement Programs For the Creation Of Credit

When credit is needed within the US financial system the US Federal Reserve may cause funds to be put in the "System" by buying back US Treasury bonds, treasury notes and other debt instruments in the open market.

The US Treasury, fulfilling its responsibilities under the Bretton Woods Agreements, developed the Medium Term Note (MTN) by employing established European financing methods through which banks and financial institutions commonly finance long-term loans by selling Letters of Credit or Bank Notes of medium term to provide funding for loans.

In the post World War II era the US Treasury and its affiliates adopted the protocols of the finance syndicates led by major European bank holding companies that would issue their

Medium Term Notes guaranteed by a matching US Treasury Guarantee.

The Treasury and the Federal Reserve developed an instrument that may be traded to create new credit, and that credit would be used in specific approved macroeconomic projects allowing such funds and credit to be applied in geographical areas requiring credit and cash infusions to survive and grow.

For example, if credit is needed for India then eligible projects in India may be approved and the credit may be created for the outlay of the approved project(s). The same goes for the Balkans, Africa, South America, for the United States, and in many areas where expertise and development are needed. Credit and cash would be made available to establish and/or expand job creation, education, health and humanitarian goals. Principals who own and can show clean and clear cash funds and who wish to partake in this method of Private Placement Deposit Financing for Approved Project Financing can apply to participate in private placement programs designed for this end.

Credit is created when the US Treasury, or its European equivalent, the European Cental Bank (ECB), can make available to approved and pre-qualified Private Placement Depositors with qualifying funds on deposit, those Bank Instruments at a discount (Primary Market Issue).

For example, the US Treasury, or the US Federal Reserve, could issue 7.5% ten-year instruments (MTN's), at a price of 80% of the face value of the instrument. The market may sell these MTNs at 100% of face value so when $1,000 US Dollars of MTNs are purchased at 80% and sold at 100% there is new credit of 20% (per 1,000 dollars) or two hundred dollars ($200.00).

Such contracts to purchase and sell these trading instruments are managed and approved by the US Treasury which are administered by prime US and European bank syndicates. The Treasury or the Fed may price these instruments at whatever price is necessary to provide the needed new credit in the geographical location or for the project they have been approved.

Not all applicants or projects are approved. Both the Applicant and the funds that will be used to purchase and sell the financial instruments must be screened according to US Patriot Act and anti-money laundering guidelines and their European equivalents.

Both US Dollars and EURO's may be used as the Private Placement Deposit. When the Private Placement Deposit is a Letter of Credit, Certificate of Deposit, Gold or a bond, these assets must be turned into cash as creation of credit trading is a cash based process. To be eligible asset items must be sold in the open market for cash or a loan facility.

The contract for the Depositor usually states a minimum amount of earnings being available to the Depositor for the financing of their projects. The Depositor may be financing more than their own projects but all of the projects must be submitted and approved. Submittals must contain a full feasibility analysis and business plan and full disclosure of all parties involved.

When the earnings are generated they will be deposited in a Bank Project Trust Account. This Project Trust Account will hold the funds for the Approved Project and will make the necessary payments for financing each phase of the proposed project according to the cash requirements of the project.

In most instances, earnings are applied to the project on a 20/80% or 30/70% ratio.

These projects, in turn, generate earnings which are paid into a local Investment Development Trust so the initial funds can be replenished and reused or rolled over into additional new projects.

Generally there is but one Principal. That Principal is the owner of the Funds and the Principal is the applicant to the approved trading foundation. The "trade entity" or "trade foundation" must also have the approval to trade from the US Treasury or the US Federal Reserve.

Velocity, Leverage, Compounding

It is well-settled that trading, when done right, invokes the fundamentals of purchasing at a discount and then selling at a premium. The "managed" aspect of the trade is predicated on the condition that any purchase is preceded and conditioned on a confirmed prearranged exit buyer that will purchase at a premium what the trader acquired at a discount.

One interesting analysis of the trade platform industry identifies three variables that work together to generate the high yields that characterize PPP trades. The three variables are velocity, leverage and compounding. The relevant portion of the article reads:

Velocity

The speed with which deals happen makes a massive difference to the overall annual return. A worst case scenario is a savings account which pays say, 4% per annum - in this example the velocity of money is annual. Let's say that you borrow money for a business. You buy stock and turn it over four times a year – the capital is now used more efficiently. If you made 12% net profit on the stock each time you sold it, you would make 48% return per year on your capital. Way better than a savings account. In this example the velocity of money is every three months.

Our third example is trading in a major market;; let's say the Forex market which is the biggest in the world. Good traders can routinely make 5% a week on the money that's at stake. If they reinvest the profits, at the end of the year the return will be 1100% of the capital employed. Now it starts to get interesting. This profit would return to the investor their original capital, plus eleven times more! In this example the velocity of money is weekly.

For my fourth example let's take a money-lender in a poor third-world country. He has just $100 available to lend. He lends money in a market to women buying and selling fruit and vegetables. His deal is that his loan has to be repaid at the end of the trading session, either morning or afternoon, and he gets back his capital plus $5. This is a completely real example that happens thousands of times every day in exactly these circumstances.

Do the math. Every day the money-lender makes $10 on his $100 capital. That's 10% a day. Suppose he works 5 days a week, that's 70% profit a week (compounded daily). Now reality diverges, because the money-lender uses his profit to live on, so his capital doesn't grow much or indeed at all. But, what if he left his profit in the deal for a year – compounding his returns? The money he would have at the end of the year is astronomic, it runs into the billions! This is simply because the velocity of money is very high – we are turning over our cash on a daily basis.

Leverage

For many investors the concept of leverage is easy to understand, particularly by reference to business deals, or real estate. Many business owners typically borrow up to 60% of the total capital from a bank, matching the 40% or so that they contribute. All this money is used to make profits and the lion's share goes to the business owner.

With real estate, leveraging has historically reached very high levels specifically in mature growing markets. In the recent past we have seen leveraging at 90% for many first time buyers in the US & Europe. This is a 9:1 leverage. All it needs is a 10% growth in the asset over a 12-month period, and the investor's return is 100%! You may think that leverage of 9:1 is very good, but it is dwarfed by our next example. You can go online right now, as a private individual, and open an account with a Forex brokerage who will allow you to trade with a leverage of 200:1, some even at 400:1, on your money. To put this in context, open a trade with just $1,000, and the money placed on the market will be either $200,000 or $400,000. This is not secret; anyone can do it. What it means is that a miniscule 0.5% move in the currency in a 24-hour period means either a 100% or a 200% gain on your Leverage. For many investors the concept of leverage is easy to understand, particularly by reference to business deals, or real estate. Many business owners typically borrow up to 60% of the total capital from a bank, matching the 40% or so that they contribute. All this money is used to make profits, and the lion's share goes to the business owner. That's why the currency, and other markets, are so dynamic and fast moving you have both velocity trading multiple times a day and leverage, up to 400:1.

Compounding

The third concept is compounding. Put simply, don't remove your weekly profits. Leave them to increase the amount of cash available for your investment activity. We have shown that just $100, compounded at 70% a week, turns into billions at the end of one year. The power of compounding is simply enormous, provided you leave your cash for long enough to have an effect.

Compounding follows a geometric progression, which means that your money doesn't grow in a straight line.

The Beauty Of A Private Placement Trade Platform

A PPTP utilizes all three concepts – velocity, leverage, and compounding – within a unique financial environment in a

Top 25 bank to create an incredibly powerful vehicle that can generate exceptional returns with no risk to your investment capital.

Money Creation

The primary reason why this business exists is to create money. The fact is that money is created by generating debt. For example, you as an individual can lend out USD100 to a friend and you can make an agreement where the interest for that loan is 10%, so that he must pay you back USD110. What you have done is to actually create USD10, even though you don't see that 10 dollars. Don't consider the legal aspects of such an agreement, just the facts. Now, the Banks are doing this every day, but with a lot more money. Banks have the power to create money out of nothing. Since PPO involves trading with discounted bank-issued debt instruments, money is created due to the fact that such instruments are deferred payment obligations (debts). Money is created from debt. Theoretically, any person/company/organization can issue debt notes (don't look at the legal aspects of it). Debt notes are deferred payment liabilities and/or debts.

Example:

A lawful person (individual/company/organization) is in need of USD100, so he writes a debt note for USD120 that matures after 1 year. He then sells it for USD100 (this is called "discounting"). Theoretically, the issuer is able to issue as many such debt notes at whatever face value he wants as long as there are those who believe that he's financially strong enough to honor them upon maturity, and thereby are interested in buying such debt notes. Debt notes like Medium Terms Notes (MTN), Bank Guarantees (BG), Stand-By Letters of Credit (SBLC), etc., are issued at discounted prices by some of the major world banks in very large amounts; Billions of USD and/or Euros every day.

In general, they do "create" such notes (debt notes) "out of thin air", so to speak. That is, they only have to write the documents. It's as easy as if you, as an individual, write a debt note. Now, the core problem: to issue such a debt note is very simple, but the issuer would have definite problems in finding a buyer, unless that buyer "is confident" that the issuer is financially strong enough to honor that debt note upon maturity. Any bank can issue such a debt note, sell it at discount and promise to pay back the full face value at the time the debt note matures. But would that issuing bank be able to find a buyer for such a debt note without being financially strong enough?

Another example: If you had USD1 Million, and had the opportunity to buy a debt note with the face value of USD1 Million issued by one of the largest banks in Western Europe for let's say USD 800,000 a debt note that matures in 1 year, wouldn't you then consider buying it if you had the chance to verify it? Now, if a "Mr. Smith" approaches you on the street and asks you if you want to buy an identical debt note issued by an unknown bank, would you consider that offer? As you see, it's a matter of trust and credibility only. And now, maybe, you will also begin to understand why there's so much fraud, and so many bogus instruments in this industry.

Normal Trading vs. Private Placement

All programs in the Private Placement arena involve trade with such discounted debt notes in one way or another. And to bypass the legal restrictions, this can only be done on a private level. This is the reason why this type of trading is so different from the "normal" trading, which is highly regulated. In other words, this business can be done and restricted on a Private level only, hence, the Private Placement.

The normal trading known by the Public is the "open market" (as the "spot market"), where discounted instruments are bought and sold with bids and offers like an auction. To participate here, the traders must be in full control of the funds; otherwise, they cannot buy the instrument and sell them off to buyers. Also, there are no arbitrage buy-sell transactions on this market, because all participants can see the instruments and their price.

However, besides this "open market", there's a "Closed-Ended, Private Market" where a restricted number of "Master Commitment Holders" are the inner circle. These master commitment holders are Trusts with huge amounts of money that enter contractual agreements with banks to buy a massive number of new issue (fresh-cut) instruments at a specific price during a specific period of time. Their job is to sell these instruments on, so they contract sub-commitment holders, who, immediately contract Exit-Buyers.

These programs are all based on arbitrage buy-sell transactions with pre-defined prices, and as such, the traders never need to be in control of the Investor's funds. However, no program can launch, unless there's enough money behind each buy-sell transaction.

It's at this point that the Investors are needed because the commitment holders and the involved banks and are not allowed to trade with their own money, unless they have reserved enough funds on the market money that belongs to the Investors which is never spent and never at risk [Riskless Principal]. This is the Master Key!

The involved banks (the Trading Banks) can lend out money to the "Trader", and it's typically 1:10. So if the Trader can "reserve" USD100M, then the bank can lend out to a Trader's Standby Letter Of Credit portfolio valued at USD1B. Actually, the bank is giving the trader a line of credit [LOC] based on how much money the trader &/or commitment holder has, since the bank doesn't lend out that much money without collateral, and not depending on how much money the Investors have.

So, if a trader says that he must be "in control" of the Investor's funds, then it means that he's not one of the "big boys", but plays on the open spot market. Lots of different "instruments" are traded, vs. if the trader only needs to reserve the Investor's funds, and doesn't need to be in control of the funds, then he's trading in this "private market".

It's because many bankers and others in the financial world are well aware of the open market, as well as being aware of the so-called "MTN-programs", but because they are closed out from the private market, they doubt that the private market exists.

Arbitrage And Leverage

The real core of the trading and its safety is due to the fact that they arrange the buy-sell transaction as arbitrage, which means that the instrument will be bought and sold at the same time with a pre-defined price; to accomplish this a chain of buyers / sellers are contracted, including the exit-buyers who often are institutions, other banks, insurance companies, big Secondary Market companies, or other wealthy individuals.

The issued instruments are never sold directly to the exit-buyer, but to a chain of 3 to 7, or even perhaps 50 Investors. The involved banks cannot, for obvious reasons, directly participate in this as in-between buyers and sellers. Still, they are still profiting from it indirectly, because they are lending out their money (with interest) to the trader, or to the Investor as a line of credit.

Furthermore, the banks profit from the commissions involved in each buy-sell transaction of debt bank instruments in the trading circle. Now, the Investor's principal doesn't have to be used for the transactions, but is only reserved as a compensating balance "mirrored", if you will, against this credit line. And . . . this credit line is then used to back up the arbitrage buy-sell transaction.

Therefore, . . . since the trading is done as arbitrage, the money (or the credit line) doesn't have to be used, but it must still be there available to back up each and every buy-sell transaction. Such programs never fail because they don't start before all actors have been contracted, and each actor knows what role to play and how they will profit from the transaction. This would embody a true representation of PPO's!

A Trader who is able to do leverage (or Ratchet Up as the British say) is able to control a credit of typically 10 times that of the principal, but even though he's in control of that money, he's not able to spend the money.

The Trader only needs to show (or 'screen') that he has the money and that he's in control of the money, and that the money is not used (or encumbered) somewhere else at the time of the buy-sell transaction.

The money is never spent. The reason is that the trading is done as an arbitrage transaction.

Let's keep it simple:

Let's say that you're offered the chance to buy a car for USD30K, and that you also find another buyer who is willing to buy it from you for USD35K. If the buy-sell transaction is done at the same time, then you don't have to spend USD30K, and then wait to earn the USD35K since it can be done at the same time you cash in USD5K in profit. However, you must still have that USD30K and prove that you're in control of it.

Arbitrage transactions with discounted bank instruments are done in a similar way. The involved traders never spend the money, but they must be in control of it.

And the Investor's principal is reserved directly for this, or indirectly, in order for the trader to leverage.

Confusion is rife because most observers seem to believe that the money must be spent.

And even though this is the traditional way of trading – buy low and sell high, and also the common way to trade on the open market for securities and bank instruments, it's possible to set up arbitrage transactions if there's a chain of contracted buyers.

Programs Structure

A trading program is nothing other than pre-arranged buy-sell transactions of discounted banking instruments designed as an arbitrage transaction. Virtually, an Investor with large amounts of funds (on the level of 100M to 1B USD) could arrange for his own program by implementing for himself the buy-sell transaction, but in this case he needs to gain control of the whole process, making contract with an *Investment

Manager with contacts with the Provider banks for the bank instruments and their exit buyers. This is not a simple task at all considering that there are many FED restrictions to be passed, and at the same time, it is very difficult to get the strong necessary connections with the related parties, i.e., the law firms/issuing banks/providers for the bank instruments and the exit-buyers/a major auditing firm/a tier one Trader's Desk.

For an Investor, it is much simpler to contract a special party known as a *Investment Manager to enter a program where the tier one level Trader with his Trading Group has everything already in place (the issuing banks, the exit-buyer, the contracts ready for the arbitrage transaction, the line of credit with the trading banks, all of the necessary guarantees / safety / a major accounting firm as pay master for the Investor, etc.) and the Investor needs only to agree with the contract/subscription offered by the *Investment Manager forgetting about any other underlying problem. Another advantage for the client/Investor is that he can enter a program with a substantially lower amount of money (although with much lower yield) against the case to proceed by himself because he could take an indirect advantage of the larger line of credit of the Trading Group.

Non-Solicitation And Non-Disclosure

As a direct consequence of the Private Placements environment where this business has to take place, a non-solicitation regulation has to be strictly followed by all of the involved parties. This factor strongly influences the way the parties, and actors can deal each other, and the way they can make contact. Sometimes, this fact can also be the cause of the origin of scams (or attempts to scam), due to the fact that at an early stage, it is often difficult for the Investors to realize if they are really in contact with a reliable source.

There is another reason why so few experienced people talk about this transaction; virtually every contract involving the use of these high-yield instruments contain very explicit non-circumvention, as well as non-disclosure clauses forbidding the contracting parties from discussing any aspect of the transaction for a long period of years.

Hence, it is very difficult to locate experienced contacts who are both knowledgeable and willing to talk openly about this type of instrument, and the extensive profitability of the transaction in which they figure. This is an extremely private business; not advertised anywhere, nor covered in the press and not open to anyone, but the best-connected, most wealthy, private entities that can come forward quickly with substantial cash funds.

How Banks And Brokers Can Earn

Banks are not allowed to act as Investors in such programs. However, they are able to profit from it indirectly in different ways, first by getting commissions on large amounts. This fact permits some private entities like facilitators, brokers, trading groups, and private Investors to take part in this business that otherwise would be a banking matter only! The private assets (in the form of a POF) coming from private clients/investors are necessary to start the process. These large, privately held cash funds are the mandatory requirement for the buy-sell transaction of banking debt instruments, and as a consequence, also the mandatory requirement for the programs through the Trading Groups.

An *Investment Manager is necessary to introduce the contacts he has developed over the span of years to the Investors and onto the trading groups! Thus, each of the involved entities takes their part in the sharing of the benefits, commissions for banks/brokers, performance fees on profit earnings, and management fees.

Project Funding

Projects are usually involved in these programs. However, the primary purpose of this type of trading is NOT to finance humanitarian projects. It's true that projects, not just People-to-People projects, can be funded as a result of this trading, and since this type of trading generates such huge amounts of money on the market, measures must be taken to hold down global inflation. One way is to adjust the interest rates (a temporary band aid). However, at this level of trading; this has little or no effect.

The best way is to finance different projects. If too much money is created, the result is massive inflation, and in order to be able to continue creating debt, different measures must be taken to keep the inflation under control.

However, . . . a much better way is to allocate some of the profit to be used for People-to-People projects which need funding, for instance; to rebuild the infrastructure in regions of the world that have experienced catastrophes, war, etc., because this creates jobs for people in those regions, as well as a trickle-down growth through community development, through funding opportunities for developers, contractors and subcontractors. Jobs are generated by applied economics and inflation is avoided.

So, . . . the reason for project funding is not only to support humanitarian organizations, even though that is wonderful, but to Fight Against Global Inflation.

Process Synthesis

The complete process involving the issuing of debt notes, the arbitrage transaction, the programs, the projects, etc., is as a final synthesis, a result of combined market forces: banks have a method of increasing their revenues and profits, Investors are able to generate substantial (Riskless) profits/earnings/income allowing them to fund & capitalise different ventures, People-to-People projects are able to access funding techniques, even without acceptable collateral.

The Law of Supply and Demand drives this unique technique. As long as the supply and demand exists, then this kind of trading will also exist (quietly and discreetly). This is finance at the highest level and not meant for everyone! Its not offered to just anyone.

As an attempt to summarize the process involved for entering a PPP transaction:

An Investor with USD10M< (Euros also) and more, can be an subscriber for a Private Placement Investment Program. The return is very good.

When the Investor that has USD100M< or more, the appreciation is very large. At the USD1B minimum< the earnings are 'through the roof', of course.

This business is entirely private. To get access to these investment programs, the Investor needs to send his preliminary documentation to an *Investment Manager whom the Investor trusts to be in direct contact with the Trading Group. There is no other way for the Investor to make contact with the Trading Group at this stage.

After the Investor has sent his KYC paperwork, the Trading Group will proceed to its Due Diligence on the applicant, and if the response is positive, and cleared, then the *Investment Manager in the trading group will contact the Investor by phone and/or email. However, usually, if the Investor is not willing to travel, everything can be done by fax, phone, and courier mail.

If not cleared, then the program manager will contact the *Investment Manager, and then advise him that the Investor did not qualify (sometimes due to laundering or other illegal activity), and the *Investment Manager forwards that information on to the Investor who often gets upset and may attempt to wrongly discredit the broker and/or intermediary, perhaps on an internet 'due diligence message boards' (they always hide behind aliases).

During the contact with the Investor, the trader, via the *Investment Manager, will explain the program's terms/conditions, the contract details, as well as the next step required to start the program. Then, it's necessary and required by the program terms; the Investor will get instructions to SWIFT into a top world bank account at the Trading Bank to subject to: the acceptance of the recipient bank officer. The Trader & *Investment Manager have prepared everything; so, the Investor is able to open the Bank account without delay (because he has already been cleared).

Otherwise, the Investor will be invited to prepare his own bank to block/reserve the funds in his own account at his own bank for one year without any transfer of money (for a Closed-Ended Company Fund, a private hedge fund company).

The Investor will receive a contract which states the total monthly gross yield, his portion (usually one quarter to one half of monthly profits); the portion disbursed to other principals; the percentage reserved for projects (projected to equal between 20 to 25% of the remainder of the earnings); a negotiated percentage for the Trading Group; and the percentage for commissions/bank fees/accounting fees/& other fees usually totaling about 4% of the remainder to be deducted for any external brokers/intermediaries.

The portion to the Investor is 25% up to 50% of the appreciation) will be wired to another Investor Returns Account at the end of the term can be located in any bank he chooses. When the Investor/Trading Associate/client accepts the contract, the contract is signed, notarised/witnessed and the program is ready to launch.

*Investment Manager lodges all Pay Orders which instructs the major Accounting firm to wire out the disbursement part to the *Investment Manager's (and all of the other's) bank coordinates. The program continues this loop for each week until the end of the program, usually 252 banking days (considered to be a yearly contract). The Trader has been able to leverage the Investor's blocked/reserved money 10 times and is able to back up the arbitrage transaction with the money, a credit line [LOC] which remains in the bank account and is screened before each arbitrage buy-sell transaction. Trading now continues, and the appropriate portion of profit is compounded each month for the year. A financial report is generated quarterly for Investors.

This program can work with cash only. This fact does not mean that the Investor will only be accepted in the case he owns cash. The Investor can be accepted by some Trading Groups as well with screenable cusip financial assets like MTNs, BGs, CDs, SBLCs, some Bonds, Bonded Promissory Notes, SKRs, and etc., which the Traders can use for enhancing his own line of credit at the Trading Bank to run these programs. In this case, the Investor will have the advantage of profiting both from the program, and still from the interest paid on the instrument/s (i.e. the interest rate of a CD or MTN).

Analysis Of Risk Involved In Ppo Contracts

Finalising PPO contracts with Investors is usually always a long stressful process because the involved parties can stumble upon many problems along the way. We will observe here a list of possible problems of behavior from the standpoint of the main parties involved at the bottom line of the process:

The Investor

The brokers/intermediaries/introducing agents
Then there will follow some hints in an addendum at the end of this educational article on possible scams and warning for scams, which cause damages to this industry by unscrupulous predators.

From the Investor's Side:

The applicant Investor will not be able to meet "a real trader" in this business directly, and without the proper introduction, and such an introduction requires that the client identifies himself and shows a certified proof (POF and Tear Sheet) that he has enough money.
The main reason why there's a broker-intermediary chain is because the people in the "Trading Groups", (we use the term

"trading groups" because there's always a small group of people that work together and not just a trader), have no time or interest in meeting all the 99% of people who are just fishing for information and/or who don't qualify because they don't have enough money, or have bogus/useless bank instruments.

If you're a qualifying Investor, then you should try to establish contracts through the *Investment Manager with his team of real players and he will be able to place you in contact with a performing trading group. Don't chase around trying to find "a real trader". Most so called 'traders' in the financial world are not involved in this kind of trading, and those who are, are keeping a very low profile (under the radar) and would never talk with an Investor/Trading 'Associate'/client which hasn't been KYC cleared first [Know Your Customer].

When it comes to non-performance, in most cases the problem is on the client/Investor side. The client doesn't qualify because he doesn't have enough money, or the bank in which he has the money is too small, or he cannot move his funds or he has a bank instrument that cannot be used, or he tries to proceed according to his own procedure and rules, and/or is located in the "wrong country", etc. Most of the client documents seen over the years have been useless! Sometimes transactions are killed because the broker and/or intermediary don't understand what to do. And the worst thing is to "shop around", trying to find the best deal. It's better to get 10% per month from a program that performs, than having to wait for 100% per week from a program that was supposed to work, but never will. There are brokers and Investors that have chased around for decades without being able to find an open door. And their main problem is that they had the wrong approach. Remember that the trading group does not have to give any explanation as to why the

Investor doesn't pass through the clearance. If they already, have a fist full of Investors awaiting clearance, then it doesn't require much to be put aside to be disqualified.

Things To Remember:

Investors must understand what is required to qualify:
A minimum of USD10+ Million in cash located in a major bank in Western Europe, USA, Canada or Australia, money which is transparent, cleared, can be traced back to origin and comes from a non-criminal history.

That the Investor and the company that he represents can be cleared [KYC]. For individuals, this is an identity control proving that the person exists. Note: individuals coming from certain countries will never qualify.

Investors are invited, and might not be accepted. They can never demand to be accepted just because they have lots of money and/or that they believe they are prominent people. Most people in the different trading groups are fed up with such inflated individuals, and are just waiting to find an excuse to turn them down.

The Investor himself must be the one, and only person that the trading group (via Investment Manager) deals with. He's not allowed to let his lawyer, or sister-in-law who is fluent in English, or whatever person, contact any person in the trading group, not even the broker. If the Investor doesn't speak English, and needs assistance, then he must sign a Limited Communication Purpose. The Investor must still be the authorized signatory on all documents.

Investors who have the least money are always placed in the queue (on the bottom of the stack). An Investor with USD100M+ will get more attention than an Investor with USD10M. Investors who have assets other than cash will also always be placed in the queue. This means that sub-USD100M clients must be patient. If they are told that they will be contacted next week, then they should accept that, and not take that as an excuse to 'shop around'.

It's not easy for an Investor to be sure that he meets the right people, i.e., intermediaries and brokers who know what to do, and what not to do, and who are working with a performing trading group. The best he can do is to educate himself and not be lured by those who claim that their program will give the highest yield. He must also be patient, and trust the seasoned *Investment Manager/Advisor. This one can be the most important initial problem from the Investor's point of view. However, there's no way that the Investor is able to come into contact directly with the trade group before he has been cleared/vetted, i.e., KYC, which requires notarized True Copies of the passport, notarized proof of residence, plus the certified True Copy of the Proof Of Funds [POF], and more. He might be able to talk with someone in the group, or at least with the broker, once the required documents have been checked. Before all of his KYC documents are cleared he will not get further.

If the Investor, for any reason, is unsatisfied with the broker and/or intermediary then he can try another one after having first sent a Cease and Desist order. In most cases where Investors have been blacklisted because they have been 'shopping around', it's their own fault. Brokers/intermediaries cannot be blamed if the Investor is 'shopping around'. And those brokers/intermediaries who once make the mistake of 'shopping around', will quickly be blacklisted as well.

These are some of the main risks the Investor can meet with these types:

- Nothing will come out of the trade; no contact and no profit, just frustration after weeks/months of waiting.
- Investors, or their Intermediaries and/or Brokers are 'shopping around' with client documents, which sooner or later will result in blacklisting.

- The Investor is told that he must move his funds out of his own control to an escrow account, etc.
- The Investor is told that he must buy a bank instrument for his money. In the worst-case scenario, this instrument is a fake, or impossible to use.
- The Investor is told that he must pay unnecessary fees for the leverage of his funds, or some bank instrument must be discounted, or banking fees must be paid, etc. These type of fees paid are lost and nothing more will happen.

From The Broker's And Intermediary's Side

There is a common misuse of such terms as a broker, intermediaries, etc. The fact is that they are not official terms in banking or finance, but such terms are used within trading groups, and in their communication between each other. The problem is that it sometimes happens that a broker, or an intermediary claims that he's in direct contact to a person with that title, but that doesn't guarantee anything, because any person can call himself a trader, or a commitment holder, or whatever. And since such positions cannot be verified, at the first stage, such titles can be meaningless as seen from the Investor's point of view.

It is imperative to go through an *Investment Manager (with years/decades of seasoning) with a team of his contacts, i.e.; formation & compliance trusts services - law firm counsels (on-shore and off-shore) – top world rated accounting firm – offshore depository top rated banks – brokers / dealers – intermediaries - trading groups – Private Placement high tier traders, and all of this is for two reasons:

First, trading groups are not allowed to solicit, nor are brokers, or even intermediaries.

However, a seasoned *Investment Manager who knows all the documents necessary to begin the formation* of a Hedge

Fund/Company Fund as an International Business Company [IBC] broker who works in connection with one, and/or several trading groups.

Secondly, to protect the involved parties on the side of the trading group, they work through several brokers, and the broker works through several intermediaries.

As an additional responsibility of the seasoned *Investment Manager, he shall screen the potential Investors and at the same time, collecting from them the correct paperwork.

After a strict checking for KYC compliance, the quality, and acceptability of the client/Investor's documentation, in a way in which the trading group receives a workable ready to launch package assembled by the *Investment Manager's professional team.

The most common risks, or problems, that a broker, an intermediary, or a facilitator can meet during their own work in this business are:

They may need to handle many clients before finding an acceptable applicant.

They could get just a part of the truth regarding the asset of the client at an early stage which may later be discovered to be unworkable, after wasted weeks or months of work on it.

They always have difficulty qualifying themselves with new clients because they cannot show any past performance (must be discreet), or past contract, and the relationship with the client is just a matter of trust at an early stage.

There could be a long list of brokers and/or intermediaries between the client and the trading group. In this case, some brokers in the middle can destroy the deal by dragging their feet and by not giving the right information to the client, or to the trading group, and/or making problems with their fee agreements (greed).

There could be several levels involved for the intermediaries: the seasoned *Investment Manager is the most important person to the Investor and the closest one to the trading group. This person must have a direct contact with the Investor and a principal in the trading group.

Any other broker beneath the referenced Investment Manager is lower on the ladder. The broker, and/or the intermediary, can have problems showing the client his level in the hierarchy at an early stage.

Essentially, this business could seem very simple! You just need clean, cleared transparent funds for a minimum USD10M+ and up in a Top Bank, a broker in direct contact with a real, and strong Trading Group, and the right client who can follow the procedure in a riskless position! One can see that this is never easy and not meant for everyone.

However, from a practical point of view, the above ideal situation is so unusual as to not equate to reality! First, of all, most of the applicant's clients usually have some problems with their funds, or they are not in full control of them, or they cannot, or do not want, to move their assets, or they are not cleared, or they are not collaborative enough to deal with the Trading Group and/or with the dealer/brokers. Or they are unscrupulous.

Any new applicant could have a challenge with the difficulties of a steep learning curve before reaching the right mindset. Most or all of this information is out of reach for the general public. Many Investors (and their 'brokers') have searched far and wide for a greater return on their money. This has remained elusive, except for an elite few.

Below Is A General Scenario Of A Private Mid-Term Buy/Sell Program:

a. The Trader's Bank communicates with the Issuing Bank as well as with the Exit Buyer's Bank, to obtain a detailed agreement with the Issuing Bank Officer and with the Exit Buyer's Bank that they are both prepared to commence the contracted series of Transactions.

The Exit Buyer's

Bank forwards a POF to the Trader's Bank for the amount of the first purchase of $100M.

(**Note** - When a POF has been issued for the Exit Buyer and forwarded to the Trader's Bank, there is a legal Funding Commitment to complete that Transaction, which may NOT be revoked while the transaction is taking place).

b. The Trader's Bank forwards to the Issuing Bank a POF in the name of the Trader and requests that an MTN be issued in the name of the Trader, along with an Invoice at a discounted price, say for example, only $97M (discounted from $100M), payable in 4 Hours.

c. A copy of the Note and an Invoice at $97M, is forwarded to the Trader's Bank, who will authenticate signatures and MTN terms to verify compliance with the Purchase Contract.

d. The Trader's Bank then forwards the certified copy of the MTN, along with a Conditional Assignment of the MTN, to the Exit Buyer's Bank, along with another Invoice at the Exit Buyer's Purchase Contract Price, $100M for example purposes, payable in 4 hours.

e. The Exit Buyer's Bank authenticates signatures, verifies compliance with the Purchase Contract, and pays the $100M Invoice price to the Trader's Bank for credit to Trader's account, within the 4-hour limit.

f. The Trader's Bank then pays the Issuing Bank's Invoice for $97M within the 4 hour limit, along with immediate instructions for the Original MTN to be sent to the Exit buyer's Bank by courier.

g. The Trader's Bank debits the Trader a Bank Fee for their services rendered, and forwards the balance, $100M minus $97M minus fee paid to the Trader, who pays the 'Trader's Associate / Investor for their Service Rendered.

h. The procedure used for this example, typically takes place 3 or sometimes 4 times each day of a four business day week, and repeats until the Trader's Purchase Contract is completed. Using this formula, the monthly profits to the Investor should be equal to a 'double digit' percentage of their POF amount.

*A hypothetical outline (applying projected fuzzy logic) utilising at least $1Bn+ as a cash deposit as Riskless Principal in Private Matched Trades assuming the following: a 3% spread per transaction X 3 (possibly 4) matched trades per day = a Gross of 9% X only 4 days (possibly 5) per week = a Gross of 36% X 4 weeks per month = a Gross of 144% minus approximately 4%± for bank, legal and contingent liability fees = a Gross of 138±% to be divided equally among 3 principal groups = 10+% Net to each group per week or Net earnings could be as much as 20% to 40±% to each principal group per month.

Of course, the Power of Compounding would be realised as the Investor's profit is added into the initial deposit (the Net Asset Value) to start the next month. This feature continues each successive month until the end of term (12 months).

An experienced Trader's Associate/Investor can safely state that with the previously listed procedure and controls for the Transactions, the only reason for a Transaction failing, once commenced, would be for the Exit Buyer's Bank to default on completing a contracted purchase of a Note, which would be considered in jeopardy to their Bank Charter. This has not been experienced but is a consideration. Should any default take place, it would be quite simple for the Trader to make the required Payment, using their own Funds, to complete their purchase of the Instrument, and to immediately sell it to a different contracted Exit Buyer. This action by the Trader eliminates any risk of loss by the Buyers and Exit Buyers as well as the 'Trader's Associate/Investor'.

NOTE: With minor variances in the connection of an Investor's Funds to a Trader's $100M (or Euros) Operating Fund, an Investor may enter into a transaction with $10M+, or more, with relatively much lower percentage payments to them. By the same token, an Investor may enter into a PPP trading operation with as much over $100M+ as they have available (and upward into the Billions+).

Now, if you have managed to read this far, congratulations, you have risen above the crowd of wanna be types. Here is the good news. In most cases, the projected appreciation/returns/profit percentages may have projections based on the Net Asset Value of the Management Fund utilizing Investors' riskless commitments into PPPs, which should average a monthly net profit of:

*Minimum Amount of Riskless Asset Commitments = 10M+

10 - 15%±

100M+ 20 - 25%±

1Bn+ 30 - 40%±

These monthly profits are utilising the power of compounding each month causing the growth to go "through the roof"!

The Beginning Of A B.V.I. Unregulated Private Closed-End Wealth Management Fund (a Hedge Fund) Follows:

*Tier 1 Ltd. Assembles & processes the following Package of Documents (there could be other documents added as well) for formation and launch of an Investor's Private Closed-End Hedge Fund (BVI), which is then delivered by Professor Rose [T1L], a seasoned *Investment Manager/Advisor, to his proprietary contacts in preparation for a targeted launch date with -m Major Top World Law Firm / Trust Services – Administrator, Major Top World Accounting Firm (BVI) & Major Top 50 Bank (Bermuda/Cayman) & a Tier One Trader's Desk (UK);

1) Offering Memorandum signed (Certified True Copies Notarised) by all Corporate Directors
2) Subscription Agreement/Booklet signed & notarised by all Corporate Directors
3) *Investment Manager/Investment Manager's Agreement signed and notarised by all Company Directors
4) K Y C compliance documents from ALL participating Parties (Certified True Copies Notarised)
5) Proof of Funds – Tear Sheet from origin/sending Bank with Corporate Resolution from Investor/s
6) Passport/s for Mandate & All Directors (Certified True Copies Notarised)
7) Proof of Residence (3 months Certified True Copies Notarised utility bills, not mobile phone bill)
8) Bank Reference Letter Notarised
9) Certified Corporate documents of Investor's and/or Corporation
10) On-shore Counsel (instructions to setup Trust forming Investor's Closed-Ended Company Fund)
11) Corporate Resolution for appointment of Investment Manager with Apostille
12) Investment Manager Agreement with Company Fund (BVI).

How Private Placement Programs / Trade Platforms Work

Many private placement programs and trade platforms are legitimate investment vehicles that are accessible to a wide variety of investors. An excellent white paper on private placement programs and trade platforms was written by MB Assets of Memphis, TN–a copy of which is available for download above. It should be noted that we have no relationship with MB Assets or its principals—their white paper is provided for educational purposes only and should not be construed as an endorsement of the firm.

Part of the confusion regarding private placement programs in particular is the term, "private placement". Private placements are used by companies to raise capital from private investors often via a set of investment documents known as a Private Placement Memorandum (PPM).

Prime Bank Programs

More often than not, when people refer to PPPs they are referring to what are more properly known as Prime Bank Programs. Prime Bank Programs, also known as Prime Bank Investments, High Yield Investment Programs (HYIPs), Buy-Sell Programs or Roll Programs, are clearly and universally fraudulent. They purport to involve the purchase and sale of medium-term notes (MTNs), Standby Letters of Credit (SBLCs), Bank Guarantees (BGs), or some similar instrument.

As the name implies, it is usually alleged that only the largest top-50 prime banks in the world are involved in this program and participation is by invitation only. There is usually a great deal of secrecy involved and the minimum investment is typically in excess of $100 million or more. Interestingly enough, prime bank programs in the US often state that only overseas banks are involved while overseas programs often state that only US banks are involved.

They are most often described as "risk-free" investments where one prime bank issues discounted instruments to a purchaser at another prime bank who has committed to purchase the notes at an agreed upon price. If this is simply a bank-to-bank transaction one might wonder where the scam comes in. Supposedly, the purchasing bank needs a large deposit from a new client to create the line of credit that will be used for the purchase. This deposit will be placed in a "blocked" account and held untouched by the bank until the transaction has been completed.

Prime bank programs have been universally condemned by the FBI, SEC and US Treasury Department as being fraudulent. In recent years, fraudsters have attempted to circumvent these governmental warnings with a clever ruse. They state that these agencies know that the programs are real, but that they are obligated to publicly deny their existence lest investors transfer large amounts of capital from deposit accounts into prime bank programs. Supposedly, this mass exodus of capital would cause the banking system to collapse, hence the official denials. This, of course, is complete nonsense.

Medium Term Notes (MTNs), Standby Letters of Credit (SBLCs) and Bank Guarantees (BGs)

Part of the reasons such frauds have been successful is that Medium Term Notes, Bank Guarantees and Standby Letters of Credit are real financial instruments. A Medium Term Note is the general name given to a debt instrument that matures in the medium term, typically 5-10 years. Bank Guarantees, as they are known outside of the US, or their US counterpart, Standby Letters of Credit, are most often used in interational commerce where a seller might be unsure about a buyer's ability to pay for goods once received. One way of overcoming this impasse is to utilize a bank guarantee or standby letter of credit.

An SBLC or BG is simply a promise to pay on the part of the bank involved in the transaction. Trading partners often have greater confidence in a transaction if the payment is backed by a commercial bank rather than a trading partner with who they might be unfamiliar. Banks are not in the business of losing depositors' money, so in order for them to issue an SBLC or BG in the first place, they would underwrite the SBLC/BG similar to an unsecured loan–meaning obtaining an SBLC/BG is a difficult endeavor to begin with.

Moreover, banks will often charge 1%-8% of the face value of the instrument, meaning a $100 million SBLC could cost the bank's client as much as $8 million to obtain, and is usually only valid for a period of one year. Which, of course, begs the question: if the borrower has sufficient standing with the bank to be approved for an SBLC/BG and sufficient funds to cover the cost of issuing it, why are they contacting us? The answer is, if this were a legitimate transaction, they wouldn't be.

Over the years many people have approached us looking for SBLCs/BGs. Most are actually looking to LEASE an SBLC/BG and use the instrument as collateral for a loan or cash investment. This is somewhat akin to leasing a new car and then trying to use the car as collateral for a loan from another lender. No automobile, SBLC, BG or any other leased asset can be used as collateral in a legitimate financial transaction, which is why these transactions never work.

Capital Funding- Capital & Credit Enhancement - "Buy Sell' or 'PPP' Our Principal is happy to take conference calls with Client Principals and issue contracts within 24 hrs upon standard compliance.

Purpose of these Programs: Project Capital Funding is an essential part of business development and finance of commercial and government approved projects.

3 Ways We Place Instruments Into Monetization And Trade:

1) MT799 Administrative Block
2) MT760 CASH BACKED SBLC, we monetize only, OR monetize and trade.
3) We can also PURCHASE MTNs and place into trade.

The following is the basic procedure for PPP Trade Programs. (Procedure for non-standard programs may vary slightly.)

1) COMPLIANCE: KYC/BANK RWA/FULL SENDER BANK DETAILS/BANK OFFICER BUSINESS CARDS
2) PRINCIPAL to PRINCIPAL call and issue of contract with receiving bank and beneficiary details.
3) CLIENT BANK SENDS CASH BACKED SBLC via MT760
4) Monetization Fund/LTV is paid out after 10-20 banking days over 3 tranches.

   - All Instruments are assigned for 366 Days and returned to the Sender 15 days before maturity or expiry date unencumbered.
   - A-AAA RATED BANKS: LTV (Loan To value) is usually 70-90% and/or CORRESPONDENT BANKS
   - AML (Anti Money Laundering) Regulations require all clients to provide full KYC/CIS information. [Principal returns their full company information in good faith]
     o The GROUP is a private investment consortium trading privately held funds and does not offer to buy or sell any public securities, and therefore does not require any licenses to trade privately held funds.
     o The Group is under exclusive signed agreements with its alliance funding partners, with its receiving banks [including JP Morgan, Bank of America and Citibank] to provide secure banking CLs [credit lines] under various account titles to activate CLs from incoming cash backed client Stand By Letter of Credit via SWIFT MT760.
     o The placement also involves HFT (High Frequency Trade) trades and does not necessarily rely on any buying and selling of financial instruments to secure margin/profit.
     o With HFT, no license is required to trade, as funds are privately held and all trades are internal, without any third parties, with the exception of our banking partners that provide private credit facilities.

- o Standard Anti-Money Laundering [AML] client assessment regulations apply on all clients.
- o In financial markets, high-frequency trading (HFT) is a type of algorithmic trading characterized by high speeds, high turnover rates, and high order-to-trade ratios that leverages high-frequency financial data and electronic trading tools.
- o We support groups in alignment with United Nation Development Programs Sustainable Development Goals in particular UNDP SDG#9: Investment in Infrastructure, Industry and Innovation.
- o We support investments at a community level to improve social and economic prosperity, and commercial development and investments in long term infrastructure projects.

Private Placement Program Details And Procedure [.;]k instruments (CD, MTN, BG, SBLCs, etc.) or liquid funds as CASH in any top bank are accepted by most PPP operatives

- Standard PPP begins with 100 million or more. Small Cap Programs accept one million and up – no top limit USD or Euros (cash or acceptable AA – AAA Rated collaterals)
- Minimum requirement is 1 million and no top limit USD or Euro (cash or acceptable AA – AAA Rated bank instruments might be used as collateral) Small Cap Programs between 1M to 10M are rarely available.
- Bank should preferably have swift capability. Any top Bank must issue Swift MT760 in favour of trader's designated bank account
- After completion of due diligence, the client's bank holding the Cash funds or issuing the bank instrument must send a free message [Swift MT 199] to the trader's designated bank confirming its readiness to either block funds or to issue a bank instrument.

- Trader's Bank will then reply to the client's bank that it is ready, willing and able to receive the bank instrument [by Swift MT 199].
- Deed of Agreement [DOA] is issued by the trader after both Banks had confirmed issuance and acceptance of the bank instrument.
- Trading occurs for a 40-Week program or as Agreed by the Trader
- Historical returns can be discussed directly with the Trader. For bank instruments with face value 100M or more, returns might be as high as 100 per cent a month shared 50:50 with the trader. But returns are never guaranteed. These are indicative historic figures. Actual returns might be lower or higher.
- Face-to-face contract signing is very rare. All Signed documents are Emailed in PDF Format. This PPP opportunity is available to legitimate investors meeting the basic criteria as listed.

Once all documentation is delivered to the program manager the compliance process begins. At that point any and all due diligence will be completed for every applicant within a week. A week after the successful verification of cash funds or the respective bank instrument, the trade might begin. Profits might be paid to the investors weekly or monthly via wire transfers Swift MT103 into their designated Bank account.

Are Private Placement Programs/Trade Platforms Real Or A Scam?

The first question we are usually asked is: are private placement programs (also known as PPPs) and trade platforms real or are they a scam? In short, they are real, but not in the way they are often described. There are many myths about these programs that we will attempt to dispel.

Perhaps the most common misconception regarding private placeent programs and trade platforms is that they are the exclusive domain of the ultra rich through secretive, invitation only investments. Often, clients are told that they must pay large, upfront fees to gain access to these exclusive instruments. In addition, they are told they must submit POF (proof of funds), a CIS (client information summary) or KYC (know your client) package, along with their passport. Nothing could be further from the truth.

How come so few investors know about these programs? Are they new?

These programs are not publicly known, and only a very small group of investors that own funds or Bank Instruments may have access to them solely and exclusively by invitation. They are not new, they are more than 55 years old.

Are they safe?

The Private Placement Programs imply no risk for the investor. The purchase/sale of MTNs is "risk-free" provided that the Trader is guaranteed the exit to the instrument that was previously acquired. If we are dealing with a real Trader, such exit will be guaranteed by contract and, therefore, there wont be any risks for the investor. Before the start of the program, the Trader will "prepare" such program planning the future purchases and sales and knowing beforehand the benefits that each of them will bring. In a second phase the program will be run, which means nothing but carrying out the purchases/sales that were previously planned and negotiated with the cut houses.

Should I deliver or transfer my funds to the Trader?

In any case. The funds will always remain on the investors' account. To carry out the program it will only be necessary to lock them. The investor must choose one of two available locking options: Swift MT-760 or the assignment of the Trader on the account. This blocking will remain for the length of the program.

Do I run any risks by submitting these documents and why are they so important?

You are not under any risk. Their presentation is imperative and important since it is the only way to check and verify the quality of the clients' funds or assets. In this business the investor always has to take the first step by providing the required documentation to avoid falling into the"soliciting" rules.

The POF (Proof of Funds) will be issued by the Bank where the investor has the resources deposited, demonstrating their quality and amount, but does not enable ANYONE to move them or dispose of them.

What procedure should I follow to deliver these documents?

Once all the required documentation is submitted (SET Compliance + bank Documentation), we proceed to verify the funds/assets the client brings and to the subsequent Düe Dilig ence (clients under study for acceptance).

Once these preliminary investigations are successfully completed, within 48-72 hs. the Program Manager will contact the client for a formal presentation and also to agree on how to block the funds. Then, the investor will receive a pre-contract to be signed and later sent to the Traders office. Then, it will be the Trader in person who will contact the client.

How and when do I collect my interests or profits?

Yields are collected weekly at the bank designated by the Trader. Ever since the collection of the first profit, this capital will be completely available for the client.

Can I partially or totally remove the invested amount?
The invested capital will remain locked for the length of the program.

How should my funds be?

Clear, clean and with a non-criminal origin. For every asset the location of the deposited resources should appear clearly stated by the bank in question. If at the time of verification, there is any doubt on this matter, the transaction will be automatically dismissed.
Can I ask for references from previous transactions?
NO, as it represents a violation of the Rules of Confidentiality and of the Non-Discovery Agreement.

Steps To Private Placement Success

1) The client provides a proof of funds and passport copy along with their compliance package

NOTE: Most of the assets that people try to apply with CAN'T be used for any REAL private placement program. These include ITR's (Irrevocable Trust Receipt), SKR's with hard asset as security (e.g., land or buildings etc), junk bonds, asset backed bonds, hard assets, real estate, and more. As you can expect, most of the applications at this stage are unacceptable, and fraudulent.

2) Trade group submits application to the compliance department for review

NOTE: Within hours, most real traders will know if the asset and owner are legitimate. Also at this time, the criminal background and origin of the funds are explored to ensure they are dealing with a clean applicant. In addition, if the client has over 100M, real trade groups typically either know of the applicant, or have seen the person try to apply before. There is a very small circle of real traders, so when someone applies with large assets, the word gets around rather fast.

3) Client passes "due diligence", speaks with the trader, and receives the contract

NOTE: Most clients have NEVER been involved with a legitimate private placement before. With that being said, many will show the contract to their attorneys, who have never been through this as well, and they may advise against proceeding due to a lack of familiarity. Needless to say, this can kill the deal, or may make the PPP investor feel uncomfortable. The problem you will run into over and over at this stage is transparency, and gaining trust from the client. Due to the private nature of the private placement business, there is only so much information the trader can reveal, and this is a common obstacle.

4) Client signs partnership agreement and the trade contract, and then the trader countersigns it to make it official

NOTE: Once the client signs the contract, there are still a number of potential obstacles before you can "close the deal". If a client signs the contract and does not complete the transaction, they may be reported to the authorities, and by doing so, they will be permanently prevented from participating in any private placement program in the future. As we said before, there is a small circle of real traders, and if they label a potential client as a non-performer, it is rare that any other REAL trader will spend their time to work with them.

5) Client contacts their bank to complete the private placement transaction

NOTE: Banks are in the business of making money, and customer requests are secondary to the profit of the bank. When a client asks to block, conditionally assign, or transfer their funds, they are cutting into the pockets of the bank, which we know they don't stand for. If the bank loses that asset off their books, they actually lose over 25x that amount

PRIVATE PLACEMENT PLATFORM | 144

in potential loans from their country's central bank (FED/ECB). With this in mind, most banks stall with excuses, since that will frustrate most customers enough to kill the transaction. Even though this may be an obstacle, this should never be a deal killer since it is the client's money, not the banks. To complete a deal, you either need a bull personality or a great relationship with the bank, otherwise you may encounter problems with the final steps.

6) Client's funds are blocked, conditionally assigned, or transferred to the trade group in accordance with the contract

NOTE: Very few trade groups request that the client transfers ownership of their assets. If they do request this, be very cautious, and expect something is not as it seems. Most private placement traders ONLY need a conditional assignment of assets, temporary beneficiary access, or the blocking of the assets in their favor for the period of the trade. This allows them to access a line of credit which they trade for the client, specific to their contract agreement. Also, so you know, PING programs are 99.9% fake, since they do not allow the trader to access the line of credit they need to start trading. No bank will loan without collateral, and since "PINGING" the account is not sufficient assurance to the bank that it has collateral in place, it never works. It is just another ignorant broker creation, and is most often part of a "bait and switch" strategy.

7) Trader accesses the line of credit from the trading bank

NOTE: The trader is the only one who can access a line of credit against blocked assets. No one who is trying to complete a scam will ever be able to draw a huge line of credit on blocked assets. The bank completes thorough due diligence on anyone it loans to, and when that loan involves millions of dollars, it is far more diligent. In short, no bank will offer a line of credit for millions to someone who they do not thoroughly trust, so there is not a lot of worry about when blocking assets in someone's favor.

8) Trader uses line of credit to have discounted bank instruments issued from bank

NOTE: First, investor issue BG, SBLC to bank of trader. Trader's bank will accept instrument and with credit department of bank trader have capabilities to monetize banking instrument and via platform connected to credit facilities of third parties banks trader have possibilities obtain credit line with purpose increase margin level with leveraged funds x10 times more than initial investor's investments accordingly profit in trading will be increased cardinally x10 times more than without credit facility. This is a key factor and advantage of PPP and benefit for investor.

9) Client receives payment of profits weekly or according to the contract

NOTE: Once everything it set up with the banking, it is a very smooth process to get continual profits into your account. Typically the first payment is made within 10-15 banking days after trading has started so they can ramp up the account to purchase larger notes. After the first payment, the client will receive disbursements on a weekly basis, or whatever their contract specifies. Most clients and brokers would be best served in setting up international bank accounts, or better yet, they can have an account at the bank where the trading is occurring. This will prevent the need to send external wires through different countries and banking systems. All profits would be internally transferred "ledger to ledger", and would not attract as much attention.

10) Client uses profits to fund projects and retains the rest for personal use

NOTE: Most real private placement programs are intended to fund humanitarian projects in underdeveloped nations. Typically, 60-70% of the program's profits must go to projects, while the remaining 30-40% is for "administrative use". In essence, the 30-40% can be used at the client's discretion, but you must make sure you are funding projects as well. The platform does not regulate this, but National Regulators may oversee companies who have applied and received money in these types of programs.

Once the client completes this 40-week trading process, they can re-enter, but they must have projects funnel the profits into. Most private placement contracts are for 2 years, and are renewed upon expiration if both parties choose.

The Basic Options:

PRIVATE PLACEMENT PROGRAMS

DIRECT INSTRUMENT BUY/SELL OPPORTUNITIES

I. PRIVATE PLACEMENT PROGRAMS

A. TWO BULLETS with the following LONG-TERM PROGRAMS. 50 M to 5 B USD/EUR/GBP. STD.

Multiple bullets followed by 40 week trade.

Trade on Cash in TOP Bank in USA, Canada, Europe, Hong Kong, Singapore.

Funds stay in owner's account. Block/Reserve, with confirmation via Swift MT-799, the client funds remain in Investor's own account and are not moved at all.

Trade on Top Bank Instrument as BG, SBLC, CD, MTN

Blocking Mode MT 760 or MT 542 Free Delivery or Euroclear Free Delivery. Submission of Instrument not before mid-July 2019.

Minimum Asset: 100 M USD/EUR. Eventually 50 M USD/EUR.

DURATION: 13 Months by Block/Reserve with confirmation via Swift MT-799

CONTRACT: The Client signs the contract with the Trader, the said contract will specifically guarantee the "principal" amount as well as the extraordinary weekly "profits" for the client during the length of the Program.

Returns:

- 3% advance in 72 hours after receiving Swift verification and authentication of MT-799
- Then First Bullet in 10 days. Return 100 % (historical)
- Then Second Bullet in 30 days. Return 400 % (historical)
- Followed by 40 week program paying up to 50 % / week net (historical)
- Then the option to enter in Trade Program (40 Week program) for 3-5 Years.

With this program, returns are exceptional. Clients can use their profits to re-enter for more trades, thus enhancing their profits further. They can participate in additional trades for 3-5 years.

Trader located in Switzerland.

No need of Project.

Trader only can accept Swift MT-799, via Brussels System Swift.

Not via Euroclear and not via Swift NET.

Comment of Platform:

The historical profit shown is the minimum of Program, because the Client signs the Trading Contract with the minimum guaranteed yields those are specified in the Trading Contract, but in reality the Client will receive higher profits. As the Program is designed to work at the maximum effort, that means that, if the Trader can do more buy & sell instruments daily than scheduled, that means more benefits for the Client.

The funds are always under the control of the Client. As an administrative lock, Investor can lock and unlock when he wants, it is for this reason that the Client does not have any risk. The Trader does not have control of the account, the

Client is the only Owner and Signatory of the account, the account does not have subaccount. The text of the Swift MT799 only speaks of administrative block in favor of the Trader."

B. ULLET Tear Sheet on min. 100 Million EUR/USD/RMB Cash. „Same Day Payment". TOP Banks World, USA and CHINA. JGA.REA.KMA.SEV

Platform:

There is no blocking of the funds. There is no movement of the funds.

The funds stay right where they have been in the owners bank account. We just mirror the owners funds and bullet trade them."

Return: Same Day Payment 1000 % gross, 700 % net. Available within 10 Working Days.

Funds MUST remain on deposit in the owner's bank account.

Investor may re-enter this Program 3 times.

C. BULLET TEAR SHEET on min. 100 Million UP TO 5 B USD, EUR, GBP, CHF, CAD Cash. One-Week Bullet. TOP Banks World.

Acceptable Banks: Top-rated World Banks (Certain other banks might be approved.)

Profit - Bullet: 98% per day for 5 consecutive banking days, payable at term end.

Optional After Bullet: 40-Weeks Long Term Program. 98% per month for 10 months over a one-year period.

D. BULLET PING PROGRAM on min. 100 Million UP TO 5 B

Major Western Currencies. Cash. One-Week Bullet.

Investor's Account is pinged for ONLY 48 hours

ROI is 5 times the invested amount, payable within 72 hours thereafter;

CHAPTER 3 | 149

Investor can re-enter the Program 2 times with all or part of the profit earned from previous transaction(s).

No project requirements

The Investor must instruct their bank officer to accommodate the trader's bank officer for the pinging of the Investor's account, and arrangements must be made by the Investor for the trader to have their bank officer verify the process with Investor's bank officer

E. LONG-TERM PROGRAM and BULLET. DIC/VEZ TRADABLE ASSET: 100 M USD/EUR OR MORE CASH
   o   Long Term Program 40 Weeks.
   o   Return 25 % per Week gross, 20 % net.

Investor's Bank sends RWA Letter to Investor for readiness. Thereafter Blocking through Swift MT 799 or MT 199.

Options:
   o   40 Weeks Trade
   o   3 Years with Trade 51 weeks yearly.

Additional:

Two to Four BULLET Programs mostly available. To be discussed with Platform after passing of Compliance. One Bullet generates 3, 4 or 5 times the asset. Can be repeated.

F. LONG TERM PROGRAM 100 M with Bullets. Mari

Tear Sheet Program with Monthly Return of 100% Minimum.

Asset Requirement:
•   Minimum 100 M USD/EUR
•   Funds Preferably in a Top-Rated International Bank
•   Tear Sheet Protocol (Other Options with Swift or Block can be discussed)

Expected Gross Return of 100% Monthly. Additionally, several Bullet Programs can be expected, depending on the market situation. Not guaranteed.

Trade Group uses its own Cash to mirror Client's Tear Sheet Value Trade Duration: 40 Weeks Trade.
•   No Project required

- Client has to sign a Profit Sharing Agreement with Trade Group

G. 100 M USD/EUR PROGRAMME 8 WEEKS NISS

Cash Asset of 100 M must be deposited on a recognized EUROPEAN bank account or transferrred to such bank account, owned by Investor, to be opened under assistance of Platform.

Internal or Administrative Hold if the funds are cash sitting in an account at a top 10 Banks like HSBC, Barclays or DB.

Trading through a Joint Venture to be established with Platform.

Returns:

- 1-2% draw within 5 business days of launching the program.
- Return: 3 Billion USD/EUR after 8 weeks. Early pay-out through pay-orders negotiable.

Platform has own project GO GREEN

No project funding by Investor.

H. NO SWIFT 1 BILLION to 500 B USD/EUR PROGRAMME LIN

The cash asset will not be split into parts to be traded on.

Platform can trade in one transaction on 50, 100 up to 500 B.

No swift, but internal hold, to be confirmed on hard copy (which must be sent by bonded courier) if cash in prime or TOP 50 Bank. If weaker, but recognizable bank, Swift MT 799 required.

Returns 10 % weekly gross, 9 % net.

Trader located in London UK. 40 weeks trade.

I. BULLET on min. 500 Million EUR/USD Cash. Same Day Payment. Major London Banks. ASAM

Same Day Payment of 900 % gross, 810 % net, prior to Trade Start.

Maximum cash asset 8 Billion.

Bank: The funds needs to be in HSBC, JPM, Deutsche Bank or Barclay's - London Canary Wharf ONLY
Cash Requirements: On ledger liquid cash only
Block Requirement: Funds blocked for 1 year
Use of Proceeds: Profits can be placed into our 40-week trade Contract presented and executed in the Table Top Meeting at the bank with pay-out deposited immediately in new VIP account in the same bank or a portion swifted to pre - arranged coordinates.
This trade program generally DOES REQUIRE the applicant to sign in the bank, but arrangements CAN BE made otherwise, if requested.
J. BULLET on min. 100 Million max. 500 M EUR/USD/HKD Cash. 3 to 5 Days. Sev
No Block No Swift No Admin Hold,
100M USD/EURO Cash Minimum (HKD Equivalent also accepted) Returns: 50% Daily (Net to Client)
Cash only, Heritage funds NOT accepted
Account Restrictions: The client is NOT required to block, hold, or SWIFT and does not need to add the trader to their account.
Distribution Schedule: Paid either at the end of Day 3 or Day 5.
No Projects required: No project funding is required and distributions are fully discretionary once received by the client.
Limitations: Funds MUST be "on-ledger" and not "off-ledger" and the client must be able to use those funds freely, and they must be unencumbered.
ANY CLIENTS WITH FUNDS AT HSBC ARE A PRIORITY (ALL TOP BANKS ACCEPTED), BUT THERE IS AN A ADDITIONAL TRADE OPTION FOR HSBC BANK FILES
K. HARD COPY BLOCKING BANK LETTER OR CLIENT PAY-ORDER SUB-PRIME BANKS LIN

Banks that can be based in PPP-difficult jurisdictions such as USA, Russia, Eastern Europe, Middle East, South East Asia, South America, South Africa, India, China will be acceptable. Other major banks (e.g., HSBC, Soc Gen etc.) that are based in major African countries will be considered on a case by case basis, but will likely be accepted.

Net returns for clients for sub-prime banks will be around 30-75% per month on the face value of the blocked funds, depending on jurisdiction, bank rating etc.

Sub-Prime Banks include:

Top 100 banks listed in the US, Russia, India, China, Brazil etc. All other commercial banks listed outside the Top 100 bank worldwide, including those in difficult jurisdictions. Private banks or unrated banks on a case by case basis.

Blocked Funds Letter via BANK TO BANK BONDED COURIER

If the Client's bank does not issue blocked funds letters, Client can also issue a bank backed corporate pay order or promissory note or some other kind of payment undertaking backed by their bank instead of a blocked funds.

If Client has other assets in custody with their bank such as marketable securities, bonds, hard assets etc then it may approach its bank to have them issue the blocked funds letter using those assets as the underlying collateral.

NOT accepted Banks: Brazilian or Venezuelan banks; Makhota Bank Indonesia; DOHA Bank; Citibank SIngapore & Indonesia. Sberbank and VTB Russia.

Submissions from „high risk fraud areas" such as Indonesia, Mexico, Taiwan, Saudi Arabia, India and others may require additional documentation.

L. 5 YEAR LONG TERM PROGRAMS LIN
- o 100 M Cash Minimum
- o BLOCKING by MT799/ MT760/ MT103
- o LTV 65% to 85%

- Returns 80% per week for 40 weeks going on to 5 years
- Bank Drafts:
- BLOCKING BY MT110 followed by Bank Bonded Courier
- LTV 65%
- Returns 80% per week of the LTV for 40 week going on to 5 years cash accounts.

M. HSBC TRADE 500 MILLION USD/EUR LIN
Bank Trade where investor meets the trader and signs in Bank HSBC London Canary Wharf.
Asset: 500 million +
The return is 10 x in one day less 25% asset management fees.
Funds need to be in / or moved to HSBC London.
Trades is followed by a 40 week program @ 50% per week on the enhanced amount less 25% Asset Management Fees.
N. Top 100 Bank BG-SBLC-MTN-CD Monetization. PEJI
Face Value Min. 100 M USD
LTV 50 % min.
Blocking per SWIFT MT 799 or MT 760 at cost of Investor required
Returns: 100 % gross per week
Platform Fees 25 %
O. HARD ASSETS – GEMSTONES
There are only very few trading entities that can monetize hard assets like gemstones and then trade on the monetization proceeds efficient and reliably. Minimum appraised value preferably 1 B USD/EUR plus.
For submission we need:
- Complete Copy of SKR or other PROOF OF ASSET
- Current Assay Report(s)/Appraisal(s)
- Proof and History of Ownership
- Full CIS
- Passport.

- o Insurance Wrap can be paid out of Monetization Proceeds.

LTV 25 to 50 % of recognized value. PP Trade on Monetization Proceeds.

II. DIRECT INSTRUMENT BUY/SELL PROGRAMS

A. LONDON "SMALL CAP" BUY/SELL 8.6 M EUR MIN

10 % gross per daily Transactions. MEM

This Minimum Entry can trigger a €500M contract.

Transactions 2-3 tranches daily over 2-3 days per week possible.

Per transaction, profit of 20 Points. The 20 points are divided as follows: The Seller gets 10 points and the Client gets 10 points less Fees of 10%. The intermediaries' fees are 15%.

Investor can make €50M after 1 month a week, and €100M a week after 2 months, from €8.6M. These are approximate figures, no guarantee.

Payments are made Fridays. All payments are commercial funds.

Procedures:

1) The amount of 8.6 M EUR to be invested into a Non-Depletion account on the client's name of the fiduciary Law-Firm in London, which is authorized and approved by HSBC Bank and Trader, is €8.6M Euro +.

2) The Client, before he sends the €8.6M to the Fiduciary, receives the Contract from the Trader with full details of the Law Firm, which will only be given after the contract is agreed and signed, and then he can make his own due diligence.

3) After the Client passes compliance successfully, the Contract will be signed between the Client and Trader.

4) Duration of the program is for one-year with rolls and ext. for 3 years or more.

B. INVESTORS WITH 100 TO 500 M CASH OR 150 M TO 500 M INSTRUMENT DIRECT BUY/SELL PROGRAMS ADAN

Depending on the issuing bank, the client can provide an SBLC, BG or Bond in the minimum amount of 150mm EUR or cash account of at least 100mm.

If an instrument, it must have a dual listing on Euroclear and Bloomberg.

If the bank is mainland Europe (with presence in Switzerland or Germany), the Commitment Holder will travel to the bank and, arrange the transaction on location at the depository bank.

There's NO SWIFT involved.

The returns to the Applicant are 10x or approximately 1B from 100 M in approximately 4 weeks.

We would simply need a CIS and proof of funds or instrument to submit.

Changes on program details, including stroner or weaker returns, are possible, as the delivering „Commitment Holders"and the market conditions change. In any case Investor will know before start of any investment exactly what he can contractually expect.

C. INVESTORS WITH 500 M CASH DIRECT BUY/SELL PROGRAMS. MEM

THE CLIENT TRANSFERS HIS CASH ASSET OF 500 M USD/EUR FROM HIS OWN ACCOUNT TO HIS OWN TO BE OPENED ACCOUNT IN TRADER'S BANK HONG KONG. TRADER WILL BECOME A CO-SIGNATORY ON CLIENT'S ACCOUNT - THE CO-SIGNATORY IS LICENSED BY THE HONG KONG MONETARY AUTHORITY (HKMA). THE CLIENT WILL NEED TO FLY TO HOG KONG FOR OPENING OF HIS OWN ACCOUNT. IF THE CLIENT IS TRANSFERRING AN INSTRUMENT, THEN THE CLIENT WILL NEED TO DEPOSIT A MILLION DOLLARS INTO HIS

OWN ACCOUNT TO COVER BANK FEES INVOLVED IN RECEIVING

INSTRUMENTS. NORMAL ACCOUNT OPENING DOCUMENTATION IS REQUIRED INCLUDING PROOF OF ADDRESS.

THE CLIENT WILL HAVE TO STATE THAT HE IS FUNDING PROJECTS.

TRADER GENERATES A COMPLIANCE FILE THAT IS SUBMITTED TO A BANK HOLDING COMPANY OR TO COMMITMENT HOLDERS / MTN PROVIDING ENTITIES, WHICH IS THEN APPROVED BY THE EUROPEAN CENTRAL BANK (ECB).

BUY/SELL OF THE MTNs OR BGs WILL BE DONE DAILY (FOUR DAYS A WEEK) UNTIL THE DELIVERY CONTRACT IS EXHAUSTED. THEN IT MAY BE APPLIED FOR A NEW DELIVERY CONTRACT.

THE MTNs OR CERTIFIED BANK INVOICE IS DELIVERED TO THE CLIENT'S ACCOUNT AT WHICH POINT PAYMENT IS MADE FOR THE MTN, WHICH IS PRE-SOLD VIA CONTRACT.

THE PROFITS ARE DEPOSITED INTO THE SAME ACCOUNT OR INTO A SEPARATE PARALLEL PROFIT ACCOUNT IN THE CLIENT'S NAME AND FULL SIGNATORY CONTROL. EVERY TRADING DAY IS PAY DAY. THE CLIENT HAS TO SIGN AND AGREE WITH EACH TRANSACTION IN THE BEGINNING. THUS, THE CLIENT IS REQUIRED TO BE IN HK FOR ABOUT A MONTH

THE CLIENT CAN COMPOUND UP TO $2B AND OPEN ADDITIONA ACCOUNTS FOR TRADE.

D. MORE MTN BUY/SELL PROGRAMS ON REQUEST (GAR)

Final Notes:

THE CONDITIONS OF ABOVE OPPORTUNITIES MAY CHANGE DAILY. THEY MUST ALWAYS BE

RECONFIRMED. THE INDICATED PROCEEDS (PERCENTAGES OR MULTIPLIERS OF USED ASSET FACE VALUE) ARE HISTORICAL.

THE TRADE PROGRAMS APPLY TO USD AND EUR CURRENCIES, AS FAR AS NOTHING ELSE IS STATED.

Investor must be signatory to the account held by him; no Power of Attorney.

WE REQUIRE A REASONABLE SHARE OF RETURNS FOR OUR HUMANITARIAN AND JOB CREATING PROJECTS. THESE ARE MANAGED BY TMT TRANSACTION MANAGEMENT TEAM. TMT CONSISTS OF FIVE SPECIALISTS, WHOSE SPEAKER IS HANSA FINANCE INTERNATIONAL LLP. OUR PROJECTS CAN TAKE THE BURDEN OF A PROJECT AWAY FROM THE INVESTOR, SUBSTITUTE, OR AT LEAST ALLEVIATE IT. TMT WILL THEREFORE REQUIRE, ACCORDING TO THE CASE, BETWEEN FIFTEEN AND TWENTY FIVE PERCENT OF ALL PAY-OUTS TO CLIENTS, NORMALLY A TWENTY PERCENT.

TMT Transaction Management Team provides a Trade Participation Contract (TPA) to Investor. Trading Entity to guarantee that Asset does not move from Investor's account.

TRADE PROCEEDS. Trade Proceeds to be paid through the Trustee/Paymaster and his Trust Account with a recognized international bank.

General Submission Requirements:
1) All documents must be currently dated. Signatures blue ink.
2) To begin with: Passport Copy, usual CIS and Proof of Funds. Rarely an old fashioned "KYC".
3) POF in form of Tear Sheet / Bank Statement, MUST be signed by two Bank Officers, to include their titles and identification numbers (PIN).

4) POF MUST be dated within 3, maximum 5 banking days before date of submission.

CHAPTER 4

The Concept Of Hedge Funds

Strictly speaking, the term "hedge fund" is not a correct definition of the institutions under consideration. The term has historical significance, as in the beginning of the second half of the last century the first institutions of this kind were engaged in buying and short-selling equities with the aim of eliminating (hedging) the risk of market-wide fluctuations. However, the possibility of using short-selling and other types of hedging is not unique to hedge funds. Moreover, over time hedge funds have started to use a wide variety of other investment strategies that do not necessarily involve hedging.

There is no legal or even generally accepted definition of a hedge fund, although the US President's Working Group on Financial Markets (1999) characterised such entities is privately organised, administered by professional investment managers, and not widely available to the public". While this definition distinguishes hedge funds from public investment companies, it does not capture many of the distinctive features of hedge funds and is so broad that it includes many other alternative investment vehicles, such as venture capital firms, private equity funds, real estate funds and commodity pools. In contrast to other pooled investment vehicles, hedge funds make extensive use of short-selling, leverage and derivatives. Nevertheless, it would be inaccurate to assign these attributes exclusively to hedge funds, as other financial companies, including banks and other registered and unregistered investment companies, also engage in such operations. The key difference is that hedge funds do not have any restrictions on the type of instruments or strategies they can use owing to their unregulated or lightly regulated nature. In addition, to single hedge funds, there are funds of hedge funds (FOHFs), i.e. funds that invest in a number of other hedge funds. In this way diversification and selection services are provided to investors that are not able to perform adequate due diligence, lack the required expertise or do not meet high minimum investment requirements. FOHFs usually charge less than single hedge funds and often offer monthly or quarterly redemption to suit institutional and retail investors. Moreover, for the even more risk-averse investor, there are also so-called F3 hedge funds or funds of FOHFs, which represent the third layer on top of single hedge funds (F1) and FOHFs (F2). To be commercially viable, F3 funds have to negotiate substantial fee rebates from underlying FOHFs.

Noting the inaccurate nature of the expression "hedge fund", the European Parliament instead decided to use the term "Sophisticated Alternative Investment Vehicles" (SAIVs), which would also encompass other alternative investment funds that differ from conventional UCITS (Undertakings for Collective Investments in Transferable Securities). A variety of similar terms have elsewhere been used by other institutions. The Basel Committee on Banking Supervision (BCBS) opted to employ the term "highly leveraged institutions" (HLIs), a label covering hedge funds as well as other institutions that are subject to very little or no direct regulatory oversight, have very limited disclosure requirements, and often take on significant leverage. The Multidisciplinary Working Group on Enhanced Disclosure (MWGED) preferred to use the term "leveraged investment funds". Interestingly, the United Kingdom's Financial Services Authority (FSA) declined to define the term because of the absence of identifiable commonality; more recently it has indicated for supervisory monitoring purposes its preference to focus on the investment techniques of hedge funds rather than on issues of legal structure.

For the purpose of this paper, the market practice of using the term "hedge fund" will be followed. This term denotes a fund whose managers receive performance-related fees and can freely use various active investment strategies to achieve positive absolute returns, involving any combination of leverage, derivatives, long and short positions in securities or any other assets in a wide range of markets. This working definition stresses the most important features of hedge funds that are likely to endure, given that all other second-tier characteristics, including regulation, registration, investor base and disclosure, will probably evolve. However, this definition does not completely separate hedge funds from private equity or venture capital funds. As a rule, the latter vehicles do not pursue active strategies that extensively employ leverage, short-selling or derivatives, and usually have much longer lock-up periods.

Features Of Hedge Funds.

1) A hedge fund is a private investment partnership; the hedge fund manager sets up a fund the hedge fund as a legal entity that allows the manager to attract money from investors and invest it according to certain rules.

2) The investments that the fund can do are not regulated by government agencies; instead, they are regulated by a private document, the Offering Memorandum, which the manager creates as part of the legal structure of the fund, and the investors accept as part of their investment. This is a key document, as it sets the boundaries of what the manager can do with the investor's money. For example,

in our snow fund, it may allow the manager to enter into snow swaps with cities and ski resorts, but it ma not allow the manager to invest in the stock market. However, it may allow the manager to invest in bonds, since the manager may prefer to obtain interest from the fund's assets while they are used as collateral for the swaps. This lack of regulation must not be confused with the fund's need to comply with investment law of each jurisdiction it participates, which of course must always be upheld by the manager; the hedge fund manager bears the full liability of compliance with securities and other laws.

3) A hedge fund seeks return niches by taking risks, which they may hedge or diversify away (or not). Hedge funds are often set up to exploit what is perceived as a market inefficiency by the manager: a possibility to make money in excess of the interest rate with low risk. This inefficiency can arise from the profitability of snow swaps, from the inability of the market to price certain bonds correctly, from opportunities created by companies on the brink of bankruptcy, or companies with potential for mergers or acquisitions, etc. A hedge fund is usually focused on one type of inefficiency, which defines their trading style and may be reflected on their Offering Memorandum. Some larger hedge funds may include a variety of styles into their trading portfolio.

4) They seeks returns independent of market movements. For example, the performance of our snow fund is likely to be independent of whether stock markets go up or down, and although they may have small correlation with bond yields perhaps due to the fact that the collateral is invested in bonds the main driver for their return the profitability of snow swaps has no relationship to interest rates. Some of the first hedge funds were created by traditional stock pickers in the 1950's who eliminated

their exposure to the broad stock market by adding a short stock index position 1 to their portfolio; in this way, the return is produced if the stocks selected outperform the market, which can happen even when the market is down.

5) Hedge funds Net Asset Value (NAV) is reported monthly. This is a key number, which reflects the value the investors own. As the investors incur into gains, this number increases, and it decreases when investor's lose money. However, this number can also increase as more investors join the fund, and decrease as they redeem their investments. This number is calculated by adding all the funds assets and removing the value of the liabilities, which include the fees payable to the fund manager and other costs. In evaluating the fund assets, the snow swap, we need a method or a model to value the snow swaps we have constructed. There is no ready valuation formulas, and the cash flow for the swap is not deterministic. The cash flows can not be foreseen accurately because our counter-parties are default-prone and not risk-free. When some counter-parties become more likely to default, the value of our swap would decrease. These factors all contribute to difficulty of reporting NAV monthly.

6) The fund management company works for the fund and therefore the fund pays the management company. The fees vary widely from one fund to another, and are stipulated in the Offering Memorandum, but they have two components: one is a flat management fee, which may vary from 1% to 2% of the NAV, and is paid whether the fund makes money or not. The second one is a performance fee, which often ranges from 10% to 20% of the net gains of the fund. Normally, the management fee is paid monthly or quarterly, while the performance fee is paid annually.

Types Of Hedge Fund Investments.

In the early times of hedge funds, investors used to invest in those funds directly. Nowadays, investors are often times invested in hedge funds, not directly, but through a variety of investment products, which we now briefly review.

Fund of funds. A management company, independent of the management company of hedge funds, but with very similar characteristics, creates a fund whose assets are invested in a portfolio of hedge funds. They are second-level hedge fund investments, where the investor acquired shares in a single fund, whose assets are then used to invest in a series of hedge funds.

The advantages of such investments are:

- Diversification
- Outsourcing to the fund-of-funds management company of proper due investment diligence tasks, analytics and other processes related to hedge fund investments
- Access to hedge funds which may be closed to other investors, or specially favorable investment terms with the underlying hedge funds

Among the disadvantages, we have;

- Higher fees: the investor will have to pay the management and performance fees of the fund-of-funds, which are over and above the ones for the underlying hedge funds
- Increased default risk: if an investor invests in a portfolio of hedge funds, and one of them bankrupts, the losses are proportional to the participation in the defaulted fund. But, if the fund-of-funds defaults (for example, due to fraud at the fund-of-funds level) then all the assets are at risk.

Hedge Fund Indices.

Hedge fund indices are composite portfolios designed to reflect hedge fund industry performance. The indices are constructed to be benchmarks that are representative of the hedge fund industry performance. Methodologies are used to select constituent hedge funds and produced weighted returns. For example, the HFRX Indices methodology combines both quantitative and qualitative processes. Statistical analysis is used to replicate statistical properties of each hedge fund, and this include correlation analysis, optimization, and Monte Carlo simulations. These methods are used to generate the highest statistical likelihood of producing a return series that is most representative of the composite hedge fund returns. Qualitative criteria such as transparency of the fund and manager's due diligence are also considered before a fund can be included.

Hedge fund indices are often classified by the strategy employed or regional focus. Examples of indices by strategy are HFRX Equity Hedge Index, HFRX Equity Neutral Index, HFRX Convertible Arbitrage Index, HFRX Distressed Securities Index, etc. Indices by regional focus include HFRX Asia Composite Hedge Fund Index, HFRX Total Emerging Market Index, and HRFX North America Index, etc.

Hedge Fund Indices, in contrast with stock or bond indices, can be investable, or non-investable. By including hedge funds that are open to investors, the hedge fund index can be turned into an investable product, and they often are. Examples of such indices are the HFRX indices, managed by HFR (Hedge Fund Research Inc.), a Chicago-based management firm. However, hedge fund indices may contain funds which are not open to new investors, in which case the indices are not investible and cannot even be replicated. Example of such indices are the HFRI indices produced also by HFR and older than their siblings HFRX indices. For an index to be investable, proper legal structures must be set up, such as a fund structure. This is another reason why many firms who publish hedge fund indices, whether closed or open to new investors, produce exclusively non-investible indices. An example of these would be the indices provided by Barclays.

Structured Products

Structured Products, in general, are pre-packaged investments that are based on and linked to some underlying benchmarks, such as equity markets, derivatives, interest rates, commodities, corporate debts, and foreign exchange markets. There is no uniform structure to these investment packages since they are tailored to meet specific financial objectives. We introduce some typical categories in structured products.

(1) Leveraged Investing

Leverage investing is a technique that invests with borrowed money. The common ones are loans and options/warrants.

• Loans

The mechanism of such leveraged investments can be shown in a simple example, as follows: an investor provides capital of $25M, and a bank provides a loan of $75M. The total amount of $100M is invested in a portfolio of hedge funds over a certain time horizon, 5 years for example. The investment pays interest to the lender, and return the principal at maturity. This principal is paid out of the liquidation value of the investment. After all the obligations are paid off, the investor who initially provided the $25M gets to keep all what is left in the fund.

The structure of such loans can be a bit more complicated, simply because in the simple example mentioned above, the bank takes too much risk and is not usually willing to give the loan without further covenants. The most usual one is one of simple protection, and the bank would chose a trigger loss level, say $5M in the example above, so that when the value of fund falls below the value of the trigger, the fund will be liquidated; in this way, the investor will lose the trigger amount, plus expenses, but the bank does not incur into any loss, provided the fund can be liquidated fast enough. When the fund performs well, the investor only needs to return the principal plus interest and keep the rest as profit. Effectively, the investor is essentially buying a call option from the bank, with the hedge fund as underlying asset, loan amount plus interest as strike price, and option premium as the investor's initial capital outlay $25M. Because of this, options, which we describe below, are used more often, as they also provide additional advantages for the issuing bank.

• Options/Warrants

Investors can purchases a call option issued as warrants, which provides positive, leveraged returns if underlying asset value increases. The underlying asset can be virtually anything, and in our case, it is the hedge fund portfolio.

For the loan example in the previous section, instead of the bank providing the $75M, collect the $25M from the investor, and then invest the total $100M in the hedge fund, the bank will prefer to issue a call option to the investor, with a value of $25M, and offer the return of a $100M investment in a fund of hedge funds above the $75M financing fee, which acts as the strike price of the call option (for the sake of clarity, we are ignoring interest rates and fees in this example). This way, the cash flow to the investor are the same, but because an option is issued, the bank does not need to invest the full $100M in the fund; banks hedge their options by taking a position in the underlying instrument equal to the delta of the option, which is less than one (usually close to 0.7) which leads to considerable savings in bank capital.

We use a small example to explain leveraged return, compared with the return if investing in the underlying directly. A hedge fund share is now worth $20. An investor buys a call warrant linked to this hedge fund portfolio. This call warrant gives the investor the right to purchase fund shares for $20 from the hedge fund. Suppose now the warrant is worth $0.5. The next day, share value of this hedge fund goes up to $21, and the warrant is worth $1.

- CPPI Options

Asset allocation between the two parts of the portfolio is done through dynamic trading strategies. One popular strategy is CPPI, which stands for Constant Proportion Portfolio Insurance. This strategy aims to deliver the same as a traditional option, with two major differences:

- Interest rate hedging. In a traditional option, the issuer of the option is in charge of hedging the interest rate risk inherent in their hedging strategy for the underlying. In a CPPI option, the interest rate risk will be passed over to the investor, or purchaser, of the option, as we will see below.

- Hedging of the underlying fund returns. In a traditional option, the issuer does not fully invest the option notional in the underlying, but the delta of the option, as dictated by the Black-Scholes strategy. As the performance of the underlying increases or decreases, the hedging strategy results in buy or sell orders of the underlying, to maintain the exposure equal to the delta, which will vary over time. This poses a problem for the issuer, as hedge funds may not have the liquidity required to adjust the hedge continuously; in other words, the hedging strategy may will typically be subject to updates every month, quarter or year, depending on the liquidity of the underlying hedge funds. In a CPPI option, this hedge risk will also be passed to the investor.

(2) Guaranteed Notes

- Definition of a guarantee

A guaranteed note is an investment strategy where the issuer guarantees the investor that, in case the underlying fund exhibits losses, the investor is guaranteed to get the original value of the investment back to the investor (without interest, though). A guarantee is a structure that combines equity or options on equity, and a fixed income instrument on the equity, in order to protect the principal invested.

(3) CFO - Collateralized Fund obligations

- Definition and structure

A Collateralized Fund Obligation is an interesting structured finance product which can be classified as a type of collateralized debt obligation, commonly known as a CDO. A CDO issues securities or notes backed on a diversified pool of loans, bond, receivables, future flows, or any type of cash flow stream that can be identified and isolated.

The capital structure of a CFO is similar to traditional CDOs, meaning that investors are offered a spectrum of rated debt securities and equity interest. The difference between CFO and CDO is the collateral that is put forward. In CFO, any managed fund can be the source of collateral. More specifically, the target collateral tends to be hedge funds, such as relative value hedge funds, event-driven hedge funds or commodity trading advisors (CTAs), along with funds that finance the needs of growing companies, such as private equity and mezzanine funds. On the contrary, collaterals of CDOs are mainly loans, structured securities, and debt. For example, the collateral can be mortgage-backed securities, corporate loans, or emerging-market sovereign debt.

Assessing the risks

Hedge fund investments share qualitative properties which are quite different from other, more traditional investments.

(1) Illiquidity

Liquidity in general refers to the ability to quickly covert securities or other assets into cash. In hedge funds, specifically, it refers to the length of notice periods that investors need to inform the fund managers before the fund share can be redeemed. This time can vary from a few weeks to a few months.

For example, in our snow fund we would have difficulty turning the swaps into their cash in mid-year, since we would have to negotiate with our counter-parties to cancel our swap contracts with them. This will invariably lead to heavy losses.

Therefore, hedge funds typically have liquidity provisions that will only allow investors to redeem their shares at certain points in time, often with an additional advance notice period required. They may also have "lock-ups", time from the initial investment that new investors have to wait before their fund shares can be redeemed, according to the usual liquidity provisions of the hedge fund. For example, a fund with an one-year lock and monthly liquidity is a fund that the investor can redeem their shares only after the first year anniversary of their investment and monthly afterwards.

(2) Valuation difficulties

Hedge funds give rise to valuation issues, because sometimes the value of the fund's assets are hard to value. In our show fund example, valuing the swap is difficult, not just because of its expected cash flows are uncertain, but also because there is no accepted accounting methodology to value the swaps. Most often, the valuation methodology is established in the Offering Memorandum, and is key to ensure investor equality, as they subscribe and redeem shares. Evaluating a hedge fund using specific methodologies is obviously more difficult and less transparent than evaluating a public company. In the case of public companies, share prices are simply their market price quoted in the stock exchange. They are determined by supply/demand relationship for the stock, which changes based on investors' perspective on the value and earning potential of the underlying company.

(3) Capacity restrictions

A fund typically has a limit as to what it can do with its money. For example, in our snow fund example we may have the ability to do 100 swaps at a value of $2M each; this means that if we attract investments much in excess of $200M, the returns will not be as good as if we limit the asset base to $200M. Because of this, many hedge funds managers put a limit to the volume of assets they accept into the fund. Investors must be careful, as some other managers may decide increase these maximums beyond the natural limits inferred from their investment opportunity, since the management and performance fee is asset based and will reward the manager independent of the percentage return of the fund.

(4) Leverage and speculative investment

Hedge funds together with other speculative investments differ from the old-fashioned investments that do not rely on borrowing capital: hedge funds are typically highly leveraged. They aggressively take large positions with only small amount of equity capital, hoping for large returns with even very small changes in favor of their positions. The high leverage gives rise to leverage risk, which means a small unfavorable change can trigger enormous losses as well, especially if positions are run unhedged.

Hedge Fund Data.

Hedge funds, as private investment partnerships, are under no obligation to disclose investment information to anyone, and the disclosure to their own investors is often limited to the NAV, monthly share price and little else. Even their investment strategies are often kept within close guard inside the management company. As a result, one of the few pieces of information that one can find about a particular hedge fund, not being an investor, is the series of monthly returns. Moreover, publications of hedge funds are considered illegal marketing materials in some jurisdictions such as the U.S, and is therefore heavily restricted to the extend that they cannot be published by the management companies in public forums, websites, etc. Marketing of hedge funds is restricted to certain individuals and cannot be brought freely to the public.

However, as a miracle of the law, publication of such data by third parties is allowed. Commercial databases are accessible to qualified users who paid a fee to use the data sets. These commercial databases exist and we name just a few:

- Hedge Fund Research Inc.
- Hedgefund.net
- Eureka hedge
- Tass

To understand the informational content of such databases, one needs to understand the following well-known syndromes:

- Backfill bias. Hedge funds are under no obligation to report to a database. Because of that, they choose when they report. They often do so when they have good performance they want to boast about, usually in times when they are looking to gather more investors.

- Survivorship bias. Hedge funds which collapse tend to disappear from the databases.

General Classification.

Equity Hedge.

This refers to hedge fund strategies that set up both long and short positions in equity and equity derivative securities. Long and short positions need to chosen so that the long position provides return to the portfolio and short position acts as a hedge against stock market decline carefully.

Ideally, it should work in the following way: in a rising market, the long-position should increase in value faster than the market returns, and the short position incur a loss less rapidly. In this case, the return from the long position is reduced by the loss in the short position. In a declining market, the short position holdings should decrease in value faster than market, generating a big return for the portfolio. The long position should decrease in value less rapidly than the market, so the loss is limited. In this case, the long position is hedged by the short position, and that is why fund managers are willing to accept return reduction in rising market for this protection when market declines.

In this general category, investment decisions are reached by applying two main techniques: identifying economic trends, and fundamental analysis. Fund managers first predict the effect of macro-economic trends on the market, and then identify industries that are attractive for long positions. Within these industries, the fund manager then seeks for well-positioned companies in the industry, usually through quantitative analysis of the company's financial status and earning prospects.

Equity hedge strategies include strategies such as Equity Long/Short, Quantitative direction, and Fundamental Value. We will discuss Equity Long/Short in more details.

Event Driven.

Event driven strategies are hedge fund strategies that exploit pricing inefficiencies caused by a wide range of corporate transactions, such as mergers, restructuring, and financial distress. The fund managers develop strategies to take advantage of special situations in corporations that change the value of its underlying assets.

Event Driven strategies include some major strategies such as Distressed Securities, Merger Arbitrage, and Regulation D.

Relative Value Arbitrage.

Relative Value Arbitrage strategies seek return from "spreads". That is, they derive return from price relationships between two related securities. The arbitrageurs seek distorted relationships between securities by quantitative analysis and valuation, take long and short positions in them, and then realized a profit when the relationship returns to normal.

Relative Value strategies include but not limited to Fixed-Income Arbitrage, Convertible Arbitrage, Asset Backed Arbitrage, and statistical arbitrage.

Global Macro

Global Macro strategies often include Active Trading, Commodity Trading, Currency Trading, and Multi-Strategy. We will introduce this category in detail later.

In the following sections, we will discuss in detail some main strategies from each of the general categories. We will introduce their hedge approaches, source of returns, and finally risk and risk controls.

Equity Hedge

Equity long/short. These funds obtain performance for their investors by buying and selling stocks. The net exposure of the long and short positions varies by funds' investment schema and managers' trading style. At first sight, they exhibit a fundamental difference with mutual funds: their ability to short sell stock.

Short Selling.

Short selling stock is a common practice among equity investors. An investor short sells stock when she believes that stock price is going to decrease. When the price does drop, she can purchase the stock at the lower price and make a profit from the difference between the short proceeds and the lower repurchase price. Mathematically, we can think of short selling stock easily by simply assuming one can buy a negative amount of stocks. However, we need to examine further the actual investment process of short selling stock, as it will have important consequences in trying to understand this particular trading style.

Stock borrowing, or short selling, is usually done through a broker. Hedge funds hires typically one or more prime brokers, who are mainly responsible for trading securities, and often they also maintain custody of the assets. When a manager wants to short sell a stock; she makes arrangements through the prime broker to borrow stock form an existing shareholder. Primer brokers typically have ample inventories of stocks from their clients that are ready to be lent. This requires prior approval of the owner of the stock, and the stock loan can be recalled anytime by the original owner. After the broker has finalized the stock lending process, typically in a matter of a few minutes (except for so-called hot securities, when it can take hours or days), the stock can be sold and the proceeds of the sale go into the fund account. The fund, at that time, has a credit equal to the cash proceeds of the sale and a debit equal to the shares they borrowed.

A short position is usually unwound when the borrower decides to buy the shares and give them back to the original owner. However, we should be aware of the potential risks in shorting stocks. If the stock price increases significantly, some sellers are forced to cover the position in case of a margin call (a monetary deposit required as collateral by the broker in situations where losses are unrealized but large). Also, the original owner of stock may decide to sell the stock and make a profit. Then the borrower is forced to buy the stock to return it to the original owner. Buying shares further increase the stock price and trigger even more position covering. This event is referred to as a short squeeze, and it usually has very negative implications for the borrower.

Equity Hedge.

This refers to hedge fund strategies that set up both long and short positions in equity and equity derivative securities. Long and short positions need to chosen carefully so that the long position provides return to the portfolio and short position acts as a hedge against stock market decline.

Ideally, it should work in the following way: in a rising market, the long-position should increase in value faster than the market returns, and the short position incur a loss less rapidly. In this case, the return from the long position is reduced by the loss in the short position. In a declining market, the short position holdings should decrease in value faster than market, generating a big return for the portfolio. The long position should decrease in value less rapidly than the market, so the loss is limited. In this case, the long position is hedged by the short position, and that is why fund managers are willing to accept return reduction in rising market for this protection when market declines.

In this general category, investment decisions are reached by applying two main techniques: identifying economic trends, and fundamental analysis. Fund managers first predict the effect of macro-economic trends on the market, and then identify industries that are attractive for long positions. Within these industries, the fund manager then seeks for well-positioned companies in the industry, usually through quantitative analysis of the company's financial status and earning prospects.

Equity hedge strategies include strategies such as Equity Long/Short, Quantitative direction, and Fundamental Value. We will discuss Equity Long/Short in more details.

Event Driven.

Event driven strategies are hedge fund strategies that exploit pricing inefficiencies caused by a wide range of corporate transactions, such as mergers, restructuring, and financial distress. The fund managers develop strategies to take advantage of special situations in corporations that change the value of its underlying assets.

Event Driven strategies include some major strategies such as Distressed Securities, Merger Arbitrage, and Regulation D.

Relative Value Arbitrage.

Relative Value Arbitrage strategies seek return from "spreads". That is, they derive return from price relationships between two related securities. The arbitrageurs seek distorted relationships between securities by quantitative analysis and valuation, take long and short positions in them, and then realized a profit when the relationship returns to normal.

Relative Value strategies include but are not limited to Fixed-Income Arbitrage, Convertible Arbitrage, Asset Backed Arbitrage, and statistical arbitrage.

Global Macro.

Global Macro strategies often include Active Trading, Commodity Trading, Currency Trading, and Multi-Strategy. We will introduce this category in detail later.

In the following sections, we will discuss in detail some main strategies from each of the general categories. We will introduce their hedge approaches, source of returns, and finally risk and risk controls.

Equity Hedge - Equity long/short. These funds obtain performance for their investors by buying and selling stocks short positions varies by funds' investment schema and managers' trading style. At first sight, they exhibit a fundamental difference with mutual funds: their ability to short sell stock.

Short Selling - Short selling stock is a common practice among equity investors. An investor short sells stock when she believes that stock price is going to decrease. When the price does drop, she can purchase the stock at the lower price and make a profit from the difference between the short proceeds and the lower repurchase price. Mathematically, we can think of short selling stock easily by simply assuming one can buy a negative amount of stocks. However, we need to examine further the actual investment process of short selling stock, as it will have important consequences in trying to understand this particular trading style.

Stock borrowing, or short selling, is usually done through a broker. Hedge funds hire typically one or more prime brokers, who are mainly responsible for trading securities, and often they also maintain custody of the assets. When a manager wants to short sell a stock, she makes arrangements through the prime broker to borrow stock form an existing shareholder. Primer brokers typically have ample inventories of stocks from their clients that are ready to be lent. This requires prior approval of the owner of the stock, and the stock loan can be recalled anytime by the original owner. After the broker has finalized the stock lending process, typically in a matter of a few minute (except for so-called hot securities, when it can take hours or days), the stock can be sold and the proceeds of the sale go into the fund account. The fund, at that time, has a credit equal to the cash proceeds of the sale and a debit equal to the shares they borrowed.

A short position is usually unwound when the borrower decides to buy the shares and give them back to the original owner. However, we should be aware of the potential risks in shorting stocks. If the stock price increases significantly, some sellers are forced to cover the position in case of a margin call (a monetary deposit required as collateral by the broker in situations where losses are unrealized but large). Also, the original owner of stock may decide to sell the stock and make a profit. Then the borrower is forced to buy the stock to return it to the original owner. Buying shares further increase the stock price and trigger even more position covering. This event is referred to as a short squeeze, and it usually has very negative implications for the borrower.

Fund of Hedge Funds:

A diversified portfolio of generally uncorrelated hedge funds and it may be widely diversified, or sector or geographically focused seek to deliver more consistent returns than stock portfolios, mutual funds, unit trusts or individual hedge funds. Preferred investment of choice for many pension funds, endowments, insurance companies, private banks and high net worth families and individuals. Provide more predictable returns than traditional investment funds

Comparison Between Hedge Funds And Private Equity:

Hedge funds are similar to private equity funds, such as venture capital funds, in many respects. Both are lightly regulated, private pools of capital that invest in securities and compensate their managers with a share of the fund's profits. Most hedge funds invest in very liquid assets, and permit investors to enter or leave the fund easily. Private equity funds invest primarily in very illiquid assets such as early-stage companies and so investors are "locked in" for the entire term of the fund. Hedge funds often invest in private equity companies' acquisition funds.

Comparison between Hedge Funds and Mutual Fund:

Like hedge funds, mutual funds are pools of investment capital. However, mutual funds are highly regulated by the SEC (U.S. Securities and Exchange Commission). One consequence of this regulation is that mutual funds cannot compensate managers based on the performance of the fund, which many believe dilutes the incentive of the fund managers to perform.

Traditionally, hedge funds also distinguished themselves from mutual funds by investment strategy (i.e. merger arbitrage, equity market neutral, but many mutual funds are now offering non-traditional investment styles

Hedge Fund Strategies:

1- *Convertible arbitrage:*

Purchase and sale strategy i.e. purchase convertible securities and at the same time sale the underlying equity.

2- Distressed Securities:

Buys equity, debt, or trade claims at deep discounts of companies in or facing bankruptcy or reorganization, with a view to capturing returns from mispricing of improved cash flow or value.

3- Hedge equities:

Long or short investments in equities and their derivatives and it may be global or country specific, hedging against downturns in equity markets by shorting overvalued stock.

4- Macro:

Aims to profit from changes in global economies typically brought about by shifts in government policy which impact interest rates, in turn affecting currency, stock, and bond markets.

5- Income:

Invests with primary focus on yield or current income rather than only on capital gains. May utilize leverage to buy bonds and sometimes fixed income derivatives in order to profit from principal appreciation and interest income.

6- Equity Market Neutral:

Using statistical techniques and valuation models to capture fundamental inefficiency in equity markets.

7- Risk Arbitrage (Merger Arbitrage):

Trading in equities of companies likely to undergo some merger and acquisition activity and there are two principle types of arbitrage: cash merger and stock merger.

8- Multi-strategy:

Investment approach is diversified by employing various Hedge Fund strategies simultaneously to realize short and long-term gains.

Regulatory Environment:

Of course financial regulators have pressed to increase their oversight of hedge fund activities as hedge funds have become more popular and more accessible to less wealthy investors. Most large hedge funds have elected to register with SEC perceiving that the SECs' somewhat onerous regulatory requirements constitute a barrier to entry an industry where such barrier are become increasingly desirable to the owners of existing successful hedge funds. Ironically, the regulators have arrived to protect small investors from the hedge funds that no longer exist as vehicle yielding extraordinary returns. The typical small American investors wish he could invest in a hedge fund because he has heard that they earn 25 percent a year rather than the 5 to 10 percent available annually from mutual funds. The truth is that most hedge funds no longer earn 25 percent a year and those that do have achieved that result by returning investors money rather than seeking additional investors.

A- SEC:

Investment companies registered with the U.S. Securities and Exchange Commission (SEC) are subject to strict limitations on the short-selling and use of leverage that are essential to many hedge fund strategies. For this and other reasons, hedge funds elect to operate as unregistered investment companies. As a result, interests in a hedge fund cannot be offered or advertised to the general public, and are limited to individuals who are both "accredited investors" (those who have total incomes of over US$200,000 per year or a net worth of over US$1,000,000) and "qualified purchasers" (who own at least US$5,000,000 in qualified investments). Further, anyone hedge fund is limited to 499 investors ("limited partners"). For the funds, the trade off is that they have fewer investors to sell to, but they have few government imposed restrictions on their investment strategies. The presumption is that hedge funds are pursuing more risky strategies, which may or may not be true depending on the fund, and that the ability to invest in these funds should be restricted to wealthier investors who are presumed to be more sophisticated and who have the financial reserves to absorb a possible loss.

In October 2004, the SEC approved a rule change, finalized in December, final rule and rule amendments2, implemented on February 1, 2006, that requires most hedge fund advisers to register with the SEC as investment advisers under the Investment Advisers Act. The requirement will apply to firms managing in excess of US$30,000,000 or more and open to new investors. The SEC has stated that it is adopting a "risk-based approach" to monitoring hedge funds as part of its evolving regulatory regimen for the burgeoning industry. This rule has been subject to challenges by U.S. courts: In June 2006, the U.S. Court of Appeals for the District of Columbia overturned it, and sent it back to the agency to be reviewed.

B- ECB3:

Banks surveyed with significant exposures to hedge funds usually had specific internal rules or controls covering their dealings with hedge funds. Other banks with less strong links to hedge funds generally relied on various risk committees and established policies to oversee their dealings with hedge funds. In some countries, parent institutions were responsible for the risk management of investments in hedge funds. In some cases, the specific policies were broader and covered either all highly leveraged institutions or all alternative investment vehicles. In those cases where specific guidelines were not in place and banks did not express an intention to develop them, supervisors might consider reviewing banks' connections with hedge funds in order to ascertain whether the scale of hedge fund-related activities warrants any specific internal rules in line with the recommendations of the Basel Committee on Banking Supervision.20 Guidelines usually included a general description of (funds of) hedge funds, due diligence procedures, credit and counterparty risk policies, the risk monitoring framework and legal documentation requirements. In some cases, such documents also included broader information on the hedge fund industry and the bank's position within it or a general business strategy visà-vis hedge funds. Some banks also had a dedicated risk management unit within their risk management columns.

In that cases where hedge funds were primarily scrutinised by various risk management committees in the framework of general risk policies, the credit or counterparty risk management units were always involved before and after engaging in lending or trading relationships. New investments often had to be approved by senior management and/or product committees. Moreover, some banks specifically highlighted that they had caps, minimum diversification, maximum concentration requirements or maximum risk levels with respect to investments in hedge funds or other hedge fund related activities.

Market Overview: Structure and Size

a) Hedge Fund Market Structure:

i) Operational Structure:

Hedge funds are usually not operated in-house by their employees. They are just investment vehicles owned by investors and sponsors (or limited and general parents) and rely on external service providers to conduct the funds day-to-day business, including managing the fund portfolio and providing administrative services. So for this type of operation structure; hedge funds establish relationships with all the necessary industry service providers:

1- The sponsors and the investors:

The sponsor is the creator of the fund and he will typically hold a member of the founder shares in the fund; that is as we talked early (page 1) the sponsor will be the general partner and the investor will be the limited partner.

2-The Manager or Management Company:

He/she is responsible for office overhead, and is usually established in a major onshore financial center as London or New York.

3-The Investment Adviser:

The role of investment advisor is simply to give professional advice on the funds investment in a way that is consistent with the funds investment objectives and policies, the investment adviser may be a part of the same overall organization as the hedge fund he serves, or he may be unrelated to it.

4-The board of directors:

The board of directory is responsible for monitoring the overall operations of the fund.

5-The fund administrator:

His primary task is to ensure accurate calculation of the net asset value at regular time interval called break periods.

6-The Custodian:

The custodian's primary responsibilities include safekeeping of the fund's assets, clearing and settlings all trades and monitoring corporate actions such as dividend payments and proxy-related information.

7-The legal advisor or lawyer:

The legal adviser or lawyer assists the hedge fund with any tax code and/or legal matters, and ensure compliance with domestic investment regulations as well as with regulations of countries where the fund is distributed.

8-The auditors:

The auditors' role is to ensures that the hedge fund is in compliance with accounting practices and any applicable laws, and to verify the annual financial statement, if any.

9-The registrar and transfer agent:

He/she keeps and updates a register of shareholders of the hedge fund. He also processes and takes necessary actions for subscriptions and withdrawals of shares in the fund, as well as for the payment of any dividends and distributions.

10-The Prime Broker:

The role of prime brokers goes beyond just replacing the hedge funds back office. Rather, they should be seen as full service providers across the core functions of execution and operation for example:

- Clearing the trades.
- Acting as global custodian.
- Margin financing.
- Securities lending.

ii)Organization Structure:

Hedge funds also need to set up efficient organizational structures.

1) Side-by-side and master/feeders:

In side by side structures, also called mirror funds or clone funds, several funds having identical or substantially similar investment policies invest in parallel in a group of cloned portfolio. These portfolios usually share a common investment adviser, portfolio managers and a custodian or administrator, and the cloning process essentially consists in facilitating bunched trades among the cloned funds and rebalancing cloned funds that have experienced different cash flows.

The master/feeder structure is an efficient alternative to side-by-side funds. In this structure a series of funds (called feeders) sell shares to investors under the terms of their prospectus and contribute their respective proceeds to another fund (called the master fund) rather than investing directly.

b) Hedge Fund Market Size:

If we are going to talk about how big is the hedge fund industry, then it will definitely a question without an accurate answer because as we know that SEC doesn't regulate hedge fund, i.e., hedge fund are not required to register but the SEC estimates, however, that there are between 6,000 and 7,000 funds that manage approximately $600 to $650 billion in assets. The report predicts that in the next five to 10 years, the assets invested in hedge funds will exceed $1 trillion.

And that is wonder us to know why hedge fund is exempt from SEC regulations, the answer is simply is of the hedge funds are only offered to wealthy individuals and institutions. A combination of statutory provisions and rules under the 1933 Act and the Investment Company Act for private rather than public offerings allow for them and the securities they issue to investors to remain unregistered. Many funds uses the safe harbor in the 1933 Act that allows them to sell to "accredited investors." These are individuals with an annual income of $200,000 or more, married couples with a joint income of $300,000 or more, or individuals with a net worth of $1 million.

2) Key Players

We can divide the key players in two categories, buyers of hedge funds and provider of hedge funds.

– a) Buyers of Hedge Funds:

Current ownership is divided between Wealthy individuals (High Net Worth Individuals or HNWI) and institutions. And it is divided as follows:

- o US HNWI and Europe HNWI.
- o US Insurance, US Pensions, Europe insurance, Europe Pensions and US non-profit.

Now let us have a close look for wealthy individual,

Wealthy individual:

Wealthy individuals (High Net Worth Individuals or HNWI) – individuals with assets in excess of US$ 1 million - account for over 60% of the approximately $600bn invested in hedge funds. There are signs that hedge funds are becoming a standard element in HNWI – not just super wealthy – portfolios.

- – Provider of Hedge Funds:
  - o Very high fees and very high profitability. The typical hedge fund manager charges a management fee in excess of 1% (versus 40-50 bp on the typical long only portfolio) and usually is entitled to 20% of the profit if a certain target return is exceeded.
  - o The vast majority of hedge fund managers are located in North America – largely in the New York and Los Angeles areas. But in Europe – London particularly- a large number of companies are starting up. Anecdotal evidence suggests US managers are opening in larger scale in London.
  - o Most advisors noted a specific life cycle for hedge funds. New start ups, to be viable, had to raise about $20m. If performance is good the fund re-opens 12 months later and grows to $60-100m. If performance is sustained, a further 12 months on, the fund can re-open and grow to $300-600m. But in practice few funds grow beyond the $25-30m size.

o The credibility of the investment decision making process is critical to fund-raising. The investment managers must have considerable experience and those with good reputations can raise $250m at launch. Experience in short selling is critical as are robust risk control measures. There are signs that with the amount of institutional money facing the market, standards and expectations on managers are falling.

Also, we can consider the players in the previous section as key player in Hedge fund even though some of them are not directly involved in such things.

Risk of Hedge Funds:

- **Political risk.** When an investment is made in a foreign nation and under the laws and sovereignty of that nation, the risk is loss due to possible nationalization.
- **Transfer risk.** This occurs when a foreign government restricts the delivery of a foreign currency.
- **Settlement risk.** A dispute between the parties to a contract could prevent the fulfillment of the contract in accordance with its stated terms.
- **Credit risk.** This happens when the counter party to a contract does not perform due to insolvency.
- **Legal risk.** This occurs when the contract is declared unenforceable due to legal problems.
- **Market risk.** Market movements can cause losses.
- **Liquidity risk.** This occurs when a market dries up and it becomes impossible to liquidate a position.
- **Operations risk.** Clerical errors can cause risk.

CHAPTER 5

Arbitrage Trading

"**B**uy low, sell high." "A fool and his money are soon parted." "Greed is good." All these adages illustrate the profit-oriented impulses of Wall Street traders, who stand ready to buy and sell. In pursuit of profits, undervalued assets are bought, and overvalued ones are sold. While risk is routine borne in trading assets, most investors prefer to exploit mispriced assets with as little risk as possible. The goal is to enhance expected returns without adding risk. Think how seductive an investment that offers attractive returns but no risk is! One approach to identifying and profiting from misvalued assets is called arbitrage. Those who do it are called arbitrageurs or simply "arbs."

Arbitrage is the process of buying assets in one market and selling them in another to profit from unjustifiable price differences. "True" arbitrage is both riskless and self-financing, which means that the investor uses someone else's money. Although this is the traditional definition of arbitrage, use of the term has broadened to include often risky variations such as the following:

- Risk arbitrage, which is commonly the simultaneous buying of an acquisition target's stock and the selling of the acquirer's stock.
- Tax arbitrage, which shifts income from one investment tax category to another to take advantage of different tax rates across income categories.

- Regulatory arbitrage, which reflects the tendency of firms to move toward the least-restrictive regulations. An example is the historic tendency of U.S. commercial banks to move toward the least-restrictive regulator state versus federal. Thus, as regulators in the past pursued a strategy of "competition in laxity," banks sought to arbitrage regulatory differences.
- Pairs trading, which identifies two stocks whose prices have moved closely in the past. When the relative price spread widens abnormally, the stock with the lower price is bought, and the stock with the higher price is sold short.
- Index arbitrage, which establishes offsetting long and short positions in a stock index futures contract and a replicating cash market portfolio when the futures price differs significantly from its theoretical value.

Even though arbitrage may be motivated by greed, it is nonetheless a finely tuned economic mechanism that imposes structure on asset prices. This structure ensures that investors earn expected returns that are, on average, commensurate with the risks they bear. Indeed, prices and expected returns are not at rest unless they are "arbitrage-free." Arbitrage provides both the carrot and the stick in efficiently operating financial markets.

Closely related to arbitrage is hedging, which is a strategy that reduces or eliminates risk and possibly locks in profits. By buying and selling specific investments, an investor can reduce the risk associated with a portfolio of investments. And by buying and selling specific assets, a target profit can be assured. Although all arbitrage strategies relies on hedging to render a position riskless, not all hedging involves arbitrage. "Pure" arbitrage is the riskless pursuit of profits resulting from mispriced assets. Hedging strategies seek to reduce, if not eliminate, risk, but do not necessarily involve mispriced assets. Thus, hedging does not purse profits.

A guiding principle in investments is the Law of One Price. This states that the "same" investment must have the same price no matter how that investment created. It is often possible to create identical investments using different securities or other assets. These investments must have the same expected cash flow payoffs to be considered identical. Indeed, the threat of arbitrage ensures that investments with identical payoffs are, at least on average, priced the same at a given point in time. If not, arbitrageurs take advantage of the differential, and the resulting buying and selling should eliminate the mispricing.

Similar to the Law of One Price is the Law of One Expected Return, which asserts that equivalent investments should have the same expected return. This is a bit different from the prior requirement that the same assets must have the same prices across markets. While subtle, this distinction will help you understand arbitrage in the context of specific pricing models.

Why Is Arbitrage So Important?

True arbitrage opportunities are rare. When they are discovered, they do not last long. So why is it important to explore arbitrage in detail? Does the benefit justify the cost of such analysis? There are compelling reasons for going to the trouble.

Investors are interested in whether a financial asset's price is correct or "fair." They search for attractive conditions or characteristics in an asset associated with misvaluation. For example, evidence exists that some low price/earnings (P/E) stocks are perennial bargains, so investors look carefully for this characteristic along with other signals of value. Yet the absence of an arbitrage opportunity is at least as important as its presence! While the presence of an arbitrage opportunity implies that a riskless strategy can be designed to generate a return in excess of the risk-free rate, its absence indicates that an asset's price is at rest. Of course, just because an asset's price is at rest does not necessarily mean that it is "correct." Resting and correct prices can differ for economically meaningful reasons, such as transactions costs. For example, a $1.00 difference between correct and resting prices cannot be profitably exploited if it costs $1.25 to execute the needed transactions. Furthermore, sometimes many market participants believe that prices are wrong, trade under that perception, and thereby influence prices. Yet there may not be an arbitrage opportunity in the true sense of a riskless profit in the absence of an initial required investment. Thus, it is important to carefully relate price discrepancies to the concept of arbitrage because one size does not fit all.

Arbitrage-free prices acts as a benchmark that structures asset prices. Indeed, understanding arbitrage has practical significance. First, the no-arbitrage principle can help in pricing new financial products for which no market prices yet exist. Second, arbitrage can be used to estimate the prices for illiquid assets held in a portfolio for which there are no recent trades. Finally, no-arbitrage prices can be used as benchmark prices against which market prices can be compared in seeking misvalued assets.

The Law of One Price

Prices and Economic Incentives:

Comparing Apples and Assets;

We expect the same thing to sell for the same price. This is the Law of One Price. Why should this be true? Common sense dictates that if you could buy an apple for 25¢ and sell it for 50¢ across the street, everyone would want to buy apples where they are cheap and sell them where they are priced higher. Yet this price disparity will not last: As people take advantage, prices will adjust until apples of the same quality sell for the same price on both sides of the street. Furthermore, a basket of apples must be priced in light of the total cost of buying the fruit individually. Otherwise, people will make up their own baskets and sell them to take advantage of any mispricing. The arbitrage relationship between individual asset prices and overall portfolio values is explored.

The structure imposed on prices by economic incentives is the same in financial markets as in the apple market. Yet a different approach must be taken to determine what constitutes the "same thing" in financial markets. For example, securities are the "same" if they produce the same outcomes, which considers both their expected returns and risk. They should consequently sell for the same prices. Similarly, equivalent combinations of assets providing the same outcomes should sell for the same price. Thus, the criteria for equivalence among financial securities involve the comparability of expected returns and risk. If the same thing sells for different prices, the Law of One Price is violated, and the price disparity will be exploited through arbitrage. Thus, the Law of One Price imposes structure on asset prices through the discipline of the profit motive. Similarly, if stocks with the same risk have different expected returns, the Law of One Expected Return is violated.

The Nature and Significance of Arbitrage

Arbitrage is the process of earning a riskless profit by taking advantage of different prices for the same good, whether priced alone or in equivalent combinations. Thus, due to mispricing, a riskless position is expected to earn more than the risk-free return. A true arbitrage opportunity exists when simultaneous positions can be taken in assets that earn a net positive return without exposing the investor to risk and, importantly, without requiring a net cash outlay. In other words, pure arbitrage requires no upfront investment but nonetheless offers a possible profit. The requirement that arbitrage not demand additional funds allows for the possibility that the position either generates an initial cash inflow or neither provides nor requires any cash initially. Consider the intuition behind this requirement. A positive initial outlay means that the arbitrage strategy is not self-financing. This would imply at least the risk that the initial investment could be lost, which is inconsistent with the no-risk requirement for the presence of an arbitrage opportunity.

Arbitrage may be considered from at least two perspectives. First, arbitrage may involve the construction of a new riskless position or portfolio designed to exploit a mispriced asset or portfolio of assets. Second, arbitrage may involve the riskless modification of an existing asset or portfolio that requires no additional funds to exploit some mispricing.

The Relationship Between the Law of One Price and Arbitrage

If the Law of One Price defines the resting place for an asset's price, arbitrage is the action that draws prices to that spot. The absence of arbitrage opportunities is consistent with equilibrium prices, wherein supply and demand are equal. Conversely, the presence of an arbitrage opportunity implies disequilibrium, in which assets are mispriced. Thus, arbitrage-free prices are expected to be the norm in efficient financial markets. The act of arbitraging mispriced assets should return prices to their appropriate values. This is because investors' purchases of the cheaper asset will increase the price, while sales of the overpriced asset will cause its price to decrease. Arbitrage consequently reinforces the Law of One Price and imposes order on asset prices.

Mispricing, Convergence, and Arbitrage

Arbitrage exploits violations of the Law of One Price by buying and selling assets, separately or in combination, that should be priced the same but are not. Implicit in an arbitrage strategy is the expectation that the prices of the misvalued assets will ultimately move to their appropriate values. Indeed, arbitrage should push prices to their appropriate levels. Thus, an arbitrage strategy has two key aspects: execution and convergence. Execution includes how the arbitrage opportunity is identified in the first place, how the strategy is put together, how it is maintained over its life, and how it is ultimately closed out. Convergence is the movement of misvalued asset prices to their appropriate values. Of particular importance are the time frame over which convergence is expected to occur and the process driving the convergence. These two are the primary factors that determine the design of the appropriate arbitrage strategy in a given situation.

The processes driving convergence fall into two categories: mechanical or absolute, and behavioral or correlation. A mechanical or absolute convergence process has an explicit link that forces prices to converge over a well-defined time period. An example is index arbitrage, in which the futures price of an index is mechanically linked to the spot (cash) value of the index through the cost-of-carry pricing relation. In index arbitrage, the convergence time period is deterministically dictated by the delivery/expiration date of the index futures contract.

A behavioral or correlation convergence process exists when there is historical evidence of a systematic relationship or a correlation in the behavior of the assets' prices. However, the mispriced assets fall short of being linked mechanically. An example of a behavioral or correlation convergence process is pairs trading. Pairs trading identifies two stocks that have historically tended to move closely, as measured by the average spread between their prices. It is common to identify pairs of stocks that are highly correlated in large part due to being in the same industry. The essence of this strategy is to identify pairs whose spreads are significantly higher or lower than usual and then sell the higher-priced stock and buy the lower-priced stock under the expectation that the spread will eventually revert to its historical average. Thus, pairs trading relies on an estimated correlation and projected convergence toward the historical mean spread. Importantly, no mechanical link guarantees this convergence, and no deterministic model indicates how long such convergence should take. Although they are commonly referred to as arbitrage, behavioral/correlation convergence process-based strategies are not true arbitrage, because they can be quite risky. This book is concerned primarily with mechanical/absolute convergence process-based arbitrage because that is the fertile soil from which modern finance has grown.

Arbitrage and the Impossibility of Time Travel.

Proving whether time travel is possible may seem the exclusive province of science. Yet some creative brainstorming by financial economist Marc Reinganum frames the issue differently. He argues that time travel is impossible because it would create arbitrage opportunities. Consider how a time traveler could engage in arbitrage. Let's say that the traveler deposits $500 in a bank account that pays 5% annually. In ten years, the value of the deposit will be $500 (1.05)10 = $814.45. Of course, the time traveler does not have to wait ten years to withdraw this amount. The traveler could immediately travel ten years into the future, collect the $814.45, and redeposit it again today. He would get $814.45 (1.05)10 = $1,326.65 in ten years, which would again be collected and reinvested immediately. So the pattern is set. Given that the interest rate remains at 5%, the time traveler could parlay the initial $500 into an infinite amount. Time travel would be the proverbial "money machine." As summarized by Reinganum:

As long as time travel is costless, and as long as the cost of transacting is nil, time travelers will drive the nominal rate of interest to zero by engaging in arbitrage transactions. Conversely, the existence of positive nominal rates of interest suggests that time travelers do not exist.

Given the nature of time travel, if the no-arbitrage principle implies that time travel is impossible today, it must be impossible in the future because there is no material distinction between the present and the future. So it seems that arbitrage is truly a timeless concept of enduring significance.

Identifying Arbitrage Opportunities

Arbitrage Situations

Arbitrage opportunities exist when an investor either invests nothing and yet still expect a positive payoff in the future or receives an initial net inflow on an investment and still expects a positive or zero payoff in the future.

This appeals to the commonsense expectation that money must be invested to result in a positive payoff. Furthermore, if you receive money upfront, you expect at the least to pay it back and certainly do not expect the investment to produce positive pay-offs in the future. It is also reasonable to expect the value of a portfolio of assets to properly reflect the prices of the underlying components of that portfolio. Thus, the situations described in this chapter indicate arbitrage opportunities in which deviations from the Law of One Price can potentially be exploited. Any one of these conditions is sufficient for the presence of an arbitrage opportunity. Consider the following examples, which indicate the presence of an arbitrage opportunity.

Arbitrage When "Whole" Portfolios Do Not Equal the Sum of Their "Parts"

What if the price of a portfolio is not equal to the sum of the prices of the assets when purchased separately and combined into an equivalent portfolio? This summons the earlier image of a basket of fruit selling for a price different from the cost of buying all its contents individually. More specifically, if fruit basket prices are too high, people will buy individual fruit and sell baskets of fruit. They would consequently "play both ends against the middle" to make a profit.

This situation could occur when commodities or securities are sold both separately and as a "packaged" bundle. For example, the Standard & Poor's 500 Composite Index (S&P 500) is a portfolio consisting of 500 U.S. stocks that can be traded as a package using an SPDR.20 Of course, the stocks can also be traded individually. Thus, an arbitrage opportunity would exist if the S&P 500-based SPDR sold at a price different from the cost of separately buying the 500 stocks comprising the index.

Consider what happens if this condition is not satisfied for a two-stock portfolio consisting of one share of Merck (MRK) selling at $31.46 and one share of Yahoo (YHOO) selling at $34.02. If the price of the equal-weighted portfolio differs from $31.46 + $34.02 = $65.48, an investor could profit without assuming any risk.

The two possible imbalances are as follows:

- Price portfolio (MRK + YHOO) > $31.46 + $34.02
- Price portfolio (MRK + YHOO) < $31.46 + $34.02

In the first case, the portfolio is overpriced relative to its two underlying components. In the second case, the portfolio is underpriced relative to its components. More specifically, assume in the first case that the portfolio sells for $75.00 and in the second case that the portfolio sells for $55.00. We expect that the sum of the prices of MRK and YHOO will equal the price of the portfolio at some time in the future. However, in light of the earlier discussion of convergence, we must admit that because there was mispricing to begin with, there is no certainty that the relevant prices will equalize in the future. We assume that such convergence will occur eventually.

If the price of the portfolio is $75.00 and therefore exceeds the costs of buying MRK and YHOO individually. In that case, the strategy is to buy a share of MRK for $31.46 and a share of YHOO for $34.02 separately because they are cheap relative to the price of the portfolio. To finance the purchases, it is necessary to sell short the portfolio for $75.00 at the same time. Because the price of the portfolio exceeds the cost of buying each of its members separately, selling the portfolio short generates sufficient money to purchase the stocks individually. The strategy consequently is self-financing. It generates a net initial cash inflow of $75.00 – $65.48 = $9.52.

Yet what will the net long and short positions yield in the future? You will have to return the portfolio at some time in the future to cover the short position, which involves a cash outflow to buy the portfolio. However, you already own the shares that constitute that portfolio. Thus, subsequent moves in the prices of MRK and YHOO are neutralized by the offsetting changes in the value of the portfolio consisting of the same two stocks. Thus, the net cash flow in the future is zero.

What does this mean? It means that you could generate an initial cash inflow of $9.52 that is like getting a loan you never have to repay! This cannot last, because everyone would pursue this strategy. Indeed, investors would pursue this with as much money as possible! Ultimately the increased demand to buy MRK and YHOO would put upward pressure on their prices, and the demand to sell short the portfolio would put downward pressure on its price. Consequently, an arbitrage-free position will ultimately be reached in which the price of the portfolio equals the sum of the prices of the assets when purchased separately.

To reinforce this result, consider the other imbalance, in which the price of the portfolio is only $55.00, which is less than the costs of buying MRK and YHOO individually for a total of $65.48. The strategy is to sell short a share of MRK for $31.46 and to sell short a share of YHOO for $34.02 separately because they are very expensive relative to the price of the portfolio at $55.00. Similarly, you would buy the portfolio for $55.00 because it is cheap relative to its underlying components.

It is obvious that selling short the two stocks individually generates more cash inflow than the cash outflow required to purchase the portfolio. Thus, the investment generates an initial positive net cash inflow of $65.48 – $55.00 = $10.48. As in the case just evaluated, it is important to consider the cash flow at termination of the investment positions in the future. Some time in the future, you will have to return the shares of MRK and YHOO to cover the short sale of each stock, which involves the cash outflow to buy each of the two stocks. However, you already own the portfolio, which consists of a share each of MRK and YHOO. Thus, subsequent moves in the prices of the long positions in MRK and YHOO are neutralized by the equivalent, mirroring price moves of the same stocks within the short portfolio. Consequently, the net cash flow in the future is zero. As observed with the other imbalance, you can effectively borrow money that never has to be paid back! This indicates an arbitrage opportunity and shows why only arbitrage-free asset and portfolio prices persist.

The Essence of Arbitrage

- In pure arbitrage, you invest no money, take no risk and walk away with sure profits.
- You can categorize arbitrage in the real world into three groups:
  - Pure arbitrage, where, in fact, you risk nothing and earn more than the riskless rate.
  - Near arbitrage, where you have assets that have identical or almost identical cash flows, trading at different prices, but there is no guarantee that the prices will converge and there exist significant constraints on the investors forcing convergence.
  - Speculative arbitrage, which may not really be arbitrage in the first place. Here, investors take advantage of what they see as mispriced and similar (though not identical) assets, buying the cheaper one and selling the more expensive one.

Pure Arbitrage

- For pure arbitrage, you have two assets with identical cashflows and different market prices make pure arbitrage difficult to find in financial markets.
- There are two reasons why pure arbitrage will be rare:
  - Identical assets are not common in the real world, especially if you are an equity investor.
  - Assuming two identical assets exist, you have to wonder why financial markets would allow pricing differences to persist.
  - If in addition, we add the constraint that there is a point in time where the market prices converge, it is not surprising that pure arbitrage is most likely to occur with derivative assets options and futures and in fixed

income markets, especially with default-free government bonds.

Futures Arbitrage

- A futures contract is a contract to buy (and sell) a specified asset at a fixed price in a future time period.
- The basic arbitrage relationship can be derived fairly easily for futures contracts on any asset, by estimating the cashflows on two strategies that deliver the same end result the ownership of the asset at a fixed price in the future.
  - In the first strategy, you buy the futures contract, wait until the end of the contract period and buy the underlying asset at the futures price.
  - In the second strategy, you borrow the money and buy the underlying asset today and store it for the period of the futures contract.
  - In both strategies, you end up with the asset at the end of the period and are exposed to no price risk during the period in the first, because you have locked in the futures price and in the second because you bought the asset at the start of the period. Consequently, you should expect the cost of setting up the two strategies to exactly the same.

a. Storable Commodities

- Strategy 1: Buy the futures contract. Take delivery at expiration. Pay $F.
- Strategy 2: Borrow the spot price (S) of the commodity and buy the commodity. Pay the additional costs.
- Investors are assumed to borrow and lend at the same rate, which is the riskless rate.
- When the futures contract is over priced, it is assumed that the seller of the futures contract (the arbitrageur) can sell short on the commodity and that he can recover,

from the owner of the commodity, the storage costs that are saved as a consequence.

b. Stock Index Futures

- Strategy 1: Sell short on the stocks in the index for the duration of the index futures contract. Invest the proceeds at the riskless rate. This strategy requires that the owners of the stocks that are sold short be compensated for the dividends they would have received on the stocks.
- Strategy 2: Sell the index futures contract.
- The Arbitrage: Both strategies require the same initial investment, have the same risk and should provide the same proceeds. Again, if S is the spot price of the index, F is the futures prices, y is the annualized dividend yield on the stock and r is the riskless rate.

Feasibility of Futures Arbitrage

- In the commodity futures market, for instance, Garbade and Silber (1983) find little evidence of arbitrage opportunities and their findings are echoed in other studies. In the financial futures markets, there is evidence that indicates that arbitrage is indeed feasible but only to a sub-set of investors.
- Note, though, that the returns are small even to these large investors and that arbitrage will not be a reliable source of profits, unless you can establish a competitive advantage on one of three dimensions.
  - You can try to establish a transactions cost advantage over other investors, which will be difficult to do since you are competing with other large institutional investors.
  - You may be able to develop an information advantage over other investors by having access to information

earlier than others. Again, though much of the information is pricing information and is public.

- You may find a quirk in the data or pricing of a particular futures contract before others learn about it.

Options Arbitrage

- Options represent rights rather than obligations – calls gives you the right to buy, and puts gives you the right to sell. Consequently, a key feature of options is that the losses on an option position are limited to what you paid for the option, if you are a buyer.
- Since there is usually an underlying asset that is traded, you can, as with futures contracts, construct positions that essentially are riskfree by combining options with the underlying asset.

Fixed Income Arbitrage

- Fixed income securities lend themselves to arbitrage more easily than equity because they have finite lives and fixed cash flows. This is especially so, when you have default free bonds, where the fixed cash flows are also guaranteed.
- For instance, you could replicate a 10-year treasury bond's cash flows by buying zero-coupon treasuries with expirations matching those of the coupon payment dates on the treasury bond.
- With corporate bonds, you have the extra component of default risk. Since no two firms are exactly identical when it comes to default risk, you may be exposed to some risk if you are using corporate bonds issued by different entities.

Does fixed income arbitrage pay?

- Grinblatt and Longstaff, in an assessment of the treasury strips program a program allowing investors to break up a treasury bond and sell its individual cash flows note that there are potential arbitrage opportunities in these markets but find little evidence of trading driven by these opportunities.

- A study by Balbas and Lopez of the Spanish bond market examined default free and option free bonds in the Spanish market between 1994 and 1998 and concluded that there were arbitrage opportunities especially surrounding innovations in financial markets.

- The opportunities for arbitrage with fixed income securities are probably greatest when new types of bonds are introduced mortgage backed securities in the early 1980s, inflation- indexed treasuries in the late 1990s and the treasury strips program in the late 1980s. As investors become more informed about these bonds and how they should be priced, arbitrage opportunities seem to subside.

Determinants of Success at Pure Arbitrage

- The nature of pure arbitrage – two identical assets that are priced differently – makes it likely that it will be short lived. In other words, in a market where investors are on the look out for riskless profits, it is very likely that small pricing differences will be exploited quickly, and in the process, disappear. Consequently, the first two requirements for success at pure arbitrage are access to real-time prices and instantaneous execution.

- It is also very likely that the pricing differences in pure arbitrage will be very small often a few hundredths of a percent. To make pure arbitrage feasible, therefore, you can add two more conditions.

  - The first is access to substantial debt at favorable interest rates, since it can magnify the small pricing differences. Note that many of the arbitrage positions require you to be able to borrow at the riskless rate.

- The second is economies of scale, with transactions amounting to millions of dollars rather than thousands.

Near Arbitrage

- In near arbitrage, you either have two assets that are very similar but not identical, which are priced differently, or identical assets that are mispriced, but with no guaranteed price convergence.
- No matter how sophisticated your trading strategies may be in these scenarios, your positions will no longer be riskless.
- If you can buy the same stock at one price in one market and simultaneously, sell it at a higher price in another market, you can lock in a riskless profit.
- We will look at two scenarios:
  - Dual or Multiple listed stocks
  - Depository receipts

a. Dual Listed Stocks

- Many large companies trade on multiple markets on different continents.
- Since there are time periods during the day when there is trading occurring on more than one market on the same stock, it is conceivable (though not likely) that you could buy the stock for one price in one market and sell the same stock at the same time for a different (and higher price) in another market.
- The stock will trade in different currencies, and for this to be a riskless transaction, the trades have to at precisely the same time and you have to eliminate any exchange rate risk by converting the foreign currency proceeds into the domestic currency instantaneously.

- Your trade profits will also have to cover the different bidask spreads in the two markets and transactions costs in each.

Evidence of Mispricing?

- Swaicki and Hric examine 84 Czech stocks that trade on the two Czech exchanges – the Prague Stock Exchange (PSE) and the Registration Places System (RMS) and find that prices adjust slowly across the two markets, and that arbitrage opportunities exist (at least on paper) –the prices in the two markets differ by about 2%. These arbitrage opportunities seem to increase for less liquid stocks.

- While the authors consider transactions cost, they do not consider the price impact that trading itself would have on these stocks and whether the arbitrage profits would survive the trading.

b. Depository Receipts

- Depository receipts create a claim equivalent to the one you would have had if you had bought shares in the local market and should therefore trade at a price consistent with the local shares.

- What makes them different and potentially riskier than the stocks with dual listings is that ADRs are not always directly comparable to the common shares traded locally one ADR on Telmex, the Mexican telecommunications company, is convertible into 20 Telmex shares.

- In addition, converting an ADR into local shares can be both costly and time consuming. In some cases, there can be differences in voting rights as well.

- In spite of these constraints, you would expect the price of an ADR to closely track the price of the shares in the local market, albeit with a currency overlay, since ADRs are denominated in dollars.

Evidence on Pricing

- In a study conducted in 2000, that looks at the link between ADRs and local shares, Kin, Szakmary, and Mathur conclude that about 60 to 70% of the variation in ADR prices can be attributed to movements in the underlying share prices and that ADRs overreact to the U.S, market and under react to exchange rates and the underlying stock.
- They also conclude that investors cannot take advantage of the pricing errors in ADRs because convergence does not occur quickly or in predictable ways.
- With a longer time horizon and/or the capacity to convert ADRs into local shares, though, you should be able to take advantage of significant pricing differences.
- Studies that have looked at ADRs on stocks in a series of emerging markets including Brazil, Chile, Argentina and Mexico seem to arrive at common conclusions. There are often persistent deviations from price parity and there seems to be potential for excess returns, sometimes of significant magnitude, for investors who exploit unusually large price divergences. Every one of these studies also sounds notes of caution: convergence can sometimes be slow in coming, there are high transactions costs and illiquidity in the local market can be a serious concern.
- Studies that have looked at developed markets such as Germany, Canada, and the UK also document occasional price differences between the local listing and the ADR, though the differences tend to be smaller and price convergence occurs more.

2. Closed End Funds

- Closed end mutual funds differ from other mutual funds in one very important respect. They have a fixed number of shares that trade in the market like other publicly traded companies, and the market price can be different from the net asset value.

- If they trade at a price that is lower than the net asset value of the securities that they own, there should be potential for arbitrage.

3. Convertible Arbitrage

- When companies have convertible bonds or convertible preferred stock outstanding in conjunction with common stock, warrants, preferred stock and conventional bonds, it is entirely possible that you could find one of these securities mispriced relative to the other, and be able to construct a near riskless strategy by combining two or more of the securities in a portfolio.
- In practice, there are several possible impediments.
  - Many firms that issue convertible bonds do not have straight bonds outstanding, and you have to substitute in a straight bond issued by a company with similar default risk.
  - Companies can force conversion of convertible bonds, which can wreak havoc on arbitrage positions.
  - Convertible bonds have long maturities. Thus, there may be no convergence for long periods, and you have to be able to maintain the arbitrage position over these periods.
  - Transactions costs and execution problems (associated with trading the different securities) may prevent arbitrage.

Determinants of Success at Near Arbitrage

- These strategies will not work for small investors or for very large investors. Small investors will be stymied both by transactions costs and execution problems. Very large investors will quickly drive discounts to parity and eliminate excess returns.

- If you decide to adopt these strategies, you need to refine and focus your strategies on those opportunities where convergence is most likely. For instance, if you decide to try to exploit the discounts of closed-end funds, you should focus on the closed end funds that are most discounted and concentrate especially on funds where there is the potential to bring pressure on management to open end the funds..

Pseudo or Speculative Arbitrage

- There are a large number of strategies that are characterized as arbitrage, but actually expose investors to significant risk.
- We will categorize these as pseudo or speculative arbitrage.

1. Paired Arbitrage

- In paired arbitrage, you buy one stock (say GM) and sell another stock that you view as very similar (say Ford), and argue that you are not that exposed to risk. Clearly, this strategy is not riskless since no two equities are exactly identical, and even if they were very similar, there may be no convergence in prices.
- The conventional practice among those who have used this strategy on Wall Street has been to look for two stocks whose prices have historically moved together – i.e., have high correlation over time.

2. Merger Arbitrage

- The stock price of a target company jumps on the announcement of a takeover. However, it trades at a discount usually to the price offered by the acquiring company.

- The difference between the post-announcement price and the offer price is called the arbitrage spread, and there are investors who try to profit off this spread in a strategy called merger or risk arbitrage. If the merger succeeds, the arbitrageur captures the arbitrage spreads, but if it fails, he or she could make a substantial loss.
- In a more sophisticated variant in stock mergers (where shares of the acquiring company are exchanged for shares in the target company), the arbitrageur will sell the acquiring firm's stock in addition to buying the target firm's stock.

Arbitrage Trading Strategies

1. Volatility Arbitrage Neutral

Volatility arbitrage neutral is a trading strategy that involves simultaneously buying and selling securities to take advantage of pricing discrepancies caused by changes in volatility. The goal is to profit from the differences in prices between the securities while keeping the overall portfolio market-neutral by maintaining a balanced exposure to the market. The strategy aims to exploit mispricing due to market inefficiencies rather than betting on the direction of the market.

Example 1: A trader buys a call option on a stock that is expected to have high volatility in the future and simultaneously buys a put option on the same stock. This strategy is called a straddle or strangle and is designed to take advantage of the expected increase in the stock's volatility without taking on significant directional risk in the price action of the underlying asset.

Example 2: A trader buys a long-dated At-the-Money (ATM) call option and sells a short-dated ATM call option on the same stock. This strategy is called a diagonal call spread and is based on the idea that implied volatility tends to be higher for options with longer expiration dates than for options with shorter expiration dates.

By taking opposing positions on the same underlying asset with different expiration dates, the trader can profit from the difference in implied volatility between the two options, whilst remaining market neutral as both options have the same intrinsic value.

2. Volatility Arbitrage Long Biased

Volatility arbitrage long biased is a trading strategy that is similar to the above strategy but with a directional bias towards the long side. The trader may take a long position in securities with high volatility and a short position in securities with low volatility, with the aim of profiting from the expected increase in the volatility of the long position. The strategy may involve using options to hedge against downside risk.

Example: A trader buys a call option on a stock that is expected to have high volatility in the future and simultaneously buys a put option on a different stock that is expected to have low volatility. The trader maintains a long bias by having a larger position in the call option. This strategy is called a ratio call spread.

3. Structured Product Arbitrage

Structured product arbitrage is a trading strategy that involves exploiting pricing inefficiencies in structured products such as collateralized debt obligations (CDOs), asset-backed securities (ABS), and mortgage-backed securities (MBS). The trader seeks to profit from the differences in pricing between the underlying assets and the structured product that contains them.

Example: A trader buys an ABS that is backed by auto loans with high credit ratings but is trading at a discount due to market inefficiencies. The trader also shorts an MBS that contains auto loans with low credit ratings that are overvalued due to market inefficiencies. The trader seeks to profit from the pricing discrepancies between the two securities as the security prices return to normal levels.

4. Capital Structure Arbitrage

Capital structure arbitrage is a strategy in which an investor seeks to take advantage of the pricing inefficiencies between different securities within a company's capital structure. This strategy typically involves buying or selling two or more securities that are related to each other, such as a company's stock, bonds, and preferred stock, in order to profit from the relative mispricing of these securities.

Example: If a company's stock is undervalued relative to its bonds or preferred stock, an investor could buy the stock and sell the bonds or preferred stock. This would allow the investor to profit from the difference in prices, as the stock price is likely to rise relative to the other securities.

To determine if bonds are undervalued relative to the stock, you need to compare the yields of the bonds and the expected returns of the stock. Typically, when bonds are undervalued relative to the stock, it means that the yield on the bonds is higher than the expected returns from holding the stock. To determine if a stock is overvalued relative to a bond, you need to compare the valuation of the stock and the yield of the bond. We could compare the price-to-earnings (P/E) ratio of the stock to the yield-to-maturity (YTM) of the bond: The P/E ratio is calculated by dividing the stock price by the earnings per share (EPS), while the YTM is the expected return of the bond if held until maturity. A high P/E ratio relative to the YTM may suggest that the stock is overvalued relative to the bond.

5. Credit Arbitrage

Credit arbitrage is a trading strategy that involves exploiting pricing discrepancies between securities that have different credit ratings or risk levels. The trader seeks to profit from the differences in pricing between the securities while taking on a calculated amount of risk. The strategy may involve analyzing credit spreads, default probabilities, and other credit-related factors to identify mispricing and arbitrage opportunities.

Example: A trader buys credit default swaps (CDS) on a company where credit default risk is increasing; perhaps the company is issuing further debt securities and increasing its leverage. Simultaneously the trader shorts CDS on a company that is expected to perform well, where credit risk is decreasing. The trader seeks to profit from the differences in pricing between the CDS while taking on a calculated amount of risk.

CHAPTER 6

Derivative Instruments

A derivative is a product derived from a basic variable and can be traded on an exchange or over the counter market. The advantage of trading on an exchange is that traders do not have to worry about the creditworthiness of their counterparties. The clearing house solves this problem by requiring both traders to keep a certain margin at the clearing house to honor their covenants.

However, the complex design of exchange traded contracts makes the valuation extremely complex, thus making exchange traded derivatives have high inherent risk. OTC transactions can allow small companies to trade without being required to go public. They can also be used for hedging, transfer trading risk, and leverage for business operations. However, the downside of OTC trading is that it is riskier relative to exchange trading because of the lack of clearinghouses and, therefore, lack of transparency. Regulator does not know the exact nature and extent of the risk to increase the credit or default risk associated with each OTC contract. The speculative nature of the transactions resulted in a lack of integrity in the market.

There are three types of derivatives: forward contracts, futures, and options.

Forward contracts are very similar to futures contracts, the biggest difference being that forward contracts are not traded on an exchange and trade standard fixed assets. In addition, the two contracts are different in form. For forward contracts, the quality of commodities and the delivery date are all decided by both parties without strict standards. The deposit payment and settlement time are different, and the participants are different. Forward contracts are typically transactions between financial institutions in the over the counter market. It is a contract to buy or sell a product at a specified time in the future at an agreed price.

Futures contracts are made on an exchange. The underlying assets of futures trading include a variety of commodities and financial assets. Commodities include pork, soup, wool, wood and so on. Financial assets include stock indexes, currencies. Financial media regularly publish futures prices, determined by the supply and demand of assets.

Options are divided into American options and European options. An American option means that the option holder has the option to exercise the option at any time before the expiration date. European option means that the option holder can only choose to exercise the option at the expiration date. Unlike the forward contracts, it does not require buying or selling the underlying asset, but it does require paying a fee to own the option.

If the spot price rises, then buying the call option may be profitable. Once the price rises above the exercise price and exceeds the number of paid royalties, the deal becomes profitable.

If the spot price falls, then buying the put option may make a profit. A trading profit is made once the price falls below the exercise price by more than the royalty paid.

Financial Derivatives

Financial derivatives are financial instruments that are linked to a specific financial instrument or indicator or commodity, and through which specific financial risks can be traded in financial markets in their own right.

Transactions in financial derivatives should be treated as separate transactions rather than as integral parts of the value of underlying transactions to which they may be linked. The value of a financial derivative derives from the price of an underlying item, such as an asset or index. Unlike debt instruments, no principal amount is advanced to be repaid and no investment income accrues. Financial derivatives are used for a number of purposes including risk management, hedging, arbitrage between markets, and speculation.

Financial derivatives enable parties to trade specific financial risks such as interest rate risk, currency, equity and commodity price risk, and credit risk, etc to other entities who are more willing, or better suited, to take or manage these risks, typically, but not always, without trading in a primary asset or commodity. The risk embodied in a derivatives contract can be traded either by trading the contract itself, such as with options, or by creating a new contract which embodies risk characteristics that match, in a countervailing manner, those of the existing contract owned. This latter activity is termed offset ability, and occurs in forward markets. Offsetability means that it will often be possible to eliminate the risk associated with the derivative by creating a new, but "reverse", contract that has characteristics that countervail the risk of the first derivative. Buying the new derivative is the functional equivalent of selling the first derivative, as the result is the elimination of risk. The ability to offset the risk on the market is, therefore, considered the equivalent of tradability in demonstrating value. The outlay that would be required to offset the existing derivative contract represents its value actual offsetting is not required to demonstrate value.

Financial derivatives contracts are usually settled by net payments of cash, often before maturity for exchange traded contracts such as commodity futures. Cash settlement is a logical consequence of the use of financial derivatives to trade risk independently of ownership of an underlying item. However, some financial derivative contracts, particularly involving foreign currency, are associated with transactions in the underlying item.

4. The value of the financial derivative derives from the price of the underlying item: the reference price. Because the future reference price is not known with certainty, the value of the financial derivative at maturity can only be anticipated, or estimated. The reference price may relate to a commodity, a financial instrument, an interest rate, an exchange rate, another derivative, a spread between two prices, an index or basket of prices. An observable market price or index for the underlying item is essential for calculating the value of any financial derivative if there is no observable prevailing market price for the underlying item, it cannot be regarded as a financial asset. Transactions in financial derivatives should be treated as separate transactions, rather than as integral parts of the value of underlying transactions to which they may be linked. This is because a different institutional unit will be the party to the derivative transaction from that for the underlying transaction. However, embedded derivatives should not be separately identified and valued from the primary instrument.

The following types of instruments are not financial derivatives for balance of payments purposes.

- A fixed price contract for goods and services is not a financial derivative instrument, unless, the contract is standardized so that the market price risk therein can be traded in financial markets in its own right.
- Timing delays arising in the normal course of business, which may entail exposure to price movements, do not

give rise to transactions and positions in financial derivatives in the balance of payments. Such timing delays include normal settlement periods for spot transactions in financial markets, and those that arise in the normal course of trade in goods and services.

- Insurance is not a form of financial derivative. Insurance contracts provide individual institutional units exposed to certain risks with financial protection against the consequences of the occurrence of specified events, many of which cannot be expressed in terms of market prices. Insurance is a form of financial intermediation in which funds are collected from policyholders and invested in financial or other assets which are held as technical reserves to meet future claims arising from the occurrence of the events specified in the insurance policies: that is, insurance manages event risk primarily by the pooling, not the trading, of risk.

- Contingencies, such as guarantees and letters of credit are not financial derivatives. The principal characteristic of contingencies is that one or more conditions must be fulfilled before a financial transaction takes place. Typically, these contingencies are not instruments that facilitate the trading of specific financial risks.

Derivative features embedded in standard financial instruments and inseparable from the underlying instrument are not financial derivatives for balance of payments purposes because the financial derivative element is an integral part of the instrument such that the underlying instrument and the derivative element involve the same counterparties. So, if a primary instrument such as a security or loan contains an embedded derivative, the instrument should be valued and classified according to its primary characteristics, such as a security or loan, even though the value of that security or loan may well be different from comparable securities and loans because of the embedded derivative. Examples are bonds that are convertible into shares and securities that carry the option of repaying the principal in a different currency from that of issuance

Classes of Financial Derivatives

There are two broad types of financial derivatives, and provided that they can be valued separately from the underlying item to which they are linked, they should be included in the financial account of the balance of payments and in the international investment position, regardless of whether they are "traded" on or off-exchange.

The two broad classes of financial derivatives are: forward-type contracts, including swaps, and option contracts.

Under a forward contract, the two counterparties agree to exchange a specified quantity of an underlying item (real or financial) at an agreed contract price strike price on a specified date. Futures contracts are forward contracts traded on organized exchanges. Futures and other forward contracts are typically, but not always, settled by the payment of cash or the provision of some other financial instrument rather than the actual delivery of the underlying item and therefore are valued and traded separately from the underlying item. If the forward-type contract is a swap contract, the counterparties exchange cash flows based on the reference prices of the underlying items in accordance with pre-arranged terms. Interest-rate, currency, and cross-currency interest-rate swaps are common types of swap contracts.

A forward contract is an unconditional financial contract that represents an obligation for settlement on a specified date. At the inception of the contract, risk exposures of equal market value are exchanged. Both parties are potential debtors, but a debtor/creditor relationship can be established only after the contract goes into effect. Thus, at inception, the contract has zero value. However, during the life of a forward contract, the market value of each party's risk exposure may differ from the zero market values at the inception of the contract as the price of the underlying item changes. When this occurs, an asset (creditor) position is created for one party and a liability (debtor) position for the other. The debtor/creditor relationship may change both in magnitude and direction over the life of the forward contract.

Under an option type contract, the purchaser of the option, in return for an option premium, acquires from the writer of the option, the right but not the obligation to buy (call option) or sell (put option) a specified underlying item (real or financial) at an agreed contract price strike price on or before a specified date. A major difference between forward and options contracts is that, whereas either party to a forward is a potential debtor, the buyer of an option acquires an asset, and the option writer incurs a liability. However, the option may expire worthless; the option will be exercised only if settling the contract is advantageous to the buyer. The buyer may make gains of unlimited size, and the option writer may experience losses of unlimited size. Options are written on a wide variety of underlying items such as equities, commodities, currencies, and interest rates (including cap, collar, and floor). Options are also written on futures, and swaps (known as swap captions), and other instruments such as caps (known as captions).

On organized markets, option contracts are usually settled in cash, but some option type contracts are normally settled by the purchase of the underlying asset. For instance, warrants are financial contracts that give the holder the right to buy, under specified terms, a certain number of the underlying asset, such as equity shares and bonds. If warrants are exercised the underlying asset is usually delivered. Warrants can be traded apart from the underlying securities to which they are linked.

Recording of Financial Derivative Transactions and Positions

The statistical treatment of financial derivatives in the balance of payments involves four steps:

- Recognizing that the exchange of claims and obligations at the inception of a derivative contract is a true financial transaction that creates asset and liability positions that have, at inception, a zero value in the case of forward instruments, and a value equal to the premium in the case of options;
- Treating any changes in the value of derivatives as holding gains or losses.
- Recording transactions in secondary markets of marketable derivatives, such as options, as financial transactions;
- Recording any payments at settlement as transactions in financial derivative assets or liabilities, as appropriate (i.e., no income arises from settlement of financial derivatives).

Valuation of Positions

A key characteristic of most derivative contracts is that transactors commit themselves forward to an agreed price at which they will or are willing to transact in an underlying item. From this, the value of the financial derivative derives from the difference between the agreed contract price of the underlying item and the prevailing, or expected prevailing, market price, appropriately discounted, of that item, and in the case of options taking into account the potential volatility of the price of the underlying instrument, the time to maturity and interest rate. In the specific case of a swap contract based on a notional principal amount, its value derives from the difference between the expected gross receipts and gross payments, appropriately discounted: that is, its net present value.

Financial derivatives are valued at their market price on the recording date. Changes in prices between balance sheet recording dates are classified as revaluation gains or losses. If market value data are unavailable, other fair value methods to value derivatives, such as options models or discounted present values, may be used.

Payments at Inception

Purchasers of options pay a premium to the seller. The full price of the premium is recorded as acquisition of a financial asset by the buyer and incurrence of a liability by the seller. In some instances, the premium may be paid at after the inception of the derivative contract. In this case, the value of the premium payment is recorded as an asset at the time the derivative is purchased, financed by an imputed loan from the writer.

The creation of a forward-type contract does not involve the recording of a financial account transaction in financial derivatives as risk exposures of equal value are being exchanged, i.e., there is zero exposure and hence zero value for both sides. Commissions and fees paid at inception or during the life of the derivative to banks, brokers, and dealers, are classified as payments for services. These are payments rendered for service activities provided within the current period, and are independent of the asset and liability relationships that are created by the derivative.

Resale of Derivatives in Secondary Markets

Resales of derivatives in secondary markets, whether exchange traded or over the counter, are recorded as financial transactions at the market price.

Settlement Payments

Net settlement payments are financial transactions, similar to transactions at maturity of other financial instruments. At settlement, either a net cash payment is made or the underlying item is delivered.

- When a financial derivative is settled in cash, a transaction in the derivative is recorded equal to the cash value of the settlement. No transaction in the underlying item is recorded. In most instances, the receipt of cash is recorded as a reduction in financial derivative assets, and the payment of cash is recorded as a reduction in financial derivative liabilities. However, when a contract involves on-going settlement, such as with an interest rate swap, a receipt of cash can be recorded as an increase in financial derivative liabilities if, at the time of the settlement payment, the contract is in a net liability position, and vice versa. If, because of market practice, compilers are unable to implement this approach, it is recommended that all cash settlement receipts be recorded as a reduction in financial assets, and all cash settlement payments be recorded as adecrseas in liabilities.

- When the underlying instrument is delivered, two transactions occur so that the transactions in both the underlying item and the derivative are recorded. The transaction in the underlying item is recorded at its prevailing market price on the day of the transaction while the transaction in the derivative is recorded as the difference between that market price for the underlying item and the strike price in the derivative contract times the quantity.

There may be practical difficulties in obtaining data to implement the preferred treatment.

Margins

Margins are payments of cash or collateral that cover potential or actual obligations under financial derivatives, especially futures or exchange traded options. The provision of margin is a feature of financial derivative markets, reflecting concern over counterparty risk.

Repayable margins consist of deposits or other collateral deposited to protect a counterparty against default risk, but which remain under the ownership of the unit that placed the margin. Although its uses may be restricted, a margin is classified as repayable if the depositor retains the risks and rewards of ownership, such as the receipt of income or exposure to holding gains and losses. At settlement, repayable margins, or the amounts of repayable margins in excess of any liability owed on the derivative, are returned to the depositor. In organized markets, repayable margin is sometimes known as initial margin.

Repayable margin payments of cash are deposits, not transactions in a derivative. The depositor has a claim on the exchange, broker or other institution holding the deposit. If securities are deposited, no entries are required because the entity on whom the depositor has a claim the issuer of the security is unchanged. Some countries may prefer to classify "repayable margins" within other accounts receivable/payable in order to reserve the term "deposits" for the monetary aggregates.

Nonrepayable margin is a transaction in a derivative paid to reduce a financial liability created under a derivative. Frequently, in organized exchanges, nonrepayable margin, sometimes known as variation margin, is paid daily to meet liabilities recorded under daily marking derivatives to market value. The entity that pays nonrepayable margin no longer retains ownership of the margin nor has the right to the risks and rewards of ownership, such as the receipt of income or exposure to holding gains and losses. A payment of nonrepayable margin is recorded as a reduction in financial derivative liabilities, (with the contra-entry of a reduction in a financial asset, probably currency and deposits); the receipt of nonrepayable margin is recorded as a reduction in financial derivative assets (with the contra-entry of an increase in a financial asset, probably currency and deposits).

Arrangements for margining can be complex, and procedures differ among countries. In some countries, repayable and nonrepayable margins are handled in a single account and it may be difficult to distinguish between them. The actual institutional arrangements must be reviewed, including which unit makes payment and the instruments used. The key test is whether the margins are repayable or involve an effective transfer of ownership between the units involved in the financial derivative contract.

Treatment of Selected Financial Derivatives

Specific Interest Rate Contracts

An interest rate swap contract involves an exchange of cash flows related to interest payments, or receipts, on a notional amount of principal, that is never exchanged, in one currency over a period of time. Settlements are often made through net cash payments by one counterparty to the other. Forward Rate Agreements (FRAs) are contracts in which the counterparties agree on an interest rate to be paid, at a specified settlement date, on a notional amount of principal of a specified maturity, that is never exchanged. FRAs are settled by net cash payments. Active financial markets exist in these contracts, allowing the generation of holding gains and losses. The creation of interest rate swaps and FRA contracts involve no entries in the financial account. Net cash settlement payments associated with interest rate swaps and with FRAs should be classified in the financial account under financial derivatives. Interest rate swaps usually involve on-going settlement during the life of the contract, whereas an FRA is usually settled at maturity of the contract.

Specific Foreign Currency Contracts

Foreign exchange swap contracts involve a spot sale/purchase of currencies and a simultaneous commitment to a forward purchase/sale of the same currencies. Forward foreign exchange contracts involve a commitment to transact in specified foreign currencies at an agreed exchange rate in a specified amount at some future agreed date. Cross-currency interest rate swap contracts, sometimes known as currency swaps, involve an exchange of cash flows related to interest payments and an exchange of principal amounts in specified currencies at an agreed exchange rate at the end of the contract; sometimes, there is also an exchange of principal at the beginning of the contract and in these circumstances there may be subsequent repayments, which include both interest payments and the amortization of principal, over time according to pre-arranged terms. All these payments are recorded as transactions in financial derivatives.

For a foreign currency financial derivative contracts, it is necessary to distinguish between transactions in the financial derivatives contract, and the requirement to deliver and receive underlying principal associated with the contract. As with other forward-type contracts, the creation of a foreign currency financial derivatives contract does not lead to the recording of transactions under financial derivatives in the financial account: any initial sale or purchase of currency is a transaction that will be reflected in the financial account, other investment at the exchange rate agreed by the counterparties. The exchange rate for the forward sale/purchase of currencies under a foreign currency derivative contract is agreed by the two counterparties at the time of the establishment of the swap contract. The derivative contract acquires value as the prevailing market exchange rate differs from the agreed contract exchange rate. At the time of settlement, the difference between the values of the currencies exchanged, measured in the unit of account and at the prevailing exchange rate, should be allocated to transactions in financial derivatives. In other words, if in the unit of account and at prevailing market exchange rates, the value of currency received (recorded as an increase in other investment, assets) exceeds that of the currency paid (recorded as a decrease in other investment, assets), a reduction in financial derivative assets is recorded (with the contra-entry of an increased in another item in the financial account, probably currency and deposits). The opposite applies for the reverse situation, i.e., when the value of the currency received is less than that of the currency paid.

Credit Derivatives

The financial derivatives described in the previous sections are related to market risk, which pertains to changes in the market prices of securities, commodities, interest and exchange rates. Financial derivatives whose primary purpose is to trade credit risk are known as credit derivatives. They are designed for trading in loan and security default risk. Credit derivatives take the form of both forward-type and option-type contracts, and like other financial derivatives, they are frequently drawn up under standard master legal agreements, and involve collateral and margining procedures, which allow for a means to make a market valuation.

Common types of credit derivatives include the following.

Total return swaps involves the swapping of cash flows and capital gains and losses related to the liability of a lower-rated creditor for cash flows related to a guaranteed interest rate, such as an inter-bank rate, plus a margin. Spread options are contracts whose value is derived from the interest rate spread between a high quality credit and a lower quality credit; for example, if the spread narrows sufficiently, the option holder benefits from exercising the option. Credit default swaps involve the swapping of the risk premium inherent in an interest rate on a bond or loan for a cash payment in the event of default by the debtor. Some credit default swap contracts require that one party make only a single payment to another in order to be financially protected against a the risk of a catastrophe befalling a creditor. For such contracts, a reference price may not be readily available, and the single premium contracts would be more properly classified as a form of insurance rather than a financial derivative.

Major types of derivatives

There are four main types of derivatives contracts: forwards; futures, options and swaps. This section discusses the basics of these four types of derivatives with the help of some specific examples of these instruments.

Forwards and futures contracts

Forward and futures contracts are usually discussed together as they share a similar feature: a forward or futures contract is an agreement to buy or sell a specified quantity of an asset at a specified price with delivery at a specified date in the future.

But there are important differences in the ways these contracts are transacted. First, participants trading futures can realise gains and losses on a daily basis while forwards transaction requires cash settlement at delivery. Second, futures contracts are standardised while forwards are customized to meet the special needs of the two parties involved (counterparties). Third, unlike futures contracts which are settled through established clearing house, forwards are settled between the counterparties. Fourth, because of being exchange-traded, futures are regulated whereas forwards, which are mostly over the counter (OTC) contracts, and loosely regulated (at least in the run up to the global financial crisis). This importance of exchange-traded versus OTC instruments will be discussed further in later section.

Options contracts

Options contracts can be either standardized or customized. There are two types of option: call and put options. Call option contracts give the purchaser the right to buy a specified quantity of a commodity or financial asset at a particular price (the exercise price) on or before a certain future date (the expiration date). Similarly, put option contracts give the buyer the right to sell a specified quantity of an asset at a particular price on a before a certain future date. These definitions are based on the so-called American-style option. And for a European style option, the contract can only be exercised on the expiration date.

In options transaction, the purchaser pays the seller –the writer of the options an amount for the right to buy or sell. This amount is known as the option premium. Note that an important difference between options contracts and futures and forwards contracts is that options do not require the purchaser to buy or sell the underlying asset under all circumstances. In the event that options are not exercised at expiration, the purchaser simply loses the premium paid. If the options are exercised, however, the option writer will be liable for covering the costs of any changes in the value of the underlying that benefit the purchasers.

Swaps

Swaps are agreements between two counterparties to exchange a series of cash payments for a stated period of time. The periodic payments can be charged on fixed or floating interest rates, depending on contract terms. The calculation of these payments is based on an agreed upon amount, called the notional principal amount or simply the notional.

Underlying assets and derivative products

While forwards, futures, options and swaps can be viewed as the mechanics of derivation, the value of these contracts are based on the prices of the underlying assets. In this section, we discuss a range of derivatives products that derive their values from the performance of five underlying asset classes: equity, fixed income instrument, commodity, foreign currency and credit event. However, given the speed of financial innovation over the past two decades, the variety of derivatives products have grown substantially.

Equity derivatives

Equity futures and options on broad equity indices are perhaps the most commonly cited equity derivatives securities. Way back in 1982, trading of futures based on S&P's composite index of 500 stocks began on the Chicago Mercantile Exchange (CME). Options on the S&P 500 futures began trading on the CME in the following year. Today, investors can buy futures based on benchmark stock indices in most international financial centres. In 2010, the authorities approved trading of futures on the China Securities Index 300, Index futures contract enabled an investor to buy a stock index at a specified date for a certain price. It can be an extremely useful hedging tool. For example, an investor with a stock portfolio that broadly matches the composition of the Hang Seng index (HSI), he will suffer losses should the HSI record a fall in market value in the near future. Since he means to hold the portfolio as a long term strategy, he is unwilling to liquidate the portfolio. Under such circumstances, he can protect his portfolio by selling HSI index futures contracts so as to profit from any fall in price. Of course, if his expectations turned out to be wrong and the HSI rose instead, the loss on the hedge would have been compensated by the profit made on the portfolio. Some investors prefer to purchase options on futures (or "futures options") instead of straight futures contracts. The option strike price is the specified futures price at which the future is traded if the option is exercised. For some market participants, the pricing of an option reveal valuable information about the likely future volatility of the returns of the underlying asset.3 One commonly cited example is the Chicago Board Options Exchange Market Volatility Index (VIX index), which is calculated based on a range of options on the S&P 500 index. When investors are concerned about a potential drop in the US stock market, they buy the VIX index as an insurance against losses in the value of their portfolio. The more investors demand, the higher the price of the VIX. As such, the VIX can be viewed as an "investor fear gauge".

Other commonly traded equity derivatives are equity swaps. Under an equity swap contract, an investor pays the total return on a stock to his counterparty and receives in return a floating rate of interest. With this equity swap, the investor can hedge his equity position without giving up ownership of his share. At the same time, the party receiving equity return enjoys exposure without actually taking ownerships of shares.

Interest Rate Derivatives

One of the most popular interest rate derivatives is interest rate swap. In one form, it involves a bank agreeing to make payments to a counterparty based on a floating rate in exchange for receiving fixed interest rate payments. It provides an extremely useful tool for banks to manage interest rate risk. Given that banks' floating rate loans are usually tied closely to the market interest rates while their interest payments to depositors are adjusted less frequently, a decline in market interest rates would reduce their interest income but not their interest payments on deposits. By entering an interest rate swap contract and receiving fixed rate receipts from a counterparty, banks would be less exposed to the interest rate risk.

Meanwhile, interest rate futures contract allows a buyer to lock in a future investment rate. For example, the Chicago Board of Trade offers federal funds futures contracts ranging from the current month to 24 months out. A by-product of these futures is that they provide useful information on the market expectations of future monetary policy decisions in the United States.

Commodity Derivatives

The earliest derivatives markets have been associated with commodities, driven by the problems about storage, delivery and seasonal patterns. But, modern day commodity derivatives markets only began to develop rapidly in the 1970s. During that time, the breakup of the market dominance of a few large commodity producers allowed price movements to better reflect the market supply and demand conditions. The resulting price volatility in the spot markets gave rise to demand of commodity traders for derivatives trading to hedge the associated price risks. For example forwards contracts on Brent and other grades of crude became popular in the 1970s following the emergence of the Organisation of Petroleum Exporting Countries. Deregulations of the energy sector in the United States since the 1980s also stimulated the trading of natural gas and electrical power futures on the New York Mercantile Exchange (NYMEX) in the 1990s.

Foreign Exchange Derivatives

The increasing financial and trade integration across countries have led to a strong rise in demand for protection against exchange rate movements over the past few decades. A very popular hedging tool is forward exchange contract. It is a binding obligation to buy or sell a certain amount of foreign currency at a pre agreed rate of exchange on a certain future date. Consider a Korean shipbuilder who expects to receive a $1 million payment from a US cruise company for a boat in 12 months. Suppose the spot exchange rate is 1,200 won per dollar today. Should the won appreciate by 10 per cent against the dollar over the next year, the Korean shipbuilder will receive only 1,090 million of won (some 109 million of won less than he would have received today). But if the shipbuilder can hedge against the exchange risk by locking in buying dollars forwards at the rate of say 1,100 won per dollar.

For thinly trade currencies or currencies of those countries with restrictions on capital account transactions, the profit or loss resulting from the forwards transaction can be settled in an international currency. This is the so-called non-deliverable forwards contract, and very often they are traded offshore.

Another type of foreign exchange derivative are cross-currency swaps. This involves two parties exchanging payments of principal (based on the spot rate at inception) and interest in different currencies. According to many market participants, having a liquid cross-currency swap market is an important for local currency bond market developments. This is because such instruments allow foreign borrowers in local bond markets to swap back their proceeds to their own currencies while hedging against the interest rate risk.

Credit derivatives

A credit derivative is a contract in which a party (the credit protection seller) promises a payment to another (the credit protection buyer) contingent upon the occurrence of a credit event with respect to a particular entity (the reference entity). A credit event in general refers to an incident that affects the cash flows of a financial instrument (the reference obligation). There is no precise definition, but in practice, it could be filing for bankruptcy, failing to pay, debt repudiation or moratorium.

The fastest growing type of credit derivatives over the past decade is credit default swap (CDS). In essence, it is an insurance policy that protects the buyer against the loss of principal on a bond in case of a default by the issuer. The buyer of CDS pays a periodic premium to the seller over the life of the contract. The premium reflects the buyer's assessment of the probability of default and the expected loss given default. In the event of a credit incident, the buyer has a right to demand compensation from the seller.

In its simplest form, the CDS is written with respect to one single reference entity, the so-called single-name CDS. Some data providers compile indices of a basket of single-name CDSs of similar ratings (e.g., the S&P US Investment Grade CDS Index consists of 100 equally weighted investment grade US corporate credits). These index tranches give investors the opportunity to take on exposures to specific segments of the CDS index default loss distribution.

The Effect Of Financial Derivatives On Enterprises

In the 1970s, after the collapse of the Bretton Woods system, the fixed exchange rate system transformed into the floating exchange rate system. Frequent fluctuations of the exchange rate and the wave of financial liberalization brought exchange rate risks and interest rate risks to countries. To meet, the need for hedging in the financial market, financial derivatives have been, developed to deal with the exchange rate and interest rate problems. Furthermore, the role of financial derivatives is more diversified.

Hedging and speculation arbitrage

Hedging is when an investor buys or sells the actual goods on the spot market and sells or buys the same number of futures contracts on the futures market. Under the domination of the supply and demand relationship, the price trend of the spot and futures markets is generally the same. However, since investors operate in the opposite direction in two markets, they could avoid risks and reduce losses through hedging.

Speculation and arbitrage refer to that investors take advantage of the price difference in different periods to buy low and to sell high. According to the interest rate, exchange rate or price risks that investors encountered, they profit by frequent buying and selling derivatives to speculate.

Function of financial derivatives

The good use of derivatives is beneficial for companies to achieve more effective risk control, reducing the risk of enterprises at the same time. Moreover, idle funds can be effectively used for enterprises and society, while risks can be controlled, transaction efficiency can be improved, and resource allocation ability can be optimized.

Since the 2008 financial crisis, the world economy has been in a state of recovery. In recent years, with the rise of global protectionism and the impact of COVID-19, corporate risk management has become an important work. According to the research, more than 60% of companies in the international financial market have used financial derivatives for risk management. The research displays that more than 62% of listed companies in China use financial derivatives, and the proportion has a significant upward trend. For China, reasonable regulation of the use of financial derivatives can promote the construction of the financial market and drive enterprises to effectively use financial derivatives to solve their own difficulties.

The high leverage of financial derivatives and complexity, as well as it's trading problems such as nonstandard information opaque in the process of operation, determines its while avoiding risk, and there is a huge risk, combined with China financial market itself is not perfect, so most enterprise use derivatives to achieve the hedging function. Only a few larger powerful capital, fault tolerance of the high rate of the enterprise to realize the function of the speculative arbitrage through financial derivatives. Therefore, the enterprise shall be an efficient use of derivatives and actively explore maximize the value of derivatives.

The Case Of The Vanke Group

Financing difficulty is a problem that most enterprises will encounter in the process of operation. Still, Vanke group has solved this problem to a certain extent by using forward foreign exchange contracts.

Vanke Group, using its own foreign debt quota to foreign banking institutions to apply for a loan, at the same time entrust domestic bank financing guarantee institutions, do Foreign Banks to Vanke group set up the special account for external debt in the lending, at the same time, the same period Vanke and signed with banking institutions within the territory of the deadline of forwarding foreign exchange contracts, and determine the amount of the purchase of foreign exchange in the future Vanke can use overseas loans to make an investment or fund allocation in China, buy foreign exchange according to the agreed amount and forward exchange rate when the contract expires, and repay the cash to the overseas bank.

Through forward foreign exchange contracts, Vanke borrows foreign funds for domestic investment, which, on the one hand, solves the situation of domestic financing difficulties, expand financing channels for enterprises and increases the domestic capital flow. On the other hand, forward foreign exchange contracts can lock in borrowing costs, carry out risk control and hedge funds for enterprises.

The Case Of Jiangxi Copper

Jiangxi Copper is one of the largest production bases of copper products in China. Due to its great demand for raw materials, it needs to purchase a large number of copper products in domestic and foreign markets to meet production requirements. Foreign exchange risks will also affect purchasing from foreign markets, which will directly affect copper prices and company profits. In short, it will bring changes in raw material prices and inconvenience to the company's production and operation activities.

In this regard, Jiangxi Copper's solution is to establish a long position in the futures market, buy the corresponding number of futures contracts in the futures exchange, and close the position after the expiration of the contracts to reduce or avoid the risk of raw material price fluctuations. But sometimes due to differences in the international environment, may make the futures market, the price of raw materials at home and abroad after the conversion, and even to the point of buying high and selling low Jiangxi copper, the solution is based on the total annual production and operation plan to determine the required raw materials, to use in the total amount divided by the number of futures contracts agreed trading days, got a plan Then use the planned quantity minus the actual quantity of raw materials delivered every day to get a difference, the difference is the Jiangxi copper industry needs to build futures positions in the futures market that amount.

In this way, Jiangxi Copper can not only avoid the uncertainty caused by the exchange rate risk of international procurement, but also balance the purchasing quantity of raw materials, reduce the related risks caused by the price fluctuation of raw materials, and make preparations for the company's production and operation.

The Case Of Roche Holdings

In 1991, Roche holding common 10-year dollar could have 8.65% according to borrow, used for business investment But to reduce the cost of financing, Roche holding hybrid securities issuance of $1 billion, is a bull market spreads debt this mixed by a 10-year bond (annual interest rate of 3.5%) and a group of three-year option certificate. Warrants give the investor a put option at a low price (sFr70 or less); when the share price is higher (more than 100 Swiss francs) to the issuer when call options; investors have the highest returns. Three years later, the company's share price rose to 125 Swiss francs, company to exercise warrants, from investors bought authority cards, for investors to maximize returns. In addition, Roche holdings by 3.5% annual interest rate of financing reduce the financing cost. The bull market spread warrants of Roche Holding not only reduce the financing cost for the company but also help the company to obtain profits, harvest the funds needed for acquisition, but also maximize the interests of investors and realize the value of financial derivatives, which has played a significant role in the development of the company.

Role Of Derivatives In Recent Credit Events And Regulatory Issues

Financial derivatives have been associated with a number of high-profile credit events over the past two decades. In the early 1990s, Procter and Gamble Corporation lost over $100 million in transactions in equity swaps. On December 6 1994, Orange County declared bankruptcy after suffering losses of around $1.6 billion from a wrong-way bet on interest rates (the so-called "inverse floaters") in one of its principal investment pools. In 1995, Barings collapsed when one of its traders lost $1.4 billion (more than twice its available capital) in trading equity index derivatives.

The amounts involved with derivatives related corporate distress in the 2000s have increased substantially. Two such events were the bankruptcy of Enron Corporation in 2001 and the near collapse of AIG in 2008. One common feature of these events was that OTC derivative tradings were thought to have played some role.

Enron's filing for bankruptcy in December 2001 took many commentators by surprise. At that time, the company was estimated to have a shareholder value of $70 billion. The core of Enron's business was dealing in derivative contracts based on the prices of oil, gas, electricity and other variables in OTC markets. Enron's derivatives transactions in these markets were largely unregulated with no reporting requirements. There was little information is available about the profitability of these derivatives activities. Some thought that speculative losses in derivatives, perhaps masked by "creative" accounting, was one of the main contributing factor to the collapse of the company.

In 2008, the US government introduced a $150 billion financial package to prevent AIG; once the world's largest insurer by market value, from filing for bankruptcy. Being an AAA-rated company, AIG was being exempted from posting collateral on most of its derivatives trading at that time. In addition, AIG was unique among CDS market participants in that it acted almost exclusively as credit protection seller. As the global financial crisis reached its peak in late 2008, AIG's CDS portfolios recorded substantial mark-to-market losses. Consequently, the company was asked to post $40 billion of collateral, partly contributed to the near collapse.

These credit events raised some important questions concerning the regulations of derivatives trading and financial stability. 5 The focus appears to centre on improvements in counterparty risk management and in favour of promoting exchange traded derivative markets. Very often, the lack of knowledge of a counterparty's financial health can lead to fears about its solvency and contagion risk. Under such an environment, OTC contracts are particularly exposed to risks of inadequate collateral and capitalisation. In this context, central clearing of derivatives transactions and more robust collateralisation are important for mitigating counterparty risk in OTC markets. In addition, financial regulators are designing new rules to improve post-trade price transparency. There are also proposals in some jurisdictions to encourage the migration of trading in some actively OTC traded products to exchanges.

CHAPTER 7

Futures Contract

A futures contract is an agreement between a buyer and a seller where the seller agrees to deliver a specified quantity and grade of a particular asset at a predetermined time in futures at an agreed upon price through a designated market under stringent financial safeguards. A futures contract, in other words, is an agreement to buy or sell a particular asset between the two parties in a specified future period at an agreed price through specified exchange. For example, the S&P CNX NIFTY futures are traded on National stock exchange. This provides them transparency, liquidity, anonymity of trades and also eliminates the counter party risks due to the guarantee provided by National Securities Clearing Corporation limited.

The standardized items in any Futures contract are:

- QQuantity of the underlying asset
- QQuality of the underlying asset
- The date & month of delivery
- The units of price quotation & minimum change in price (tick size)

From the above, it is evident that financial futures termed as a notional commitment to buy or sell a standard quality of a financial instrument at a specified price on a specified future date. It means that this market is rarely used for the exchange of financial instruments. In fact, financial futures markets are independent of the underlying assets.

In general, financial futures are not different from commodity futures except of the underlying asset; for example, in commodity futures, a particular commodity like food grains, metals, vegetables, etc. are traded whereas in financial futures, instruments like equity shares, debentures, bond, etc. traded. The fact that the terms of futures contracts are standardized is important because it enables traders to focus their attention on one variable, price. Standardization also makes it possible for traders anywhere in the world to trade in these markets and know exactly what they are trading. This is in sharp contrast to the cash forward contract market, in which changes in specifications from one contract to another might cause price changes from one transaction to another. One reason futures markets are considered a good source of commodity price information is because price changes are attributable to changes in the commodity's price level, not changes in contract terms.

Unlike the forward cash contract market, futures exchanges provide:

- Rules of conduct that traders must follow or risk expulsion
- An organized market place with established trading hours by which traders must abide
- Standardized trading through rigid contract specifications, which ensure that the commodity being traded in every contract is virtually identical
- A focal point for the collection and dissemination of information about the commodity's supply and demand, which helps ensure all traders have equal access to information
- A mechanism for settling disputes among traders without resorting to the costly and often slow U.S. court system

- Guaranteed settlement of contractual and financial obligations via the exchange clearinghouse

TYPES OF FINANCIAL FUTURES CONTRACTS

Depending on the type of underlying asset, there are different types of futures contract available for trading. They are

Interest rate futures

Interest rate futures are traded on the NSC. These are futures based on interest rates. In India, interest rates futures were introduced on August 31, 2009. The logic of underlying asset is the same as we saw in commodity or stock futures. In this case, the underlying asset would be a debt obligation, debts that move in value according to changes in interest rates (generally government bonds). Companies, banks, foreign institutional investors, non-resident Indian and retail investors can trade in interest rate futures. Buying an interest rate futures contract will allow the buyer to lock in a future investment rate.

Foreign currency futures

They trade in the foreign currencies, thus also known as Exchange rate futures. The MCX-SX exchange trades the following currency futures:

- Euro-Indian Rupee (EURINR),
- Us dollar-Indian rupee (USDINR),
- Pound Sterling-Indian Rupee (GBPINR) and
- Japanese Yen-Indian Rupee (JPYINR).

Stock index futures

Understanding stock index futures is quite simple if you have understood individual stock futures. Here the underlying asset is the stock index. For example – the S&P CNX Nifty popularly called the 'nifty futures'. Stock index futures are more useful when speculating on the general direction of the market rather than the direction of a particular stock. It can also be used to hedge and protect a portfolio of shares. So here, the price movement of an index is tracked and speculated. One more point to note here is that, although stock index is traded as an asset, it cannot be delivered to a buyer. Hence, it is always cash settled. Both individual stock futures and index futures are traded in the NSE.

Bond index futures

These are based on particular bond indices, that is, indices of bond prices. As we know that prices of debt instruments are inversely related to interest rates, so the bond index is also related inversely to them. Example is the Municipal bond index futures based on US Municipal bond that is traded on the Chicago Board of Trade (CBOT).

Cost of living index futures

This is also known as Inflation futures. These futures contracts are based on a specified cost of living index, for example, consumer price index, wholesale price index, etc. these futures can be used to hedge against the unanticipated inflation which cannot be avoided. Hence such future contracts can be very useful to certain investors like provident funds, pension funds, mutual funds, etc.

Specifications of the futures market exchanges

All the futures contracts are initiated through a particular exchange. When a new futures contract is developed, an exchange must specify the underlying asset, size of the contract, how price will be quoted, where and when delivery will be made, and how price will be determined.

Stock exchanges perform the following functions:

1) They provide and maintain a physical market place known as the floor where futures transactions are sold and purchased by the members of the exchange.
2) They maintain and enforce ethical and financial norms applicable to the futures trading undertaken on the exchange.
3) They make efforts to promote business interests of the members because the exchange's main objective is to extend the facilities for such trading to its members.

Each exchange has usually membership organization whose members can be individuals or business organizations. Membership is limited to a specified number of seats. The members of the exchange have the right to trade on the floor of exchange, in turn, they agree to follow and abide by the rules of the exchange.

The Clearing House

An agency or separate corporation of a futures exchange responsible for settling trading accounts, clearing trades, collecting and maintaining margin monies, regulating delivery and reporting trading data. A clearing house is a financial institution that provides clearing and settlement services for financial and commodities derivatives and securities transactions. These transactions may be executed on a futures exchange or securities exchange, as well as off-exchange in the over the counter (OTC) market. Clearing houses act as third parties to all futures so that clearing house stands between two clearing firms (also known as member firms or clearing participants) and its purpose is to reduce the risk of one (or more) clearing firm failing to honor its trade settlement obligations. A clearing house reduces the settlement risks by netting offsetting transactions between multiple counterparties, by requiring collateral deposits (also called "margin deposits"), by providing independent valuation of trades and collateral, by monitoring the credit worthiness of the clearing firms, and in many cases, by providing a guarantee fund that can be used to cover losses that exceed a defaulting clearing firm's collateral on deposit. Also, it acts as a clearing firm.

Some of the important functions performed by the clearing house

- As clearing house give guarantee for all the transactions and acts as counterparty for all the transactions it will never have open positions in the market.

- It ensures that all parties adhere to the system and procedures so that various parties in the market can do trading smoothly which in turn leads to more confidence of the players on the markets and hence it increases liquidity in the market.

- It ensures a proper risk management system in place by stipulating that margin is maintained which is of two types initial and maintenance margin and hence accounting is done for all the gains and losses on daily basis and hence chances of default are reduced considerably.

- It ensures that delivery of the underlying asset is consistent in terms of quality, quantity, size etc. so that there is no confusion among parties, in other words all contracts are standardized.

Hedging using futures contract

Noting the shortcomings of the forward market, particularly the need and the difficulty in finding a counter party, the futures market came into existence. The future market basically solves some of the shortcomings of the forward market. Futures contracts are one of the most common derivatives used to hedge risk. A futures contract is an arrangement between two parties to buy or sell an asset at a particular time in the future for a particular price. The main reason that companies or corporations use future contracts is to offset their risk exposures and limit themselves from any fluctuations in price. The ultimate goal of an investor using futures contracts to hedge is to perfectly offset their risk. In real life, however, this is often impossible and, therefore, individuals attempt to neutralize risk as much as possible instead. For example, if a commodity to be hedged is not available as a futures contract, an investor will buy a futures contract in something that closely follows the movements of that commodity. To enter into a futures contract a trader needs to pay a deposit (called an initial margin) first. Then his position will be tracked on a daily basis so much so that whenever his account makes a loss for the day, the trader would receive a margin call (also known as variation margin), i.e., requiring him to pay up the losses.

There are basically two types of hedges using futures contract;

Short hedge: Short hedge is taking a short hedge position in the futures market. It is appropriate when someone expects to sell an asset he already owns and wants to guarantee the price. In general being short means having a net sold position, or a commitment to deliver. Thus here the main objective is to protect the value of the cash position against a decline in cash price.

For example, Company X must fulfill a contract in six months that requires it to sell 20,000 ounces of silver. Assume the spot price for silver is $12/ounce and the futures price is $11/ounce. Company X would short futures contracts on silver and close out the futures position in six months. In this case, the company has reduced its risk by ensuring that it will receive $11 for each ounce of silver it sells.

Long hedge: long hedge is taking a long position in the futures market. It is a situation where an investor has to take a long position in futures contracts in order to hedge against future price volatility. A long hedge is beneficial for a company that knows it has to purchase an asset in the future and wants to lock in the purchase price. A long hedge can also be used to hedge against a short position that has already been taken by the investor. It is appropriate for someone who expects to buy an asset and wants to guarantee the price.

For example, assume it is January and an aluminum manufacturer needs 25,000 pounds of copper to manufacture aluminum and fulfill a contract in May. The current spot price is $1.50 per pound, but the May futures price is $1.40 per pound. In January the aluminum manufacturer would take a long position in May futures contract on copper. This lock in the price the manufacturer will pay.

If in May the spot price of copper is $1.45 per pound the manufacturer has benefited from taking the long position, because the hedger is actually paying $0.05/pound of copper compared to the current market price. However if the price of copper was anywhere below $1.40 per pound the manufacturer would be in a worse position than where they would have been if they did not enter into the futures contract.

Example of hedging strategy using futures

A farmer who has been on the fence about hedging decides to hedge his corn crop. He thinks that prices will remain around the current level or decrease in late August when he anticipates selling his new crop. The cash price for new crop corn is $5.52 and the September futures price is $6.28. The farmer anticipates that he will have 10,000 bushels of corn to sell. Since the farmer wants to protect himself against a decrease in prices, he will be a short hedger. His goal is to lock in the price of $5.52/bu for corn. Each corn futures contract contains 5,000 bushels. The farmer sells two September 2011 corn futures contracts at $6.28 on 2/23/11. It is now September and the farmer's instincts held true.

Payoff Of Futures Contract

The payoff of futures contract on maturity depends on the spot price of the underlying asset at the time of maturity and the price at which the contract was initially traded. There are two positions that could be taken in futures contract:

Long position: One who buys the asset at the future price take the long position. In general, the payoff for a long position in a futures contract on one unit is ST-F Where F is the traded future price and ST is the spot price of the asset at expiry of the contract. This is because the holder of the contract is obligated to buy the asset. The following figure depicts the payoff diagram of investor who is long on a future contract.

Figure shows that investor makes a profit in long position if spot price at the expiry exceeds the future contract price and losses if opposite happens.

Short position: One who sells the asset at the future price takes the short position. In general the payoff for the short position in a futures contract is F- ST Where F is the traded future price and ST is the spot price of the asset at expiry of the contract. The figure below depicts the payoff diagram of investors who is short on a future contract.

Types of Futures Traders

Speculators and hedgers are the two main types of investors in futures contracts.

Hedgers

Hedgers are commodity producers, such as mining corporations or a farmer. The companies utilizes futures contracts to protect themselves from future price volatility. For example - A cocoa grower may believe that come harvest time, the commodity's price will have dropped. He could sell a futures contract at current rates to protect against perceived losses, then exit the deal by buying cocoa at lower prices near harvest time. In essence - he sold the cocoa at a higher price before purchasing it at a lower price when it was actually produced, being an advantage from the difference in selling and buying prices. Other hedgers are pension fund corporations, insurance companies, and banks.

Speculators

Private investors and independent floor traders are the ones that make up this category. These companies are primarily interested in making money by buying contracts that are predicted to get higher in the future and selling contracts that are expected to decline in the future.

The Futures Contract And The Futures Exchange

A significant difference between futures and forward contracts arises because futures contracts are legally required to be traded on futures exchanges while forwards are usually created by individual parties operating in the decentralized OTC markets. Because a futures contract is transacted on an exchange, the traders originating the contract use the exchange clearinghouse as the counter-party to their trade. While both a short trader (seller) and long trader (buyer) are required to create a futures contract, both traders execute the trade with the clearing-house as the direct counter-party. This allows a futures contract to be created without the problems associated with forward contracting, which typically depends on the creditworthiness of the counter-party. By design, futures contracts are readily transferable via the trading mechanisms provided by the exchange. Because forward contracts depend on the performance of the two original parties to the contract, these contracts are often difficult to transfer. One practical implication of this difference is that if a futures trader wants to close out a position, an equal number of offsetting contracts for that commodity month is transacted and the original position is canceled. Forward contracts are usually offset by establishing another forward contract position with terms as close as possible to those in the original contract. Unless the forward contract provides a method for cash settlement at delivery, this will potentially involve two deliveries having to be matched in the cash market on the delivery date.

To facilitate exchange trading, futures contracts possess a number of key features, especially standardization and marking to market. The elements of standardization provided by the futures contract and by the rules and regulations of the exchange governing such contracts involve the deliverable grade of the commodity; the quantity deliverable per contract; the range of quality within which delivery is permissible; the delivery months; and, the options associated with the specific grade and date of delivery that is permissible. Standardization is achieved by making each futures contract for a given commodity identical to all other contracts except for price and the delivery month. In addition to standardization, forwards and futures also differ in how changes in the value of the contract over time are handled. For futures, daily settlement, also known as marking to market, is required. In effect, a new futures contract is written at the start of every trading day with all gains or losses settled through a margin account at the end of trading for that day. This method of accounting requires the posting of a "good faith" initial margin deposit combined with an understanding that, if the value in the margin account falls below a maintenance margin amount, funds will be transferred into the account

Forward and Futures Markets

To prevent the contract from being closed out. On the other hand, settlement on forward contracts usually occurs by delivery of the commodity at the maturity of the contract. Hence, futures contracts have cash flow implications during the life of the contract while forwards usually do not.

Modern Usage Of Forward And Futures Contracts

In modern markets, considerable variation is observed in the relative use of forward or futures contracting across commodity markets. For example, in currency markets, the large value and volume of many individual trades has the bulk of transactions for future delivery conducted in the currency forward market. Exchange traded currency futures contracts are an insignificant fraction of total trading volume in the global currency market. As trading in forwards is closely integrated with cash market transactions, direct trading in forward contracts is restricted to the significant spot market participants, effectively the largest banks and financial institutions. Because currency forward contracts do not have regular marking to market, restricted participation is needed to control default risk. As such, differences in the functioning of futures and forward markets impacts the specific method of contracting selected for conducting commodity transactions. For example, in contrast to forward trading, futures markets are designed to encourage participation by large and small speculative traders. The increased participation of speculators not directly involved in the spot market provides an important source of additional liquidity to futures markets not available in forward markets. In order to achieve this liquidity certain restrictions are imposed on trading, such as limits on position sizes and the imposition of filing requirements. By restricting participation to large players in the commodity market, many of the restrictions required for the functioning of futures markets are not present in forward markets.

Advantages Of Futures Contract

Futures are highly leveraged investments: To own a futures contract, an investor only has to put up a small fraction of the value of the contract (usually around 10%) as margin. In other words, the investor can trade a much larger amount of the commodity than if she bought it outright, so if she has predicted the market movement correctly, her profits will be multiplied (ten-fold on a 10% deposit). This is an excellent return compared to buying a physical commodity such as copper or wheat.

Speculating with futures contracts is basically a paper investment: The actual commodity being traded in the contract is only exchanged on the rare occasion that delivery of the contract takes place. Since the average individual investor is a speculator, a futures primarily comprised of businesses that actually use the commodities they are trading. The hedgers' objective is to lock in a favorable contract price that protects them against unforeseen fluctuations in the spot market. Hedgers are willing to give up the possibility of lower spot prices to avoid the detrimental effects of exorbitantly high spot prices. Farmers, mining companies, and oil drillers are examples of hedgers who use futures contracts as a kind of cost insurance policy for their businesses.

In contrast to the hedger, the speculator never uses commodities in any manufacturing capacity. Speculators trade strictly for the prospect of acquiring profits. By watching the markets closely every day, a speculator can take advantage of small fluctuations in a futures contract's price by buying and selling at lower or higher points during the life of the contract. trade is purely a paper transaction and the term "contract" is only used as the futures contract has an expiration date.

Liquidity: Since there are huge amounts of futures contracts traded every day, futures markets are very liquid. This ensures that market orders can be placed very quickly as there are always buyers and sellers of a commodity. For this reason, it is unusual for prices to suddenly jump or fall dramatically, especially on the nearer contracts (those which will expire in the next few weeks or months).

Commission charges are small: compared to other investments and are paid after the position has ended. Commissions vary depending on the level of service given by the broker widely.

Disadvantages Of Futures Contract

High risk of loss: Before becoming too excited about the substantial returns possible from commodity trading, it is a good idea to take a long, sober look at the risks. Reward and risk are always related. It is unrealistic to expect to be able to earn above-average investment returns without taking above-average risks as well. Commodity trading has the reputation of being a highly risky endeavor. It is true that a high percentage of traders eventually lose money. Many people have lost substantial sums. Leverage is a double edge sword, it can either make you rich or make you lose your shirt and more.

Margin Call: In the futures market, rather than providing a down payment like on a house, the initial margin required to buy or sell a futures contract is solely a deposit of good faith money that can be drawn on by your brokerage firm to cover losses that you may incur in the course of futures trading. They are typically about five percent of the current value of the futures contract. If and when the funds remaining available in your margin account are reduced by losses to below a certain level known as the maintenance margin requirement your broker will require that you deposit additional funds to bring the account back to the level of the initial margin. Or, you may also be asked for additional margin if the exchange or your brokerage firm raises its margin requirements. Requests for additional margin are known as margin calls.

Difference Between Forwards And Futures Contract

The main differentiating feature between futures and forward contracts are as given below:

Definition: A forward contract is an agreement between two parties to buy or sell an asset (which can be of any kind) at a pre-agreed future point in time at a specified price. On the other hand, a futures contract is a standardized contract, traded on a futures exchange, to buy or sell a certain underlying instrument at a certain date in the future, at a specified price.

Structure & Purpose: Forward contracts are customized to customer needs. Usually no initial payment required. These are usually used for hedging while in case of futures they standardized, initial margin payment required and are usually used for speculation.

Transaction method: Forwards are negotiated directly by the buyer and seller but futures are quoted and traded on the Exchange.

Guarantees: In case of forwards no guarantee of settlement until the date of maturity only the forward price, based on the spot price of the underlying asset is paid. On the other hand both parties must deposit an initial guarantee (margin) in case of futures. The value of the operation is marked to market rates with daily settlement of profits and losses.

Contract Maturity: Forward contracts generally mature by delivering the commodity. Its expiry datedepends on the transaction. But future contracts may not necessarily mature by delivery of commodity. Its expiry date is standardized.

Closing a Position: To close a position on a futures trade, a buyer or seller makes a second transaction that takes the opposite position of their original transaction. In other words, a seller switches to buying to close his position, and a buyer switches to selling. For a forward contract, there are two ways to close a position — either sell the contract to a third party, or get into a new forward contract with the opposite trade.

Liquidity: It is easy to buy and sell futures on the exchange. It is harder to find counterparty over the counter to trade in forward contracts that are non standard. The volume of transactions on an exchange is higher than OTC derivatives, so futures contracts tend to be more liquid.

CHAPTER 8

Investing In CFD Contract

Investing in contracts for diffeRence (CFDs) is a relatively recent development in the Australian retail investment market. The number of CFD providers has grown from a couple of pioneers early in the decade to around 20 today. Because providers operate independently of a securities exchange, there are no hard figures on the number of active CFD traders in Australia, nor the volume of transactions. But a survey of the CFD market by market research company Investment Trends puts the number of active CFD traders at about 30,000. Contract size is between $30,000 and $40,000. Investors trade twice a week and hold their positions from three to five days.

Some estimates of the United Kingdom market, where CFDs have been established much longer, show that CFD traders account for 20 per cent or more of turnover on the London Stock Exchange. In Australia, the current industry estimate is that 10 to 15 per cent of the daily transactions on the Australian Securities Exchange (ASX) are due to CFD trades. CFD providers range from specialists such as CMC Markets, IGMarkets and MF Global to big groups such as CommSec. Last year the ASX entered the market with exchange traded CFDs.

In its early days the market was largely the domain of professional traders looking for a leveraged product for share trading that was simpler and more efficient than options and warrants. These traders held short-term positions and could go long or short.

By the middle of the decade, the range of products available through CFD providers had broadened to include overseas share markets, currencies, commodities, indices and sectors. As providers built more sophisticated risk management tools, such as guaranteed stop loss facilities, CFDs started to attract a wider range of investors. In recent times, short-term traders have been joined by long-term investors who have come to see them as an efficient way of investing and as a way to hedge established holdings.

The most recent trend on the market is the development of structured investment products that combine CFDs with capital protection. CFD providers are joining forces with financial planners, stockbrokers and fund managers to design products that adapt CFDs for a bigger group of investors, including wealth accumulators.

What is a CFD?

A contract for difference (CFD) is a form of derivative that involves a contract between an investor and a CFD provider to exchange the difference between the value of a security at the time the contract is opened and the time it is closed. The underlying security might be a stock on a local or overseas share market, a local or overseas stock index, a currency, a commodity, an interest rate or a debt security. Rather than owning shares or other securities, the investor is buying and selling the price movement of the security. The contract represents a theoretical order to buy or sell security. When the position is closed, the profit or loss is set by the difference between the opening and closing price. In practice it works like a margin loan in giving investors leverage. When an investor opens a CFD position they put down a deposit on the value of the shares, which can be as little as 5 percent. The CFD contract mirrors the performance of the shares the profit or loss is determined by the difference between the buy and the sell price of the underlying shares.

CFD providers report that popular trades include the top local stocks and some big Wall Street stocks, the S&P/ASX 200 index, gold and the Australian dollar against the US dollar.

One of the attractions of CFDs is that they give an investor the ability to trade long or short. An investor who takes a view that a stock is going to fall can sell it (short it) using a CFD contract.

Conventional trading instruments can make short selling costly and complicated. A stockbroker must borrow stock to cover the investor's position and this adds substantial cost to the transaction. CFD providers allow their clients to enter a short position at the same cost as a long position. Compared to other derivative instruments, CFDs are simple. Options and warrants have a pricing structure that incorporates some arcane financial concepts such as time decay, but the price movement of a CFD contract is directly linked to the change in the value of the underlying security. This is what CFD providers are talking about when they say the contract mirrors the underlying asset.

The emergence of CFDs is due, in part, to the development of the internet as an information and trading resource. Retail investors have access to sophisticated trading platforms that were once the preserve of institutional investors.

Clients watch their stocks being traded in real time, with bids and offers on display. When they place an order they can see their trading account being debited and, if they make a profit on a transaction, their account being credited instantly. A lot of the competition between CFD providers is about who has the best platform.

Features And Benefits Of CFDs

CFDs are familiar to traders who want cost-effective, leveraged access to markets where they can use short-term trading techniques to take advantage of market volatility. They are less familiar as a tool for people accumulating wealth through private portfolio or self-managed funds, and for retirees who are looking for an efficient risk management tools.

One big difference between CFDs and other derivative trading instruments is that CFDs, unlike options and warrants, have no expiry date. Investors can keep their CFD contracts open for as long as they like.

This gives CFDs a great deal of flexibility; they are not just short-term trading tools. CFD providers have been developing their products to cater to investors who want leverage and hedging as part of their longer term strategies.

One example is CMC Markets' Shield Account, which allows trustees of self-managed funds and other investors to trade in the ASX200, other indices, and currencies. The product has a built-in stop loss facility that covers the investor if the market moves against their contract position.

Long-term investors can use CFDs of this type in a number of ways: n hedging. To protect a portfolio against adverse market movements, an investor can take a CFD position that is opposite to the portfolio position. If the portfolio is long Australian shares, which is a typical exposure for self-managed super funds, the trustee can use a CFD contract to short the ASX 200. If the market falls the gains on the short position will offset the losses in the physical portfolio and defeR caPital gains. An investor may have built up an overweight position in a stock that has performed very well. The investor wants to diversify away from what has become a high-risk exposure but does not want to sell down the stock and create a capital gains tax liability. CFDs can be used to sell against that stock position. The sale of a contract has the effect of locking in a selling price and frees up cash for other investment and leveRage. Many investors approach retirement with less in their retirement savings portfolios than they would like. CFDs can be used in the same way as a margin loan to gain greater market exposure with limited exposure. With a stop loss in place, losses can be controlled. A stop loss operates like an insurance premium. A guaranteed stop loss provides an additional layer of protection by providing a guarantee that the contract will be closed out at the set price. For example, an investor takes out a CFD contract on a stock at $17 and places a guaranteed stop loss at $16.50.

It is possible that the stock will hit $16 without trading at $16.50. A guaranteed stop loss will get the trader out at $16.50, but a stop loss won't. Some CFD providers charges a premium for that level of protection.

It is important to remember that the liability for a holder of a CFD contract is not limited to the deposit paid. In the case of some derivatives, such as warrants, if the underlying share price moves against the investor the derivative will expire worthless. All that is lost is the money invested in the warrant.

In the case of a CFD contract, if the market moves against a position the holder of that position may be called upon to pay additional funds. That is where the stop loss and guaranteed stop loss facilities come in; they unwind contracts once a certain loss level has been reached.

The Cost Of Using CFDs

CFD providers charge commission on transactions, interest on the leveraged-up amount of the portfolio and, in some cases, monthly account fees and commission is charged on the initial deposit. Some providers have flat commission rates, regardless of the size of the transaction. The most commonly occurring flat commission rate is 0.10 per cent. On a $10,000 initial deposit, the commission would be $10. Providers that charge commissions on a sliding scale have rates that are as low as 0.05 per cent and as high as 0.2 per cent.

A commonly occurring scale is 0.125 percent for small transactions down to 0.08 per cent for initial deposits of $100,000 or more. Some brokers have different rates for online and phone transactions, with higher charges for phone services. financing costs are charged on the portfolio balance above the initial deposit. Securities can be traded by putting up as little as three per cent of the value of the underlying asset. The investor gains exposure to the whole amount of the transaction; the CFD provider offers exposure to the balance. The provider protects its own exposure to the underlying asset by taking out a hedge and the cost of that hedge is passed on to the investor as a financing charge.

The cost of financing is calculated as a margin over the cash rate. Margins varies from 1.25 to 2 per cent. Interest is calculated daily and the investor's account is rebalanced daily. When the investor takes a short contract, the CFD provider pays interest. Monthly fees vary widely. Some providers have no monthly fee and no fee for live market feeds. Other have no monthly fee but charge separately if the client wants a live feed. Some charge a monthly account fee, with a charge of around $40 the norm, but will waive it for frequent traders.

Minimum opening balance requirements vary from nil, in the case of a couple of providers, and up to $5,000. The most commonly occurring minimum opening balance is $5,000.

How CFDs Work A Step-By-Step Guide

Most successful CFD traders have a few things in common. They have a well-developed trading strategy, they have a risk management plan and they are prepared to commit time every day to monitor the market and their trading positions. This is as true of the investor who lets a CFD contract run for months or years as it is of the trader who opens and closes multiple contracts in a day.

There is no single trading strategy that works best. Traders use a variety of techniques: straightforward fundamental analysis that allows them to look for cheap stocks; momentum indicators that track the market's support for a stock through price movement and volume; and technical and quantitative trading systems.

Traders set aside a certain amount of time each day. They set up watch lists and have a list of criteria for taking action. Traders also keep a diary of their trading activity; this allows them to keep track of what works for them and what doesn't.

Investment guidelines should include the types of assets that will go into the CFD portfolio, the degree of leverage, target returns and risk tolerance. The guidelines might stipulate only trading in Australian shares with daily volume greater than $350,000 (volume is important to ensure the investor can get out of the position). Is the investor going to trade long only or go short? How much capital is the investor prepared to put at risk?

Investors who are planning to trade a variety of different assets should look at the trading platforms offered by CFD providers to make sure they can monitor their positions in share CFDs, index CFDs and currency CFDs with a single view.

Traders allocate a set amount of their trading portfolio to each trade. This is an important element of the risk management process. Small exposures of one or two per cent reduce risk for two reasons: if the contract results in a loss it is only a small loss; and it is easier to get out of a small position. Many small positions with limited risk are better than one big position. Most CFD traders allocate around two per cent of capital to a contract.

Investors have different levels of risk tolerance. To assess their level they need to ask certain questions. How much is at risk on each trade? How much is at risk across the whole portfolio? How much are you making for each dollar at risk? Some traders set a level at which they will take profits to ensure they make a return on their investments. Other traders oppose this approach, arguing that the market should decide when the trend is over. These traders prefer to use a stop-loss. A stop-loss order is an order you place either online or by calling the provider, to close your position when it reaches a certain point.

Stop-loss orders are trading insurance. The investor will be taken out of a trade when the nominated stop-loss level is reached. The key is to use the stop-loss to keep losses small and under control.

Stop-loss positions can be adjusted as the price of the underlying security rises. If the shares are worth $30 when they are purchased the stop-loss might be set at $25. If the share price goes up to $40, the stop-loss can be adjusted up to $35. This is called a trailing stop.

It is important for investors to understand that with CFDs, they are trading on margin. Stocks can be traded by putting up as little as three per cent of the value of the shares. This leverage allows investors to take big positions with small outlays, but it is important to note that the investor is exposed to the whole amount of the transaction. The investor puts up three per cent and the CFD provider offers exposure to the balance supported by derivative contracts.

If the contract results in a loss, the investor is liable for the whole amount. That is why it is so important to have a strong risk management strategy in place before trading. Many seasoned traders do not trade unless they have set a stop-loss position first.

Trade in rising or falling markets

CFD's allow you to trade LONG or SHORT. A Long Trade is where you BUY an asset with the expectation that it will rise, just as you would when buying a normal share. A Short Trade is where you SELL an asset that you do not own in the expectation that the price will fall and you can buy the asset back at a cheaper price. Shorting in the ordinary share market is almost impossible. With CFD's, however, you can go short as easily as you go long. Giving you the ability to profit even if a share price falls if you trade the right way.

No Stamp Duty

Because with CFD's, you don't actually physically buy the underlying shares, you don't have to pay stamp duty. Saving 0.5% when compared to a traditional share deal.

Commission

Commission is charged on CFD's just like on an ordinary share trade, the commission is calculated on the total position value not the margin paid.

Overnight Financing

Because CFD's are traded on margin if you hold a position open overnight, it will be subject to a finance charge. Long CFD positions are charged interest if they are held overnight, Short CFD positions will be paid interest. The rate of interest charged or paid will vary between different brokers and is usually set at a % above or below the current LIBOR (London Inter Bank Offered Rate).

The interest on position is calculated daily, by applying the applicable interest rate to the daily closing value of the position. The daily closing value is the number of shares multiplied by the closing price. Each day's interest calculation will be different unless there is no change at all in the share price.

Contracts for Difference (CFD's)

The disclosure rules are as follows:
- Physical holdings in shares
- Physically settled long derivative positions (as per current rules)
- Positions in cash settled financial instruments providing exposure to the economic performance of shares that give rise to a long position (including long call options, short put options, swaps, CFD's, convertible bonds, rights, etc.). This includes any financial instruments that entitle the holder to acquire shares that have not yet been issued (such as convertible bonds and warrants) and basket trades (such as ETCS) subject to the exemption set out below
- No netting of longs and shorts in the physically settled and/or cash settled instruments is permitted
- The rules require calculation on a delta basis. A transitional period, permitting disclosure on a nominal basis (provided there is full disclosure of the strike price)

Disclosure Thresholds:

- Disclosure at 3% and 1% increments thereafter. The denominator remains the issued share capital of the Company (free float)

Exemptions:

- Baskets: exempt if exposure to the economic performance of the shares is less than 1% of the relevant share class and such exposure comprises less than 20% of the value of the basket (subject to anti-avoidance measures). N.B. Baskets include ETCS, indices, and similar instruments.

No requirement to disclose if these conditions are not met due to passive changes.

- Client Serving Intermediaries: exempt where regulated intermediaries are acting in a client facilitation capacity. To take advantage of this, certain conditions need to be met and a certification sent both initially, and on an annual basis to the FSA
- Certain intragroup transactions: where undertaken for tax or accounting reasons

Revised Rules:

- an underwriter does not need to disclose any long position in the economic performance of shares held by virtue of obligations under a "conventional" underwriting or sub-underwriting contract in relation to a rights issue;
- a person who passively receives rights on a rights issue solely by being an existing shareholder and who does not change their proportionate interest will not have to include those rights in the calculation of their position in the shares; and
- any person who actively acquires or disposes of rights during a rights issue (so that their proportionate holding will change after the new shares have been issued) will be expected to include all the rights, whether acquired actively or passively, in their calculation of their position in the shares..

CFD positions in share register analyses

With regard to CFD, holdings in a share register it is not our practice to include the client who has taken the position, The Market Maker that has sold the CFD to their client will often hedge their position by buying shares in the market. As a result, they are required to disclose this holding and therefore it is often the banks acting as counterparty to CFD trades that appear on the share register. These holdings will appear on the register as Market Maker accounts (even though they are proprietary desk trades/holdings), and can sometimes be registered in a stock lending account if they are larger holdings.

It is only when the CFD is exercised that the shares will be registered into the clients name and will acquire subsequent the voting rights. Hedge funds will often go to management claiming they hold a 5 or 10% stake through CFDs in order to get a meeting. These requests often overstate their true holding / exposure for effect, though increasingly shareholder activists have taken small (~1%) stakes and try to instigate change, breakup or takeover bids in certain cases.

Notwithstanding the above, although the shares do not belong to the client until the contract is exercised there may be a certain element of control in the voting rights of those shares.

Investment Market Capitalization

Market capitalization, or market cap, is one measurement of a company's size. It's the total value of a company's outstanding shares of stock, which include publicly traded shares plus restricted shares held by company officers and insiders.

To calculate market cap, you take the total number of a company's shares outstanding and multiply that figure by the company's current stock price. For example, if a company has 5 million shares outstanding and its current stock price is $20, it has a market capitalization of $100 million.

You may hear companies described as large-cap, mid-cap or small-cap—or even mega-cap or micro-cap. The delineation between each group can vary, but generally, you'll see them broken down like this:

- **mega-cap:** market value of $200 billion or more;

- **large-cap:** market value between $10 billion and $200 billion;
- **mid-cap:** market value between $2 billion and $10 billion;
- **small-cap:** market value between $250 million and $2 billion; and
- **micro-cap:** market value of less than $250 million.

Certain stock indexes or investment funds will use this measure to group companies together by size. For example, the S&P 500 is made up of mega-cap and large-cap stocks and is weighed by market cap, so companies with a higher market cap account for relatively more of the index than companies with a comparatively smaller market cap. Meanwhile, the Russell 2000 Index is a small-cap stock market index.

Newer investors might mistakenly believe that stock price alone could be a good indicator of how large a company is, but what's most important in determining a company's size is the number of shares outstanding.

Take Company A and Company B, for example. Both have stocks trading at $50 a share, but Company A has 5 million shares outstanding, and Company B has 5 billion shares outstanding. That means Company A has a market cap of $250 million, making it a small-cap company, whereas Company B has a market cap of $250 billion, meaning it's a particularly large, large-cap company—often called a mega-cap company.

Why Market Cap Matters

For starters, market cap can give you a general idea of where a company stands in the business development process. Is it a relatively new public company, for example? If so, it might have room for growth. After all, access to investor capital to expand the business is why many companies decide to go public in the first place.

Market cap can also provide a rough gauge of a company's stability. Large-cap companies tend to be less vulnerable to the ups and downs of the market than mid-cap companies, and mid-cap companies are generally less susceptible to volatility than small-cap companies.

That's in part because larger companies typically have greater financial reserves and therefore often can absorb losses more easily and bounce back more quickly from a bad year. At the same time, smaller companies might have greater potential for fast growth in economic boom times than larger companies. This is why some dividend seekers will use market cap as a filter when looking for companies that pay consistent dividends.

These generalizations are no guarantee that any particular large-cap company will weather a downturn well or that any particular small-cap company will or won't thrive. Still, market cap can be a useful gauge, particularly when it comes to diversifying your portfolio. When you diversify, you aim to manage your risk by spreading out your investments. You can diversifies by investing among different asset classes; for example, by investing in both stocks and bonds. And you can also diversify within asset classes. Investing in small-cap and large-cap stocks is one example of diversifying within one asset class (stocks).

What Are Large-Cap Stocks?

Large-cap companies are businesses that are well-established and have a significant market share, like market caps of Rs 20,000 crore or more. These companies dominate the industry and are very stable. They hold themselves well in times of recession or during any other negative event. Besides, they usually have been functioning for decades and have a good reputation. If you want to invest in a company's stocks by taking less risk, then large-cap stocks are a good option. These stocks are less volatile in comparison to mid-cap and small-cap stocks, and lower volatility makes them less risky. However, since they come with low-risk, the returns here can be relatively lower than mid and smallcap stocks.

Reliance Industries and Infosys are examples of some large-cap market companies that are listed on the stock exchanges of India. Their strong foothold in the market and consistent good performance makes them good choices for long-term investors.

What Are Mid-Cap Stocks?

Mid-cap companies are those with market caps above Rs 5,000 crore but less than Rs 20,000 crore. Investing in these companies can be riskier than investing in large-cap market companies, because mid-caps tend to be more volatile. On the other hand, mid-cap companies also have the ability to turn into large-cap companies in the long run. These companies can offer a higher growth potential than large-cap stocks do, hence, more investors are attracted to investing here.

Metropolis Healthcare, Castrol India, and LIC Housing Finance are some examples of mid-cap companies that are listed on the stock exchanges of India.

What Are Small-Cap Stocks?

Small-cap companies are those that have a market capitalization of less than Rs 5,000 crore. These companies are relatively smaller in size and have significant growth potential. What makes them risky is the low probability that they will be successful over time. This makes the stocks of such companies volatile in nature. Small-cap companies have a long history of underperformance but when an economy is emerging out of a recession, small-cap stocks often prove to be out performers.

Bajaj Consumer Care, Shobha Ltd, and VST Industries are some examples of small-cap market companies that are listed on the stock exchanges of India.

Difference Between Large-Cap, Medium-Cap and Small-Cap companies

Company type and stature

Large-cap companies are companies that are big and well-established in the equity market. These companies have reliable management and rank among the top 100 companies in the country. Mid-cap companies sit somewhere between large-cap and small-cap companies. These companies are compact and rank among the top 100–250 companies in the country. Finally, small-cap companies are much smaller in size and have the potential to grow rapidly.

Market capitalisation

Large-cap companies have a market cap of Rs 20,000 crore or more. Meanwhile, the market cap of mid-cap companies is between Rs 5,000 crore and less than Rs 20,000 crore. Small-cap companies have a market cap of below Rs 5,000 crore.

Volatility

Your investment risk in the stock market is closely related to volatility. If the price of a stock remains reasonably stable even in turbulent markets, it means the stock has low volatility. On the other hand, stocks that see significant price fluctuations at such times are termed as highly volatile. The stocks of large-cap companies tend to be less volatile, which means their prices remain relatively stable even amid turbulence. This makes them relatively low-risk investment options. Mid-cap stocks are slightly more volatile than large-cap stocks and carry somewhat more risk. Small-cap companies are highly volatile and their prices can swing considerably, which increases the risk for investors.

Growth potential

The growth potential of large-cap stocks is lower than that of mid- and small-cap stocks. That being said, large-cap stocks are a stable investment option, especially if you have a longer investment horizon. This makes large-caps well suited to investors with low risk appetites. If your risk appetite is moderate, you could look into mid-caps, as these have a slightly higher potential for growth. The highest growth potential lies with small-cap stocks, but you should invest in these only if you have a high tolerance for risk.

Liquidity

The term 'liquidity' means that investors can buy or sell large-cap shares quickly and easily without affecting the share price. Now, large-cap stocks tend to have higher liquidity as there is a high demand for large-cap shares in the stock market. Thus, squaring off positions is easier when you purchase such shares. In comparison, mid-cap companies have lower liquidity as the demand for their stocks is slightly lower. Small-cap companies have the least liquidity, which can make squaring off positions more difficult.

Mutual Funds And Market Capitalisation

Mutual funds are an integral part of the Indian financial system. Mutual fund schemes are categorized into large-cap, mid-cap, or small-cap funds based on their investment allocation. For example, a large-cap mutual fund scheme will mainly invest in large-cap stock, while mid-cap and small-cap schemes will invest in mid-cap and small-cap stocks, respectively.

The Limitations of Market Cap

Something important to keep in mind is that market cap is the perceived value of a company because stock price is determined by investors. It isn't necessarily the actual value of a company and all of its parts. Some of that perceived value may stem from expectations of future growth or the introduction of a product, but those expectations may not pan out, in which case the share price of the company—and thus its market cap—is likely to adjust accordingly.

That's why it's a good idea to look at a number of metrics when considering an investment. Market cap can be one tool you use to develop a diverse portfolio, but it shouldn't be your only tool.

CHAPTER 9

What Is Money?

Most people use money every day, and many go to great lengths to acquire it. Yet despite its central nature in our lives, very few people think about what money is, how it is created, how its design impacts our economy, or whether the monetary system could be improved.

Most economists define money in terms of what it does, and that is usually divided into the four core functions that it performs.

- A medium of exchange allowing us to pay for goods and services.
- A unit of account, allowing us to understand the relative price of several different things.
- A store of value, giving people security that the money will still be worth the same in the future.
- A means of making final payment or settlement.

The physical form that money takes has evolved over time across different parts of the world, and has included tally sticks, clay tablets, cattle, and various forms of precious metal, such as gold and silver.

Today, however, money takes the form of what is referred to as 'fiat' money – money that derives its value from state regulation and law, rather than any physical commodity. In modern economies, money takes one of three forms.

Cash (notes and coins)

The simplest form is cash – the £5, £10, £20, and £50 notes and the metal coins that most of us have in our wallets at any time. Paper notes are created under the authority of the Bank of England and printed by specialist printer De La Rue. Metal coins are produced under the authority of the Treasury by the Royal Mint. Although cash is being used for fewer and fewer transactions as electronic payment becomes more popular, the Bank of England expects the total amount of cash in circulation in the economy to keep increasing over time because prices tend to rise and the population keeps on growing. It is estimated that there are currently £67,818 million in notes17 and £4,011 million in coins in circulation.

Central bank reserves

Central bank reserves are an electronic form of money created by the Bank of England. Unlike cash, however, members of the public cannot access or use central bank reserves. Only high-street and commercial banks, building societies, and a small number of systemically important financial institutions that have accounts with the Bank of England can use this type of money. Commercial banks use central bank reserves to settle payments with other banks at the end of each day. Whenever payments are made between the accounts of customers at different commercial banks, they are ultimately settled by transferring central bank money (reserves) between the reserves accounts of those banks.

Commercial bank deposits

The third type of money is what is in your bank account. In banking terminology, it is referred to as bank deposits or demand deposits. Whenever you make a purchase in a shop using your debit card, you are doing so using bank deposits. In such an instance, your bank will debit your current account according to the value of your purchase, and will tell the shop's bank to credit its account by the same value.

In technical terms, bank deposits are simply a number in a computer system; in accounting terms, they are a liability of the bank to you. The terminology is slightly misleading, as a bank deposit is not a deposit in the sense that you might store a valuable item in a safety deposit box. Instead, it is simply an electronic record of what the bank owes you. Although not widely recognised, any cash you deposit in a bank does not legally belong to you it belongs to the bank.

As will be discussed in the next section, this third type of money is not created by the Bank of England, the Royal Mint, or any other part of government. Instead, it is created by commercial banks such as Barclays, Lloyds, RBS, and HSBC, in the process of making new loans Bank deposits are not legal tender in the strict definition of the term. Legal tender has a very narrow and technical meaning in the settlement of debts. It means that a debtor cannot successfully be sued for non-payment if they pay in court in legal tender. In England and Wales, only notes and coins are legal tender. In Scotland and Northern Ireland, notes are technically not considered legal tender, leaving coins as the only form of legal tender in these parts of the UK.

In modern economies, however, bank deposits function as money – they can be used to pay for things, including government taxes, and banks will usually convert them into cash on demand. In addition, in most countries a large sum of an individual depositor's holdings of money is guaranteed by the government in the UK it is currently the first £75,000. For this reason, most members of the public would consider bank deposits to be as good as cash.

Traditionally, economists have only focused on the first two types of money cash and reserves (hereafter referred to as 'central bank money') in considering the level of seigniorage in the economy. The Bank of England's standard definition of the money supply, bank deposits now make up 97.4% of all the money used in the economy. As a result, aside from a tiny fraction of cash, today money is mainly digital information. Huge volumes of money are moved around our economies simply by people typing data into computers.

The current monetary system is therefore characterised by two separate 'circuits':

- The (relatively small amount of) central bank reserves which are created by the Bank of England and used by commercial banks to settle payments with each other.
- The (much larger amount of) bank deposits which are created by commercial banks in the process of making loans and used by the public to make transactions
- Commercial banks sit at the centre of these two circuits. For commercial banks, central bank reserves are assets and bank deposits are liabilities. Cash operates outside of these circuits as it is used by both commercial banks and the general public as a form of money (i.e., it is a liquid asset used as a means of payment). As we will see, this is because commercial banks will convert bank deposits into cash on demand (e.g. through ATM withdrawals), and the Bank of England will convert central bank reserves into cash so that commercial banks can meet the public's demand for cash. As the Bank of International Settlements notes:

Contemporary monetary systems are based on the mutually reinforcing roles of central bank money and commercial bank monies. What makes a currency unique in character and distinct from other currencies is that its different forms (central bank money and commercial bank monies) are used interchangeably by the public in making payments, not least because they are convertible at par.

In order to fully understand how this system operates in practice, it is helpful examine how new money is created and introduced into the economy.

Massive Confusion Exists About Money

The Quantity Theory of Money (QTM), widely taught in universities, is blatantly false. The QTM teaches us that money is neutral; it has no effects other than on prices. In other words, money is a veil which must be lifted to uncover the workings of the real economy. The Keynesian view is a partial correction to the QTM; Keynes says that money does have real effects, both in the short run and in the long run. Insufficient money leads to recession and unemployment, while excess money leads to inflation. Currently, there exists a wide range of alternative heterodox theories of money, including the Chartalist view, Modern Monetary Theory of money as debt, State Theory of Money (Sovereign Money), Commodity Money (Gold and Silver) and many others.

There Is Reason For This Confusion.

As Zarlenga and Poteat (2016) write: "The battle to control money has raged for millennia." An essential element in this battle is confusion about the nature of money. Those who derive extreme benefits from this system perpetuate confusions and myths regarding money. The authors correctly state that as long as the system is not understood, steps to create a fair and equitable system cannot be taken. Confusion about money exists not just because the nature of money is complex, but because there are deliberate attempts to conceal how the system works. In order to create a better system for the Islamic world, it is essential to educate Muslims about the nature of money and the financial system.

According to the standard QTM, money is linked only to prices and not to the workings of the real economy. More money means higher prices and less money means lower prices. Accordingly, money is a veil which we must look through in order to uncover the real economy. Nothing could be further from the truth. The circulation of money is of utmost importance in understanding how the economy works. The QTM is part of the effort to mislead people, and take attention away from how money actually works within an economy. In other words, QTM itself is a veil to hide the truth about money.

The QTM is just one example of numerous confusions about money which are widespread and widely believed. Understanding the present monetary system requires simultaneous understanding at two levels the domestic currency system and the international system. The fact that the international system is exceedingly unfair is transparently obvious to all. The US Dollar is equivalent to gold in the present system, which permits the US to print any quantity of money it wants. Trillions of dollars have been printed to finance the Iraq war, bailouts of bankers and other extravagant expenses. No other country in the world can do this since such excessive printing of money would cause hyperinflation. However, since the dollar is the reserve currency for the rest of the world, this excessive printing of money has had only a trivial and minor impact on the US domestic inflation rate. Incidentally, this immediately shows how the QTM is false, the price levels in the USA have not responded to the massive amounts of money created in past decades. This puts the US in a position of being able to buy up real resources, including human beings, from the rest of the world in return for printed paper. This is a key to current US political power. Understanding how this system works is essential to finding solutions to our current problems on economic, political, and social fronts.

Money is not Gold

A very important consequence of the research of Zarlenga in 2002 and others is to lay rest to the myth that the only viable form of money is Gold. This is a natural confusion which is addressed in detail both in the current paper of Zarlenga and Poteat in 2016 and much more extensively in Zarlenga's book the Lost Science of Money. It is important to understand this since Muslims who see the serious problems with the current monetary system immediately turn to gold as the solution. I will not repeat the extensive arguments of the authors, but briefly summarize them as follows.

The amount of money needed by an economy expands rapidly in a growing economy. Gold cannot keep pace. Historically, it has always been supplemented by money creation to allow the economy to grow. In situations where this was not done, economic damage in the form of deep and serious recessions have resulted. Furthermore, the price of gold has not been stable, notwithstanding assertions to the contrary by authors who support gold.

Sovereign Money

To understand the nature of money, it is necessary to remove the misconception that money derives value from being backed by gold, or by any other valuable commodity. In fact, money derives value from the authority of the state. The definition due to Aristotle is endorsed by Zarlenga and Poteat (2016): "Money exists not by nature, but by law." It is the guarantee of the state that "money will be legal tender in all transactions" that creates value in money. Money comes into being by state decree and the force of the law. In his book, The Lost Science of Money, Zarlenga provides a large amount of historical evidence to illustrate and explain this connection between money and sovereign authority.

This understanding of money has several radical implications. First, because money is created by sovereign authority, only the state should have the power to create money. Second, because money is a public good, useful for all, the benefits from money creation should be made available to the public, and not restricted to any small group. This is the central message and reform that is needed to create a good monetary system for use in Islamic countries. There are many myths that have been manufactured to prevent the public from coming to this realization. Not one but many major barriers have been created in the public mind so that they would reject any move towards such a system.

The Myth of Corrupt Governments

There is no doubt that there is a lot of corruption in many governments. However, public and private institutions are run by people coming from the same society, and so there is no differential between public and private corruption. Just as government officials can cheat, so private shopkeepers can dilute the milk. If we look at the history of the past fifty years, we find that private sector corruption has been responsible for a huge amount of world-wide damage. The global financial crisis, caused by criminal profit seeking by the private sector, led to millions being homeless and hungry in the richest countries in the world. There is very strong evidence that carpet bombing and wars in Iraq, Libya, Afghanistan and Syria were all done to protect private oil interests and provide profits to the private sector. Thus, the idea that governments are somehow more corrupt than the private sector is contrary to historical facts.

Government control of money supply will lead to hyper-inflations Since Zarlenga and Poteat (2016) have already addressed this issue, I will not discuss it further. It is worth noting that the QTM tells us that money does not matter. If this was believed, then there would be no harm in turning over money creation to the state. So the myth of governments causing hyperinflations has been created to prevent us from thinking about placing the control of money in the hands of the government. Actually, government control of money provides the most effective solution to problems of unemployment, but this key economic insight has been buried and forgotten in this debate.

The Government already controls the money supply

This widespread myth based on the deposit multiplier and the fractional reserve has been explored in papers discussed in detail in Zarlenga and Poteat (2016). This can be called the theory of "exogenous" money, where money is created outside the control of the private sector. In fact, this myth conceals the real nature of modern money, which is mainly bank credit. This is called "endogenous" money – that is, money which is created by the private sector. The orthodox and dominant economic theories endorse exogenous money, while heterodox economists generally favor the endogenous money theories.

Bank Created Credit as Money

After disposing of the myths about money, we must consider the nature of money as it exists today. In the wealthier economies, the majority of the money is created by banks. The nature of the fractional reserve banking system is such that they are required to keep a certain amount of cash – say 5% – of the total amount of credit that they extend. So if a bank has cash in its reserves of 5,000 Rupees, it can extend credit of 100,000 Rupees. The extra 95,000 is credit which is created by the banks.

Even though bank credit is dramatically different from state-issued money in both its origins and on its effects upon the economy, standard textbooks of monetary theory pass over this difference in silence and consider both as equivalent monies. This issue is of great importance from the Islamic perspective. This is because the real nature of money has not been put forth before the religious scholars, and they have given rulings about money without understanding the difference between credit created by the bank and genuine money created by the government. It seems likely that credit creation would not be permissible Islamically since the bank is lending what it does not have. When customers come to demand the money the bank has created, the bank borrows – either from other banks or from the Central Bank – in order to fulfill this demand. This transaction, selling something which is not in your possession, is explicitly prohibited in Islamic teachings.

As we shall see, banks have captured the money- creation function which belongs to the state, and are making huge and unjustified profits from this function. The banks' capture of this public service puts an extremely heavy burden on the entire society. It is similar to the private capture of the provision of essential utilities like water, electricity. This allows privateers to extort huge amounts of money from the public since everyone must buy these services, regardless of cost. This is why these services are provided by the public sector all over the world. In recent times, there was some experimentation with switching to public provision of such services, but this resulted in the predicted private extortion, and many of these privatizations were reversed. Creation of money is an essential public service and cannot be placed in the hands of the private sector for similar reasons.

How the Bank of England Came Into Being

The history of the world can be seen as a history of the battles to control the power of money creation. Even though it naturally belongs to the state, there have always been financiers who have sought to capture this power and take it away from the state to use it for their personal ends. An understanding of these battles is essential to understanding the nature of modern money, and the power struggles currently going on for its control globally. We provide a brief sketch of some key historical episodes. A mixed system with both public and private creation of money was in effect in 1600, when Queen Elizabeth issued relatively worthless base metal coins as legal tender in Ireland. She also annulled all other types of coinage, effectively abolishing private creation of money. This action was challenged in the highest courts, and the courts ruled in favor of the Queen, along Aristotelian lines, as follows: what the sovereign declared to be money

Historian of money Alexander Del Mar, cited by Zarlenga (2002), details the many conspiracies by wealthy financiers which were carried out in order to reverse this decision, to put the power of money creation back in private hands. The end result of these manipulations was the creation of a private Bank of England which was authorized to issue money on behalf of the state of England. When King William came to power in 1689, he needed money to carry out a war with France. A powerful group of financiers provided him with the required money, 1.2 million pounds on easy terms, provided that he would authorize them to charter the Bank of England, which would give them the sole power to issue money. In return for this privilege, the Bank would be obliged to provide loans to the government whenever required.

This led to what appears to be a completely absurd situation. The Bank of England creates money out of nothing on the authority of the sovereign state of England – this is the nature of money. However, it lends this created money to the state itself and charges interest to the state for this loan. Generously, the Bank of England offered to collect the interest itself in the form of taxes on the public. Why didn't King William print the money himself, using his own sovereign authority, and avoid interest payments and taxes on the public? This was partly due to widely believed defective theories of money which equated money with gold. King William was provided with a loan in the form of gold. The Bank of England issued notes which were believed to be backed by gold. However, the nature of the fractional reserves system is such that only a small amount of gold is required to create a huge amount of paper money. As long as the public does not understand the nature of money, and believes money must be backed by gold, they will not understand that it is possible for the sovereign to issue fiat money by decree, creating money out of nothing. There is another factor which makes for was money, and it was treason for anyone else to create it.

This is exactly in line with Islamic rulings on the private creation of money, which is declared as a fasād fi al-arḍ the necessity of gold, and that is international trade. While domestic money can be created out of nothing, this money creation can have serious repercussions internationally, and of course, purchases of foreign goods requires more than fiat currency.

However, the general template of banking remains the same to this day. Banks create money, and lend it to the government, even though it is the government which creates the value of money by its sovereign authority. While the government can create money for free, the banks charge for this privilege, and everyone in the general public pays the price in the form of taxes and interest.

Private Control of Money Creation

Ellen Brown and Stephen Zarlenga provide details of the many battles fought between the state and private financial interests for the control of money creation. There have been many victories and losses on both sides, and an essential element in the battle has been deception – the public in general, and politicians and rulers in particular, have not understood the nature of money, and have allowed banks to acquire the privilege of printing money without realizing the power that they have given to the private sector banks. We omit this long and complicated history, even though it is of great importance to understanding the current structures of financial institutions.

In the modern world, the power of money creation has been taken away from governments and given to private banks. This has happened gradually since the movement for financial liberalization started in the 1980's. However, the process has been gaining momentum. We now discuss the consequences of this takeover and privatization of a vital public service. The first important point to note is the creation of many myths about money to conceal the nature of the system.

The Myth of Financial Intermediation: According to the widespread common public understanding, the banks gather money from diverse sources and make it available to investors. Thus, they perform a vital function. Funding investments is essential for the growth of an economy. This myth then justifies the earnings of the banks as a return for the service they provide.

The Truth of Money Creation: In fact, banks do not lend money which they gather from depositors. They create the money they lend. Suppose a bank has a deposit of $1,000 and makes a loan of $5,000. It does so by simply opening an account in the name of the borrower and making an electronic entry for $5,000 in that account. This money is not taken out of the money deposited; it is created out of nowhere. What happens when the borrower demands money, in cash, which the bank does not have? The bank simply borrows from the Central Bank, which is required by law to cover such emergencies. The interest rate on borrowing from the Central Bank is much lower than the rate at which loans are made, so the bank makes a profit on this deal.

The Truth about Investments: Even if banks create money, and lend it at interest, they can perform a useful function if they fund productive investment. However, over the past thirty years, there has been a dramatic increase in "financialization". That is, loans are provided for property, stocks, derivatives, and fancy financial instruments, which earn profits but do not create productive capacity in the economy. Keynes recognized that banks provide loans on a speculative basis, looking for a quick and high return, rather than funding long term productive projects which would produce a benefit for the nation. He stated that: "Speculators may do no harm as bubbles on a steady stream of enterprise. But, the position is serious when enterprise becomes the bubble on a whirlpool of speculation. When the capital development of a country becomes a by-product of the activities of a casino, the job is likely to be ill-done".

The Function of Banks

The myth of financial intermediation has been invented to distract attention from the real function of banks. When we think about banks gathering money from depositors to give to investors, the real function of banks is completely hidden from public view. Strangely enough, these functions are ignored by economic textbooks, and macroeconomic models make no mention of the banking sector. Yet, banking is at the heart of modern economies, and understanding the real function of banks is essential to understanding contemporary economic events.

The core and central function of banks is the creation of money. This money is created when the bank gives a loan to a borrower. The banks earn profits by lending money that they don't have and earning interest on the loan. The fractional reserve system allows the banks to maintain cash reserves which are only a small fraction of the money they lend. If there is a cash demand on the bank which is more than their reserves, they borrow from other banks, or from the central bank, to meet this demand. The inter-bank borrowing rates are low compared to commercial rates, which ensures that banks always make profits. They borrow money at low rates to lend to others at higher rates, and even then, they only borrow a small fraction of what they lend – the rest of the money is artificial money created by the bank. While this is a very lucrative business, there is one fly in the ointment. Money can only be created if borrowers demand loans. There is a huge potential demand for investment loans on a participatory basis – people would like to invest in business, and pay back out of the returns generated. However, the modern institutional structure does not conform to this type of lending. This is because banks are lending money which they don't have and therefore they cannot afford profit loss sharing. This explains why we don't see mushārakah contracts in Islamic banks, which work on the same principles. It is not only the institutional structure which does not favor profit-loss sharing, there is also a conservative banker mindset. Financing of real and productive investment projects involves taking certain types of risks and acquiring certain types of specialized knowledge which bankers don't have experience with. This means that one major source of demand for credit, which is for productive investments, is not available to bankers.

Nonetheless, banks must make loans in order to carry out their business of money creation. But throughout the ages, creditors have insisted that they should receive payment with interest, regardless of the circumstances of the borrower whether or not the borrower is in distress, and whether or not his business made a profit. Uncertainties of the real world and the weak financial position which leads to borrowing, ensures that some borrowers will end up in distress. Bankers take advantage of this distress to seize collateral and to effectively enslave borrowers, ensuring that they provide financial benefits to banks far in excess of the amount borrowed. Islamic laws address precisely this problem and provide a beautiful solution. However, genuine Islamic solutions, do not suit the mindset and framework of modern financial institutions. Instead of making radical changes required to the institutional structures, Muslim economists have focused on making radical modifications to the Islamic laws in order to create "Islamic" equivalents to western financial institutions.

Bankers' Stratagems

The main and central concern of banks is to make more and more loans, from the money they create from nothing. This is an extremely profitable business because the good they manufacture has zero cost of creation, yet they charge a hefty price to sell it. However, as mentioned earlier, they can manufacture money only when there is demand for it. Bankers employ a lot of different strategies in order to generate demand for loans. As a result, people acquire the habit of taking interest based loans, and the amount of debt in the society increases, sometimes dramatically.

It is very important to understand that a situation where money is scarce and hard to get, is very pleasant for bankers. The greater the scarcity of money, the easier it is for bankers to sell their product. Also, in such situations, it is also possible to put a greater price for providing this service. This price is the interest rate. The higher the commercial interest rate, the more profit the banks make, provided that there are borrowers who are willing to borrow at that rate.

The interests of the bankers are in conflict with the needs of the society and the nation. In order to have economic prosperity and growth, money should be easily available to finance good productive projects. At the same time, one has to ensure that money is not available to finance socially harmful activities. In order to protect the interests of the bankers, textbooks of modern economic theory project the myth that the most productive activities are the ones which have the highest returns. Thus, textbooks teach that the interests of the bankers are aligned with social interests. The bankers will provide loans to finance activities which have the highest payoffs, and which are the most beneficial socially. This is emphatically not true. In fact, the highest payoff to society comes from investing in people – providing for basic social needs, health, education, and jobs. However, there is no private profit in these investments. Furthermore, if the government does a good job of providing for needs, then a large portion of the populace will have no need to borrow from the banks. Economic distress, high taxes, unemployment, low productivity, etc. are in the interests of the financiers as they create situations where people are forced to borrow. With exigent needs, they will even be willing to borrow at high interest rates.

Not only is public prosperity bad for bankers, but also investment in future productivity is not very profitable. The investments which are the most socially beneficial, like education, have very long run payoffs with a lot of variability. Productive investments in genuine medium or short term projects tend to have low returns. Real work brings honest returns of say 5 to 10 percent. However, there are many strategies that banks can use to earn far higher returns. One of the most common is to create speculative fever. If people start buying stocks or properties, then these start appreciating in value. Seeing this price appreciation leads more people to become interested in buying. If prices of lands or stocks appreciate at 25%, while bank loans have interest of 10%, people become interested in taking loans to buy stocks or land. As more people take loans to buy, prices appreciate even faster, creating an even greater incentive for people to take loans. There are two factors which make this speculative cycle extremely dangerous. One is the ability of banks to create money at will. This means that once the price boom starts, if people want to get in on the apparently easy profits available, money will be made available to them by banks. The second is the use of leverage. You can use $100 to buy $1000 worth of stocks on the margin. If the stock appreciates only 1%, you make a 10% gain on your money. This process of leveraging pours petroleum on the fires of speculation, and ultimately leads to collapse. A technical exposition of the various stages of this speculative cycle is available in the form of Hyman Minsky's Financial Fragility Hypothesis.

One very important point which is missed by many analysts is that bankers have no skin in the game. The money that they lent did not exist in the first place. So, if there is a complete collapse of the financial system, the bankers, lose nothing. It appears to the world that the bankers loaned money and are now not getting anything back. This generates enough sympathy to allow governments to bail out the banks. But in fact, the banks created the money they lent at zero cost. Hiding the mechanism of money creation is essential to playing this game, since after the collapse, the banks generally get the government to refund their losses on the pretext that the world will collapse if the financial institutions fail.

Some Crucial Historical Facts

We have described the big picture of how current financial institutions are built on exploitation through interest based debt. We now describe very briefly how the opposing interests of banking and the public have shaped economic events since the twentieth century.

The Great Depression of 1929: While minor banking crises were a routine occurrence, the biggest system wide financial crisis that the world had ever seen occurred in 1929. More, detailed expositions of the, causes are available from many sources, so here we just provide a very brief introduction. In the roaring 20's, banks managed to provide huge amounts of credit to buy stocks, lands, houses, and even commodities on installments. The price appreciation of the stocks became unsustainable and the stock market crash wiped out many banks. The modern system of money creation depends on credit created by banks to stimulate the economy since the power of money creation has been taken away from the government. Since many banks went bankrupt, while there were not enough people with collateral available for loans, there was a massive contraction in the money supply. This contraction meant that the economy could not recover from the crisis, and the recession persisted until World War II changed the rules of the game.

After the Great Depression, the true nature of money and banking became clear to many economists. Keynes said that the government could eliminate the recession by printing money or by providing jobs even valueless jobs like having one party dig ditches and the other party fill them up. The money created as payment for this activity would solve the economic problems. The Chicago Plan was widely endorsed by leading economists and struck at the root of the problem. It proposed to take the power of money creation away from banks by requiring 100% reserve banking. This would lead to a shortfall in the money supply and a recession unless the government steps in to fill the vacuum. Accordingly, the plan gave extensive powers of money creation to the government.

Many elements of the plan were adopted, but the financial lobby successfully blocked the crucial idea of taking the power of money creation away from private banks. Despite this important success, they could not block a vast range of regulations and restrictions placed on banking activities, which were designed to prevent a repeat of the Great Depression. Among the many rules and regulations on banking, a crucial piece of legislation was the Glass-Steagall Act of 1933, which prevented banks from making speculative investments of any type. This was extremely important in preventing speculative bubbles in the stock market and in property values for several decades.

This chaining of the financial industry led to an era of widespread prosperity in the West. For fifty years, there were no system wide banking crises. Income inequality improved as the share of the bottom 90% in national income increased, while the share of the top 1% decreased. Bankers and financiers also prospered but made profits at normal rates of 5% to 10% like the real sector. This state of affairs was not satisfactory to them, and the financial elites plotted to reverse this setback created by the Great Depression. For present purposes, it is sufficient to note that this plotting resulted in a successful outcome with the start of the Reagan-Thatcher era.

The Reagan-Thatcher Era: There was a minor economic downturn in the USA and European economies when Arab countries imposed an oil embargo in retaliation for US support of Israel in the Yom Kippur War. The financiers had been waiting for such an event and seized the opportunity to blame all economic problems on the regulation of finance, and on an oversized government. Massive pre-planned propaganda campaigns deceived and scared the public into supporting programs and policies designed to harm the public interest and provide profits to the finance industry.

These tactics of deceiving and scaring the public were first designed and advocated by Machiavelli, and many political scientists remarked on how these have been extensively adopted for use by politicians in the USA and Europe. As the first step of an extensive program of financial de-regulation, Reagan de-regulated the Savings and Loan (S&L) industry (a small sub-sector of the banking industry) in 1982. The S&L industry behaved exactly as predicted by Minsky and others, and went on an orgy of speculative credit creation. In consequence, between 1985 to 1995, more than 1,000 out of a total of 3,234 S&L banks went into bankruptcy. The total cost of the crisis, which was paid for by taxing the public, was more than the entire earnings of the banking industry for the previous fifty years. However, this time, the finance industry was very well prepared for this fallout. As an indicator of public knowledge about the event, we find that the Wikipedia entry on the S&L Crisis mentions at least seven different reasons for the crisis but barely mentions the financial deregulation as a side issue. The public was not allowed to perceive the direct linkage between the de-regulation and the S&L crisis so that the de-regulation could proceed smoothly, despite this disastrous outcome of the first step.

De-Regulation and the GFC: The final two steps of financial de-regulation came with the repeal of the Glass-Steagall act in 1999 and the enactment of the Commodity Futures Modernization Act in 2000(9), which was added as a rider to an 11,000 page conference report, and passed without being read by congressmen(10). These bills allowed banks to engage in speculation and also created a trillion-dollar market for derivatives which was completely unregulated. As anyone familiar with Minsky could have easily predicted, banks created a huge excess of credit which fueled wild speculation in properties and stocks and led to a crash in a short span of seven years. Massive amounts of fraud and criminal activities were done by bankers in order to allow them to sell loans to unqualified people while knowing in advance that these loans would fail.

Moneyless Economy

There is a group of researchers on moneyless economy, which proposes economic policies without consideration of monetary aggregates. But our subject in this section is different. In the paper Ross (Starr, ND) discusses a moneyless economy, without any price attached to any product or labor, and shows how an existing style market can be implemented. In the following section, we present a moneyless economy, similar to Ross, but with a different philosophy. We shows that the structure and the management of the economy will change in a moneyless system. We discuss three approaches to create a moneyless economy.

In the present economy, a product is created jointly by an entrepreneur and a financier and then imposed on the people. The cell phone, face book, cigarette, airbags for automobiles, etc. are such technologies. This kind of technology creates an environmental pollution on human behavior. People become smokers and create health hazards. Face book and cell phone produced a new generation that is constantly talking lost all capabilities of attention, focus, tenacity, dedication etc. These new generations do not even understand what these human qualities are. They get frustrated if someone does not twit, or does not get any email. As a result, we are getting low quality education. Students are running away from math, science, and engineering. They do not think, want to think, does not know what thinking is.

If we can remove money then it will be possible to create an economy where product will be created by people and will not be imposed on them to make money. Greed will be removed from humanity. We will come back to ourselves, we will learn to think again, find ourselves within ourselves, and decide what are our desire, our work, and our need. Nobody will impose anything on us. A true democracy will be created. Environmental pollution will be eliminated both from nature and from human character. So, the first approach is based on the following concept.

Assume that I need some money now. Also, assume that I have the machines and I have the freedom to print them. Then I will not have any money problem. I will be able to buy whatever I want and whenever I want. Because I will not have to give the money back to any one, because I printed it. I will not have poverty any more.

The same will be true for the US government. Suppose the government wants to build a high speed train, from Los Angeles to New York. Let us say it will cost 500 billion dollars. The US Government can print the money and give it to all the people, the contractors, and the corporations who will work for the project. The government will not have to give back the money to anyone. For, it has printed it, out of nothing, out of thin air. Since the government will not have to give it back, so there will be no need for tax on the people. This printing method will eliminate deficit, tax, and poverty. But ironically, the government cannot print it. This printing power has been taken away by the central bank (The Fed), a private bank. Therefore the government will have to borrow it from the Fed and return it with interest. There lie all the problems – deficit, tax, and poverty. Know that the Fed is printing just the way I would have printed it, out of thin air. There is no gold standard now.

Thus you can see that the root cause of deficit is the central bank. If we take that power back from the Fed, then we will not have any deficit. The deficit is completely artificial, and is imposed on us by some people who tricked the government in 1913 when the Fed was established. In the absence of central bank there will be no poverty anywhere in the world, there will be no deficit and therefore no taxes. So the whole world has been taken hostage by few people, who are the owners of the central banks.

Thus, if the governments had the power to print money, then clearly it, becomes a money less economy. It is just paper, we can print any time and any amount to keep all of us happy. Let us examine what is money now. We are all dealing with electronic money these days. Our employment checks are deposited electronically by our employers in our banks. We have credit cards, which are electronic money; we use them to buy our things. We pay the credit cards from the website using our own home computers. We rarely see any dollar bills any more. It is not necessary to have them anymore. Very soon we will authorize our credit card companies to directly deduct their money from our accounts automatically, without even asking them to tell us what is happening. Thus the money is just a number in some database on some computers. That number will go up and down and will control our fate and expenditure. Now we ask do we need that number to control us. Why do we need such a number?

The main reason for having this number is that some people want to control all of us, deprive us from equal share of wealth. Consider the second approach now. Suppose we decide to ignore that number and create a system where we all start working free like slaves. That is, we all become slaves of our country. We do what we are doing now, but only for free. I go to my work every day, work sincerely and carefully for full eight hours, and come back home. Only difference is that we work free. I go to the grocery store, buy whatever I need, and get out without paying any money. I want to travel somewhere; I book the flight, if it is available, free of charge, and fly. I want to live in a big house, I ask a contractor, he builds the house free of charge and I live there, no money is involved anywhere. All I have to ensure is that I work somewhere for eight hours, free of charge, every day, five days a week. We use the hours as money and not use any multiplier of hours as a number or salary as we do now. We will still have unequal wealth if we want, but now our views about wealth will change because it is free.

One possible contradiction may rise, because the above model ignores the value of education and knowledge. The answer to this problem is pretty simple. All the great people who changed our society by bringing new technology, like Thomas Edison, Benjamin Franklin, Wright Brothers, Bill Gates, and Steve Jobs, etc. were not formally educated. Thus education is not necessary to create a new technology. If we observe our work carefully you will see that we are not using our education in building our technology. Capitalism is using our education as a factor for discrimination.

One may conclude also that people will stop working because money power forces the people to work. But that may change once people get the freedom. People will be able to do their own thing in their own way. Human life may completely get transformed once freedom is achieved from money. Now we do not have that, we are forced to work in defense companies, being fully aware that we are making war machines that will kill people; we are forced to work in cigarette companies knowing that it causes cancer, we are being highly paid in Wall Street to create various schemes to transfer wealth. All these will change, and a much cleaner, spiritual society may eventually evolve. Another advantage is that money based economy violates the sigma law thus causing environmental pollution. A moneyless system, which inherently adheres to sigma law, will eliminate all kinds of physical and psychological pollution.

The third option is the following. If you can install a voting system with secret ballot in the US house of congress and senate, then you will have a perfect democracy. You probably know that we do not have a secret ballot system in Washington DC now. And that is why we do not have democracy in USA. Capitalism does not like democracy. If you try to implement such a system, then you will be destroyed. This true democracy will eventually eliminate capitalism and the central bank.

So, how we can be saved? How do we implement a moneyless system? There is no alternative, and an external catastrophe is needed. It may be possible to destroy the computer database of the banking system. That is in the hands of hackers. Very soon that will happen. We have seen this happening in a James Bond movie. But the database can be recreated. So it is not a solution.

Essentially all the approaches are going against central banks. They are all powerful, they will kill you. President Abraham Lincoln wanted to print money to finance the civil war. President Kennedy created an executive order (Woolley, ND) to print money. Many say they were assassinated because they went against the central bank. If the central bank senses that you are threatening them then you will be gone too. They have the guns, and we do not. Note that we have central banks in almost all countries now.

The war in Afghanistan started on October 7, 2001. In the middle of this war the central bank planned a meeting in Bonn, Germany, started printing new currency, and by Jan 2, 2002 replaced all old Afghan currencies. The PBS news reporter Margaret Warner asked (PBS, 2003) the advisor to the new central bank why it was so important to change the currency at this critical war time. The Iraq war started on

March 20, 2003. By January 15, 2004, all Iraqi currencies were replaced by new currency and the central bank (CBI, 2010) was installed on March 6, 2004.

These events should indicate why we went to war in Muslim countries. We can see that the war drum is beating against Iran and North Korea because they do not have central banks. Thus we can see that the central banks are not focused in running the economy and in the well being of citizens, but in acquiring control of financial systems of all countries and is willing to do so at any cost. Observe that the installation of central banks was carried out in the middle of turmoil, before even people, politicians, and governments realize what they are going to lose.

The Three Key System Entities

The Board of Governors, the Federal Reserve Banks, and the Federal Open Market Committee work together to promote the health of the U.S. economy and the stability of the U.S. financial system.

The Federal Reserve Board: Selection and Function

The Board of Governors—located in Washington, D.C.—is the governing body of the Federal Reserve System. It is run by seven members, or "governors," who are nominated by the President of the United States and confirmed in their positions by the Senate. The Board of Governors guides the operation of the Federal Reserve System to promote the goals and fulfill the responsibilities given to the Federal Reserve by the Federal Reserve Act.

All of the members of the Board serve on the FOMC, which is the body within the Federal Reserve that sets monetary policy. Each member of the Board of Governors is appointed for a 14-year term; the terms are staggered so that one term expires on January 31 of each even-numbered year. After serving a full 14-year term, a Board member may not be reappointed. If a Board member leaves the Board before his or her term expires, however, the person nominated and confirmed to serve the remainder of the term may later be appointed to a full 14-year term.

The Chair and Vice Chair of the Board are also appointed by the President and confirmed by the Senate, but serve only four-year terms. They may be reappointed to additional four-year terms. The nominees to these posts must already be members of the Board or must be simultaneously appointed to the Board.

The Board oversees the operations of the 12 Reserve Banks and shares with them the responsibility for supervising and regulating certain financial institutions and activities. The Board also provides general guidance, direction, and oversight when the Reserve Banks lend to depository institutions and when the Reserve Banks provide financial services to depository institutions and the federal government. The Board also has broad oversight responsibility for the operations and activities of the Reserve Banks. This authority includes oversight of the Reserve Banks' services to depository institutions and to the U.S. Treasury and of the Reserve Banks' examination and supervision of various financial institutions. As part of this oversight, the Board reviews and approves the budgets of each of the Reserve Banks.

The Board also helps to ensure that the voices and concerns of consumers and communities are heard at the central bank by conducting consumer-focused supervision, research, and policy analysis, and, more generally, by promoting a fair and transparent consumer financial services market

The Federal Reserve Banks: Structure and Function

The 12 Reserve Banks and their 24 Branches are the operating arms of the Federal Reserve System. Each Reserve Bank operates within its own particular geographic area, or district, of the United States.

Each Reserve Bank gathers data and other information about the businesses and the needs of local communities in its region. That information has then factored into monetary policy decisions by the FOMC and other decisions made by the Board of Governors.

Reserve Bank Leadership

As set forth in the Federal Reserve Act, each Reserve Bank is subject to "the supervision and control of a board of directors." Much like the boards of directors of private corporations, Reserve Bank boards are responsible for overseeing their Bank's administration and governance, reviewing the Bank's budget and overall performance, overseeing the Bank's audit process, and developing broad strategic goals and directions. However, unlike private corporations, Reserve Banks are not operated in the interest of shareholders, but rather in the public interest.

Each year, the Board of Governors designates one chair and one deputy chair for each Reserve Bank board from among its Class C directors. The Federal Reserve Act requires that the chair of a Reserve Bank's board be a person of "tested banking experience," a term which has been interpreted as requiring familiarity with banking or financial services.

Each Reserve Bank board delegates responsibility for day-to-day operations to the president of that Reserve Bank and his or her staff. Reserve Bank presidents act as chief executive officers of their respective Banks and also serve, in rotation, as voting members of the FOMC. Presidents are nominated by a Bank's Class B and C directors and approved by the Board of Governors for five-year terms.

Reserve Bank Branches also have boards of directors. Pursuant to policy established by the Board of Governors, Branch boards must have either five or seven members. All

Branch directors are appointed: the majority of directors on a Branch board are appointed by the Reserve Bank, and the remaining directors on the board are appointed by the Board of Governors. Each Branch board selects a chair from among those directors appointed by the Board of Governors. Unlike Reserve Bank directors, Branch directors are not divided into different classes. However, Branch directors must meet different eligibility requirements, depending on whether they are appointed by the Reserve Bank or the Board of Governors.

Reserve Bank and Branch directors are elected or appointed for staggered three-year terms. When a director does not serve a full term, his or her successor is elected or appointed to serve the unexpired portion of that term.

Reserve Bank Responsibilities

The Reserve Banks carry out Federal Reserve core functions by;

1) supervising and examining state member banks (state-chartered banks that have chosen to become members of the Federal Reserve System), bank and thrift holding companies, and non-bank financial institutions that have been designated as systemically important under authority delegated to them by the Board;

2) lending to depository institutions to ensure liquidity in the financial system;

3) providing key financial services that undergird the nation's payment system, including distributing the nation's currency and coin to depository institutions, clearing checks, operating the Fed-Wire and automated clearinghouse (ACH) systems, and serving as a bank for the U.S. Treasury; and

4) examining certain financial institutions to ensure and enforce compliance with federal consumer protection

and fair lending laws, while also promoting local community development.

In its role providing key financial services, the Reserve Bank acts, essentially, as a financial institution for the banks, thrifts, and credit unions in its District that is, each Reserve Bank acts as a "bank for banks." In that capacity, it offers (and charges for) services to these depository institutions similar to those that ordinary banks provide their individual and business customers: the equivalent of checking accounts; loans; coin and currency; safekeeping services; and payment services (such as the processing of checks and the making of recurring and nonrecurring small and large-dollar payments) that help banks, and ultimately their customers, buy and sell goods, services, and securities.

In addition, through their leaders and their connections to, and interactions with, members of their local communities, Reserve Banks provide the Federal Reserve System with a wealth of information on conditions in virtually every part of the nationinformation that is vital to formulating a national monetary policy that will help to maintain the health of the economy and the stability of the nation's financial system.

Certain information gathered by the Reserve Banks from Reserve Bank directors and other sources is also shared with the public prior to each FOMC meeting in a report commonly known as the Beige Book. In addition, every two weeks, the board of each Reserve Bank recommends discount rates (interest rates to be charged for loans to depository institutions made through that Bank's discount window); these interest rate recommendations are subject to review and determination by the Board of Governors.

The Federal Open Market Committee:

Selection and Function

The FOMC is the body of the Federal Reserve System that sets national monetary policy. The FOMC makes all decisions regarding the appropriate position or "stance" of monetary policy to help move the economy toward the congressionally mandated goals of maximum employment and price stability. The Committee raises and lowers its target range for the policy rate, which is the federal funds rate (the rate at which depository institutions lend to each other), to achieve these dual objectives. At times, as an additional policy measure, the FOMC has used forward guidance about its policy rate to influence expectations about the future course of monetary policy. In addition, the Committee sometimes leans on balance sheet policy, where it adjusts the size and composition of the Federal Reserve's asset holdings, to assist with market functioning and help foster accommodative financial conditions. Congress enacted legislation that created the FOMC as part of the Federal Reserve System in 1933 and 1935.

FOMC Membership

The FOMC consists of 12 voting members—the 7 members of the Board of Governors; the president of the Federal Reserve Bank of New York; and 4 of the remaining 11 Reserve Bank presidents, who serve one-year terms on a rotating basis.

All 12 of the Reserve Bank presidents attend FOMC meetings and participate in FOMC discussions, but only the presidents who are Committee members at the time may vote on policy decisions.

By law, the FOMC determines its own internal organization and, by tradition, the FOMC elects the Chair of the Board of Governors as its chair and the president of the Federal

Reserve Bank of New York as its vice chair. FOMC meetings are typically held eight times each year in Washington, D.C., and at other times as needed.

FOMC Responsibilities

Once the FOMC determines the appropriate stance of policy, it must then make sure this stance is effectively transmitted to financial markets. The Board and FOMC have many monetary policy implementation tools at their disposal. Key tools include the Federal Reserve's administered interest rates and open market purchases and sales of securities. The FOMC also directs operations undertaken by the Federal Reserve in foreign exchange markets and authorizes currency swap programs with foreign central banks.

Other Significant Entities Contributing to Federal Reserve Functions

Two other groups play important roles in the Federal Reserve System's core functions:

- Depository institutions—banks, thrifts, and credit unions; and
- Federal Reserve System advisory committees, which make recommendations to the Board of Governors and to the Reserve Banks regarding the System's responsibilities.

Depository Institutions

Depository institutions offer transaction, or checking, accounts to the public and may maintain accounts of their own at their local Reserve Banks. Depository institutions receive interest on the reserve balances they hold in their Reserve Bank accounts. Interest on reserves is a key tool for monetary policy implementation.

Advisory Councils

Five advisory committees assist and advise the Board on matters of public policy.

1) Federal Advisory Council (FAC). This council, established by the Federal Reserve Act, comprises 12 representatives of the banking industry. The FAC ordinarily meets with the Board four times a year, as required by law. Annually, each Reserve Bank chooses one person to represent its District on the FAC. FAC members customarily serve three one-year terms and elect their own officers.

2) Community Depository Institutions Advisory Council (CDIAC). The Board of Governors to originally established the CDIAC obtain information and views from thrift institutions (savings and loan institutions and mutual savings banks) and credit unions. More recently, its membership has expanded to include community banks. Like the FAC, the CDIAC provides the Board of Governors with firsthand insight and information about the economy, lending conditions, and other issues.

3) Model Validation Council. This council was established by the Board of Governors in 2012 to provide expert and independent advice on its process to rigorously assess the models used in stress tests of banking institutions. Stress tests are required under the Dodd-Frank Wall Street Reform and Consumer Protection Act. The council is intended to improve the quality of stress tests and thereby strengthen confidence in the stress testing program.

4) Community Advisory Council (CAC). This council was formed by the Federal Reserve Board in 2015 to offer diverse perspectives on the economic circumstances and financial services needs of consumers and communities, with a particular focus on the concerns of low and

moderate-income populations. The CAC complements the FAC and CDIAC, whose members represent depository institutions. The CAC meets semiannually with members of the Board of Governors. The 15 CAC members serve staggered three-year terms and are selected by the Board through a public nomination process.

5) Insurance Policy Advisory Committee (IPAC). This council was established at the Board of Governors in 2018 by section 211(b) of the Economic Growth, Regulatory Relief, and Consumer Protection Act. The IPAC provides information, advice, and recommendations to the Board on international insurance capital standards and other insurance issues. Reserve Banks also have their own advisory committees. Perhaps the most important of these are committees that advise the Banks on agricultural, small business, and labor matters. The Federal Reserve Board solicits the views of each of these committees biannually.

Historical Evidence And Current Practice

Before we look at the treatment of the subjects: central banks, banks, and money creation by leading textbooks, we will first take a look at the history of important central banks, to see if Weidmann's narrative is correct. We will see that it is not. Neither did or do governments have a monopoly on money creation, nor did they routinely abuse any power they had in this regard. The insinuation of Weidmann and Issing that it is only central banks who create money will turn out as just as wrong.

Paper money in early China

It is no coincidence that Weidman goes back to 13th Century China to give us an historical example of government-controlled money creation that went wrong. He has to do so because, contrary to his claim, the important central banks in the west historically were created by private bankers for private gain. It is true that bankers created them in cooperation with the government as a new scheme to give credit to the government. This usually involved privileges conferred on these commercial banks, notably the privilege that their notes would be accepted for payment of taxes and duties. But still, central banks were not government controlled entities, issuing money on behalf of the government. The bulk of the seignorage, i.e. the direct monetary gain from printing money, usually went to private bankers. There was a lot of political controversy, historically, about whether commercial banks or the government should issue money, and for a long time, the commercial banks prevailed in this fight even as far as banknotes are concerned. As far as deposit money is concerned, the largest part of the money supply, banks have prevailed until today. So Weidmann is clearly giving a badly distorted account.

Not even the Chinese example that Weidmann chooses is a good one to make his point. Contemporary reports about the economy of Kublai Khan's empire and of his successors stress how wealthy and well organized it was. China was far ahead of Europe at that time. The system of paper money might or might not have been instrumental, but it is far from straightforward to argue that this monetary system was a failure. The devaluation of this paper money over 150 years, that Weidmann alludes to, amounts to a hardly spectacular five or six percent inflation annually. According to Werner (2007), this paper money system worked well for decades, if not centuries, as all available research reports the Chinese economy as flourishing during that time.

The Bank of England

The Bank of England was founded in 1694 as a private enterprise. A consortium led by the Scottish businessman

William Paterson had suggested the scheme. It would afford
King William and Queen Mary a large loan. The consortium
was granted the right to found the privately owned Bank of
England and to create money by issuing banknotes. They
lent those "Notes of the Bank of England" and some gold to
the crown against interest of 8%. (Rothbard, 2008). The Bank
of England was awarded the monopoly of issuing banknotes
in London by the Bank Charter Act of 1844, only in the 20th
century did the Bank of England move away from
commercial endeavors. It was nationalized in 1946. Until
then it was a private institution working mostly for the
financial benefit of its private shareholders.

No evidence here for the theory of central banks as creatures
of governments over issuing money for the benefit of the
government.

The US Federal Reserve And Its Predecessors

The merchant banker Alexander Hamilton, the first United
States Secretary of the Treasury, successfully promoted the
chartering by Congress of the privately owned First Bank of
the United States in 1791, a bank with special money creation
privileges. He staunchly opposed the idea that the
government itself should issue the money needed to fund
manufacturing and the settling of the west. He wanted
commercial banks to do it, but they should have the strong
backing of the government. This backing consisted, among
other privileges, in accepting the notes of the First Bank in
duties and taxes (Nettels, 1962).

The bank faced stiff political opposition. The fight was not
about fears of over-issuance, though. It was about the
constitutionality of outsourcing the regulation of money to
a private company and about the privileges conferred to
private bankers at the expense of farmers and other
producers and the public at large.

Private bankers' highly privileged role remained a source of political controversy for more than a century. After its 20 year charter ran out in 1811, a bill to recharter the First Bank of America failed. Five years later, the banker Alexander Dallas, in his other capacity as Secretary of the Treasury, initiated the chartering of the Second Bank of the United States. He endowed the – again – predominantly privately owned bank with the same privileges as the First Bank had had (Rothbard 2008).

President Andrew Jackson eventually was successful in his campaign to take away the privileges of the Second Bank in 1836. Jackson insisted that it was improper for Congress to pass the important task of creating money and regulating its value to a private corporation. Thus, the predecessors of the Federal Reserve offer nothing in evidence for the theory of central banks as creatures of governments, over-issuing of money for the benefit of the government.

For eight decades the US would not have a central bank. Banknotes were still printed and circulated in the economy, though. They were printed by a multitude of competing commercial banks. As Issing pointed out in this speech, such a system has the potential advantage that competition of banks might prevent over-issuance in such a system and the palpable disadvantage that transaction costs are very high, if notes of more than a thousand banks with different discounts from their nominal value are circulating.

In 1862, Salmon Chase, who had been installed as Treasury Secretary by banker and financier Jay Cooke and his newspaper owning brother, pushed through Congress a national banking law that alleviated the competitive limit to money creation that banks had faced in the absence of coordinating central bank.

The new layered system had New York City based national banks at the top, designated as central reserve city banks.

They could give loans and thus create deposit money as a multiple of the amount of Treasury bonds, gold and silver they held. Other nationally chartered banks in big cities, the reserve city banks, could hold their reserves in the form of deposits at central reserve city banks or in Treasury bonds. They could create a multiple of these reserves as checking accounts. National banks in smaller places called country banks could hold more modest reserves also at reserve city banks to back up the loans they gave.

One can see that money creation in the national banking system was driven mostly by the interests of the banking community in the early United States. While it is true that the idea behind the national banking laws were, besides creating a national currency, to help the government finance the civil war. However, the money that the government created was only a fraction of the money that commercial banks were allowed to create on top of the government bonds that they were forced to hold. The result of the new system from which initiator Cooke benefitted very handsomely was a great expansion of the number of banks and of deposits and also a series of severe financial crises in fairly short order. There were panics and bank runs in 1873, 1884, 1893 and 1907, because banks, notably those in New York at the top of the money issuing pyramid, repeatedly had difficulty to meet demand for redemption of their deposits.

As a reaction to these crises, the Federal Reserve System was created in 1913, again upon private bankers' initiative. At a secret meeting at Jekyll Island, Georgia in December 1910, they hammered out the essential features of the new Federal Reserve System. Bankers representing the interests of Rockefeller, JP Morgan and Kuhn, Loeb & company, the most powerful institutions of the time, dominated the meeting. The continental European, notably the German system served as a model for the basic structure. The idea was to make the process of money creation more disciplined and orderly and to have a deep pocketed institution to bail out the banks if the public lost confidence in the notes they had issued. The bankers wanted the government only as paymaster, though. Otherwise, it was supposed to have as little influence over the process as possible.

To this day, the twelve regional Federal Reserve Banks, which are in charge of regulating banks, are owned and governed by their member banks. Before the subprime crisis, this fact was never advertised and often concealed by the pretense that the Federal Reserve System was a public institution.

The Federal Reserve Bank of New York is the one in charge of regulating, overseeing and bailing out Wall Street banks with public money. Wall Street banks chose the President of the New York Fed and charged him with regulating and controlling them. A board chosen and dominated by bankers makes sure he does it right. Only during the subprime crisis did the Federal Reserve give up the pretense of being a public institution. The New York Fed, managing US\$1.7 trillion of emergency lending programs for banks and brokerages, was called upon to inform the public of the whereabouts of the public funds going to Wall Street. At this point, the Federal Reserve of New York insisted – ultimately in vain – that as a private institution it is not bound by the Freedom of Information Act.

Central banking in Germany

In Prussia, the political powerhouse of mid-19th Century pre-unification Germany, a central bank called Preussische Bank was created in 1846 as a hybrid institution, which was run by government representatives but with a capital base which was mostly provided by wealthy businessman and private bankers, who would have a right to a dividend as long as the bank was profitable.

The reason for founding the central bank was a dearth of money in circulation in a period of beginning industrialization. There were coins circulating and small denomination treasury obligations, but not enough. In stark contrast to Weidman's account, the Prussian bureaucracy under-issued the debt certificates that served as small denomination paper money rather than over-issuing them and the Royal Bank was stingier with credit than the business community in the commercial centers wanted them to be. The Prussian bureaucrats were loath to give commercial banks the freedom to emit currency, because they feared that too much money would be issued. Their mistrust was fuelled by the fact that none of the bankers' proposals for the licensing of private note issuing central banks had a provision of unlimited liability of the banks' owners as prevailed in the Scottish free banking system. The contemporary US-system with private note issuing banks and correspondingly many different notes trading at varying discounts was regarded as a bad example to be avoided.

The fight in Prussia over the right to issue notes had an important political dimension. The fact that private shareholders were invited to provide the capital for the Preussische Bank was a compromise between the preference of Prussian bureaucrats like Minister Christian von Rother, who wanted to keep note emission in public hands and mistrusted profit-oriented private bankers in this respect, and the King's perceived need in pre-revolutionary times to appease a dissatisfied moneyed citizenry, which was pressing for the right to issue banknotes.

From 1871 to 1876, the Prussian Bank would serve as the central bank of the newly unified German Reich and eventually would become the Reichsbank, which was also run by the government and owned by private shareholders.

The German model of giving a (near) monopoly of note issuance to a government run central bank was considered highly successful and would later, together with the Bank of England, become the blueprint for the Federal Reserve System.

Money Creation By Commercial Banks Today

We have seen that for much of history, government was only indirectly involved in issuing banknotes, and had nothing like a monopoly on it. Over time, most governments took over the responsibility for central banks and the issuance of banknotes, which functioned as means of payment. (Some of that control they have relinquished again recently by deciding to let independent technocrats, often with commercial banking backgrounds make the relevant decisions.) However, even where the government had or has this monopoly to issue notes, this is far from being a monopoly to issue money. Today, only a fraction of the money which circulates in the economy consists in cash issued by the central banks. M3, the preferred definition of money of the European Central bank is 11 times larger than the sum of currency in circulation and reserves of commercial banks at the central bank, i.e., base money. We make by far the largest part of our payments without using any government issued banknotes. We pay by transferring deposits at commercial banks to someone else and we receive our paychecks in the form of deposits in the bank, i.e., in electronic money, created by commercial banks.

This money is created any time a commercial bank gives credit to a non-bank or buys an asset from a non-bank. If I take a mortgage loan from a bank of €100,000, the bank will credit my account with a deposit of €100,000 in exchange for my obligation to pay back, say €150,000 over time. €100,000 in new deposits has been created by a few keystrokes and signatures. It might soon leave my bank account, as I pay my house with it, but it will remain in the banking system, as I will transfer the money to somebody else's account at another bank. (The money market, on which commercial banks exchange liquidity, will in normal times make sure that my bank will be able to obtain the central bank deposit needed to make the transfer.

This deposit money created by commercial banks is equivalent to legal tender for all practical purposes. The government accepts a transfer of this deposit money as taxes, and everybody is obliged to accept it for payment in normal business. That these deposits created by commercial banks are "money" is also recognized by the fact that all major central banks, like the Federal Reserve, the European Central Bank and the Bank of England count them as money in the monetary statistics they compile.

Even when commercial banks were refused the privilege to issue banknotes in 19th Century Prussia; they were able to create money by issuing fungible deposit slips on current account balances of their customers. Whoever presented these deposit slips had the right to have the balance paid out in cash. This enabled commercial banks to lend out much more money than they had in deposits, since most customers would leave the deposits in the bank and transfer the deposit slips to pay their bills.

The Reserve Position Doctrine (RPD), also called Monetarism, which was first propagated by the Federal Reserve (Bindseil 2004) and later also by the Deutsche Bundesbank and, for a few years, by the ECB, rests on the assumption that central banks control the process of money creation. They issue so-called base money in the form of currency and bank deposits at the central bank, i.e., reserves. Banks use this base money to give credit and thus create a more or less fixed multiple of the monetary base in deposits, according to the money multiplier.

In reality even central banks ostensibly adhering to the Reserve Position Doctrin, have not been steering the monetary base, but have been occupied with setting an interest rate on the money market, with which they try to influence and smooth short-term interest rates in the economy in general. Goodhart (2001) claims that the Fed continued to use interest rates as its fundamental modus operandi, even if it pretended to pursue monetary base control. He talks of play-acting and even deception in this regard.

Ulrich Binseil, who used to be head of liquidity operations of the ECB and currently is Deputy Director General of financial market operations, makes it clear that interest rate targeting, which has long been the norm for all major central banks, and control over base money are incompatible: "Today, there is little debate, at least among central bankers, about what a central bank decision on monetary policy means: it means to set the level of short term money market interest rate that the central bank aims at in its day-to-day operations." And he quotes Goodhart a renowned academic economist with central banking experience, saying "Central bank practitioners, almost always, view themselves as unable to deny setting the level of interest rates, at which such reserve requirements are met, with the quantity of money then simultaneously determined by the portfolio preferences of private sector banks and non-banks." In other words: the central bank will normally feel obliged to provide whatever demand for monetary base is created by the interaction of private borrowers and banks, because otherwise, short term interest rates would gyrate wildly.

Thus, according to this view prevailing among central banking practitioners, central banks fulfill the task of supporting money creation by commercial banks by providing reserves as needed and disciplining the process in such a way that runaway inflation does not erode the public's trust in the money thus created.

Even if one should be of the opinion that the central bank is able in our current monetary system, to control the amount of money that commercial banks create, it is certainly not justified to give the impression, as Mr. Weidmann and Mr. Issing do, that only (government owned) central banks create money and that all money creation is for the benefit of the government. Even if the central bank were to control commercial banks' money creation, it would still be done by commercial banks for the benefit of commercial banks (and at the risk of taxpayers who have to bail them out, if it goes wrong). Central bankers never, ever talk about the hugely profitable privilege that the ability to create legal tender means for commercial banks.

CONCLUSION

Once you have a clear understanding of what investing in this kid of programs involves and how fractional reserve banking comes into play, you must discover a way to get into a trading platform. This step near the beginning of the process can be the most difficult of all. This is because private placement trading is exactly that private and secret. If you want to get involved with these programs or other alternative investment opportunities, you need to get in touch with an investing and trading company.

The best way to make money with trading programs is to find a genuine opportunity. The last thing you want, after all, is to be strung into a deal that ends up being illegal or illegitimate in some way. To spot an opportunity that you want to avoid, see if national brokerage firms refuse to become involved in the private placement program. When this happens, it may be the case that the brokerage firm has been bitten when investing in private placement trading programs before and they want to avoid a repeat occurrence. The reality is that there is a multitude of ways that growth investors can find investments to complement their existing portfolio. In the end, it is always up to each individual to choose the methods that work best for them personally, but it is also always helpful to be aware of different approaches to identifying investments with the greatest potential for providing future profits.

Acknowledgement

First and foremost, praises and thanks to God, the Almighty, for his showers of blessings throughout my research work to complete this book successfully.

My thanks go out to all those who have supported me and helped complete this book directly or indirectly. I am overwhelmed in humbleness and gratefulness to acknowledge the depth of all those who have helped me put my ideas above the level of simplicity and into something tangible.

I cannot express enough thanks to my committee for their continued support and encouragement.

My completion of this project could not have been accomplished without the support of my great and talented editor Bilal Qureshi. Thank thank you for putting up with me and the countless hours. I would also like to thank him for his friendship, empathy, and great sense of humour.

Special acknowledgement to my Daughter Isabella and my sister Paula for the love, understanding and support they have shown me over the years. My late parents, Esther and Eric, are no longer here, but they are always in my heart and thoughts.

To my loving partner Janice. Your encouragement when the times got rough is much appreciated and duly noted. It was a great comfort and relief to know that you were willing to provide management of our household activities while I completed my work. My heartfelt thanks.

To my special dogs Beau and Baby Myla, who have put up with me and behaved themselves during the writing of this book. They are also an inspiration in my life.

Finally, thanks go to all the people who have supported me in completing this book directly or indirectly.

OTHER BOOKS BY THE AUTHOR

Cryptocurrency Millionaire Make Money
With Cryptocurrency

Secret Of Wealth Creation: Principle Lessons On The
Secrets Of Building A Long Lasting Wealth

Guide To Private Placement Project Fundingtrade
Programs: Understanding High-Level Project Funding
Trade Programs

Make Money Doing Nothing

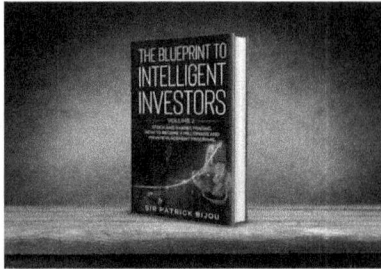

The Blueprint To Intelligent Investors

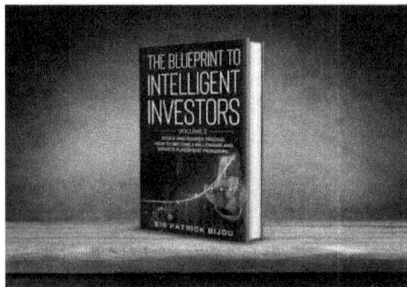

The Blueprint To Intelligent Investors Volume 2

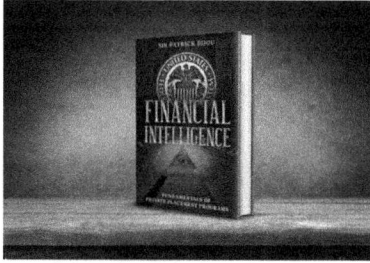

Financial Intelligence: Fundamentals Of Private Placement
Programs (PPP)

Private Placement Programs - The Holy Grail

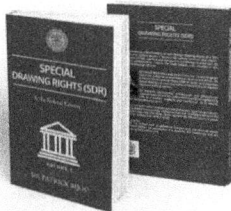

Special Drawing Rights (SDR) And The Federal Reserve

Special Drawing Rights (SDR) And The Federal Reserve Volume 2.

Cryptocurrency: The Next Level For Banking Reform

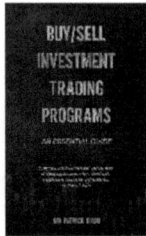

Fundamentals of Buy/Sell Investment Trading Programs

Unsurpassed Relationships In Wealth Management

www.ingramcontent.com/pod-product-compliance
Lightning Source LLC
Chambersburg PA
CBHW071541210326
41597CB00019B/3074